TYRANNY UNMASKED

JOHN TAYLOR

Tyranny Unmasked

John Taylor

Edited by F. Thornton Miller

Liberty Fund

INDIANAPOLIS

This book is published by Liberty Fund, Inc., a foundation established to encourage study of the ideal of a society of free and responsible individuals.

The cuneiform inscription that serves as our logo and as the design motif for our endpapers is the earliest-known written appearance of the word "freedom" (amagi), or "liberty." It is taken from a clay document written about 2300 B.C. in the Sumerian city-state of Lagash.

Foreword and other editorial additions © 1992 by F. Thorton Miller. All rights reserved. All inquiries should be addressed to Liberty Fund, Inc., 8335 Allison Pointe Trail, Suite 300, Indianapolis, IN 46250-1684. This book was manufactured in the United States of America.

Frontispiece from Virginia State Library and Archives. Oil painting attributed to William J. Hubard.

Library of Congress Cataloging-in-Publication Data

Taylor, John, 1753–1824.
Tyranny unmasked / John Taylor : edited by F. Thornton Miller.
   p.   cm.
Includes bibliographical references and index.
ISBN 0-86597-104-8 (hardcover). — ISBN 0-86597-105-6 (pbk.)
1. Tariff—United States.   2. United States—Politics and
government—1817–1825.   I. Miller, Frederick Thornton.   II. Title.
HF1754.T4   1992
382'.7'0973—dc20   92-26255
                                                                        CIP

C   10   9   8   7   6   5   4   3   2   1
P   10   9   8   7   6   5   4   3

CONTENTS

FOREWORD

When John Taylor supported James Monroe's campaigns for president, he informed the candidate that upon taking office he would find his old friend in the opposition. Taylor stated that he intended to live and die a "minority man." He made the frequent inquiring into the measures of government his life's work. To fulfill this task, he wrote *Tyranny Unmasked*. He and other Old Republicans believed that, without their vigilant watch over the federal government on behalf of the people, individual liberty would be sacrificed.[1]

John Taylor of Caroline County, Virginia, was born in 1753. Orphaned as a young boy, he was adopted by his maternal uncle Edmund Pendleton. One of Virginia's most distinguished citizens, Pendleton served from the Revolution to his death in 1803 as head of the state's highest court. Taylor studied at William and Mary and then read law in his uncle's office. He served as an officer in the Continental army and the Virginia militia during the Revolution. After the war, he had a successful law practice. Following marriage to Lucy Penn, daughter of the signer John Penn of North Carolina, he retired from the law to spend the remainder of his life as a planter. His home was Hazlewood, on the Rappahannock River near Port Royal.

Taylor was an advocate of scientific farming. He wrote the agricultural treatise *Arator* and was the first president of the Virginia Agricultural Society. Like other members of the Virginia gentry, he fulfilled his public duty, serving in the state legislature (1779–81, 1783–85, and 1796–1800) and as a representative of Virginia in the United States

1. Taylor, *A Pamphlet Containing a Series of Letters* (Richmond: E. C. Stanard, 1809). See "Letters of John Taylor," Taylor to Monroe, 22 February 1808, 15 January and 8 November 1809, 10 February, 12 March, and 26 October 1810, and 31 January 1811 in *John P. Branch Historical Papers of Randolph-Macon College*, ed. William E. Dodd, vol. 2 (1908): 291–94, 298–306, 309–311, 315–19.

ix

Senate (1793–94, 1803, and 1822–24). He was serving as a senator when he died on 21 August 1824.

Taylor was a leading espouser of Country, or agrarian, republicanism, which derived mainly from the writings of the eighteenth-century English Country opposition. Advocates of the ideology included Viscount Bolingbroke [Henry St. John], and Cato [John Trenchard and Thomas Gordon]. This perspective originated in a provincial outlook toward London and the central government and in a belief that there was a division between the simple, virtuous farmers in the country and the wealthy noble courtiers at the king's court. While the former looked to the best interests of the whole, the latter, corrupted by wealth and power, thought only of their self interests. The opposition believed this corruption violated the principles of the ancient English constitution, altered the checks and balances, and, unless opposed, would end English liberty.

The Country opposition rose against the corrupt Court and believed it had won with the glorious Revolution of 1688. But William III and the Whigs had their financial revolution, the English banking system was developed, and the national debt became an institution. A Court party was created and became established under the leadership of Robert Walpole. The opposition now added bankers and financial speculators to the list of those at Court who it believed wished to grow wealthy by robbing the country.[2]

By the time of the Revolution, many Americans were using the Court-Country paradigm to explain to themselves and the world what they feared and why they resisted the imperial government. From this perspective, the American revolutionaries waged a successful Country

---

2. Perez Zagorin, *The Court and the Country: The Beginning of the English Revolution* (New York: Atheneum, 1970); Isaac Kramnick, *Bolingbroke and His Circle: The Politics of Nostalgia in the Age of Walpole* (Cambridge: Harvard University Press, 1968); and Caroline Robbins, *The Eighteenth-Century Commonwealthman: Studies in the Transmission, Development, and Circumstance of English Liberal Thought from the Restoration of Charles II until the War with the Thirteen Colonies* (Cambridge: Harvard University Press, 1959).

opposition.[3] In the 1780s, however, the republican Patriots divided. Now that the distant threat to their liberty was removed, some Americans, many of whom became Federalists, began devising plans to restructure and strengthen the republic. Anti-Federalists, Taylor among them, responded to the reform movement—and its main result, the Constitution—with the same distrust they had shown earlier toward London. They feared that a new central government (eventually in Washington, D.C.) would replace the old one, and that, again, there would be a concentration of power over which they would have little control.

Along with many Anti-Federalists, Taylor had wanted only a revision of the Articles of Confederation (basically wanting things to stay as they were). They wanted to keep a purely federal government wherein the states were sovereign, with power remaining at the state and local levels. After the Constitution was ratified, they hoped for a new convention, or for amendments that would undermine the power of the federal government.[4] In the meanwhile, they advocated the strict construction of the Constitution in order to restrict the administration of the federal government as much as possible. They developed an interpretation that denied that the Constitution was a fundamental or supreme law of the land. This view would be further developed and amplified in Taylor's writings, including *Tyranny Unmasked.*

During the 1790s, Taylor was among the many Anti-Federalists who joined with the Republican opposition of James Madison and Thomas Jefferson in its effort to drive Alexander Hamilton and the Federalists out of power. Drawing upon the Court-Country paradigm, the Republicans portrayed Hamilton as modeling his policies on Walpole's and building the Federalists into a Court party in America. Taylor publicized the view of the new Country opposition to Hamil-

3. Bernard Bailyn, *The Ideological Origins of the American Revolution* (Cambridge: Harvard University Press, 1967); Gordon S. Wood, *The Creation of the American Republic 1776–1787* (Chapel Hill: University of North Carolina Press, 1969).

4. Richard E. Ellis, "The Persistence of Antifederalism after 1789," in *Beyond Confederation: Origins of the Constitution and American National Identity,* ed. Richard Beeman, Stephen Botein, and Edward C. Carter (Chapel Hill: University of North Carolina Press, 1987), 295–314.

ton's Court in his pamphlet *An Enquiry into the Principles and Tendency of Certain Public Measures.*[5]

Although Taylor joined in Madison's efforts during the 1790s to organize the Republican opposition to Hamilton, he and other agrarian Republicans did not simply wish to replace the Federalist administration. They opposed a strong national government and blamed the Constitution for allowing Hamilton's success. Taylor wrote that "the public good, in the hands of two parties nearly poised as to numbers, must be extremely perilous."[6] The concomitant conflict between parties and interest groups would divide America and lead to disunion. Americans must return to those who represented the whole.

A concern for upholding state rights was at the heart of Taylor's political thinking and runs through all of his writing, including *Tyranny Unmasked.* Taylor was an advocate of state rights, first, as an end in itself—in each state, Americans made up a single people and should be allowed to legislate for themselves in internal matters. The closer the exercise of power was to the citizen body at the local level, the more it could be trusted. Second, he believed state rights served as a means to watch and restrict the federal government, keeping it constrained and weak. A state could act as a buffer between its citizens and the federal government.[7]

In Taylor's view, states should function in the federal system like

5. Taylor, *An Enquiry into the Principles and Tendency of Certain Public Measures* (Philadelphia: Thomas Dobson, 1794); Lance Banning, *The Jeffersonian Persuasion: Evolution of a Party Ideology* (Ithaca, NY: Cornell University Press, 1978). Banning states that Taylor's 1790s pamphlets established him as "the most interesting and important Republican publicist" at the time, provided historians with "the most important source for an understanding of Republican thought," and they also "reveal more obviously than any other the Republicans' debt to English opposition thought," 192–3.

6. Taylor, *A Definition of Parties: Or the Political Effects of the Paper System Considered* (Philadelphia: Francis Bailey, 1794), 2–3.

7. Taylor, *New Views of the Constitution of the United States* (Washington: Way and Gideon, 1823).

Parliament functioned in the British system, acting to protect itself, the people, and the constitution against Stuart kings. The British had not resisted their government, but had used one part of government, Parliament, to oppose another, the Crown. Parliament was the traditional institution where grievances could be heard, petitions could be made to the king, and resolutions of protest could be drafted. That was the role that the lower houses of the thirteen colonies performed. State righters drew upon this tradition of going through the states to counter the federal government.[8]

As an active politician, Taylor made his greatest contribution in the service of state rights: he presented the Virginia Resolutions of 1798 and led the Republicans in the Virginia legislature as they sought to rally the opposition to the Federalists. The Republicans charged that the Sedition Act violated the First Amendment by imposing a censorship on the press. Federalists responded that its purpose was not to prevent publication but to punish publications libeling the government. This was in the Anglo-American common law tradition and—the Federalists pointed out—the Sedition Act was an improvement since truth was made a defense. Republicans answered by denying that America had a federal common law. They held that the English common law had been brought to the colonies and then was modified by statute, first by the colonial, and then by the state, legislatures. There were, accordingly, as many common law systems in America as there were states.[9]

Taylor believed that the Federalists were using the Sedition Act to expand centralized power, which would subvert individual liberty. He

8. John M. Murrin, "The Great Inversion, Or Court Versus Country: A Comparison of the Revolution Settlements in England (1688–1721) and America (1776–1816)," in *Three British Revolutions: 1641, 1688, 1776*, ed. J. G. A. Pocock (Princeton: Princeton University Press, 1980).

9. See the speeches of Taylor in *The Virginia Report of 1799–1800, Touching the Alien and Sedition Laws, Together with the Virginia Resolutions of December 21, 1798, Including the Debate and Proceedings Thereon in the House of Delegates of Virginia* . . . (1850; reprint, New York: Da Capo Press, 1970), 24–29, 111–22.

warned that "one usurpation begat another."[10] The states granted certain power to the federal government and, he argued, if the federal government acted unconstitutionally and tyrannically, the states and the people must act to check the concentration of power. He believed disunion was better than oppression. Taylor told his fellow Virginians that liberty was their country and they must be ready to protect it.[11] His later works, especially *Tyranny Unmasked*, were efforts to further identify the tyrant.

In the 1800 election, Taylor and other Republicans who had taken a Country opposition stand could hope that they had been victorious. Yet, although Jefferson spoke of reforming Federalist abuses and of reducing the size of the government, he also took a moderate course between the Federalists and the extreme wing of his own party. None of the acts establishing the Hamiltonian system was repealed. Taylor saw the refusal by the Jefferson and Madison administrations to advance the "revolution of 1800" as a betrayal. The Republican party continued to gain support, but Taylor believed republican principles had been abandoned. He wrote that an "adherence to men, is often disloyalty to principles." Taylor and others who continued in the tradition of the Country republican ideology, now calling themselves the "Old Republicans," believed that those who were attracted to power—"majority men" tended always to become corrupt and to abuse the trust and betray the best interests of the people. For this tendency, they had to be watched by "minority men."[12]

In 1820, after the Marshall Court's opinions in *Martin v. Hunter's Lessee* and *McCulloch v. Maryland*, Taylor attacked the Court's broad construction of the Constitution in *Construction Construed, and Constitutions Vindicated*. He described two kinds of constitutional construction: one to maintain principled government and the other to corrupt

10. Ibid., p. 25. Taylor was so infuriated by the Alien and Sedition Acts and the Federalist defense of them that he advocated secession. See Jefferson to Taylor, 1 June 1798, in *The Writings of Thomas Jefferson*, ed. Andrew A. Lipscomb (Washington: The Thomas Jefferson Memorial Association of the United States, 1903–1904), 10:44–47.

11. *The Virginia Report*, 24–29, 111–22.

12. Taylor, *A Pamphlet*, quote from 12.

government. He believed the latter was used by those in power to extend that power and the founders never intended "this pernicious species of construction."[13] He felt that the Supreme Court used a broad construction to assert its supremacy over Constitutional interpretation and over state courts. Because state and federal courts were separate, he felt state courts should also interpret the Constitution. Taylor wrote that constitutional uniformity was not necessary. Separate constitutional opinions would preserve liberty and keep "our system for dividing, limiting, and checking power."[14]

As he went on to explain in *Tyranny Unmasked*, the Constitution was of value only to keep the federal government operating in accord with what Taylor called the principles of 1776 or 1798. "We need only recollect that the intention and end of the constitution was to 'secure the blessings of liberty to ourselves and our posterity.' "[15] For Taylor, the Constitution was of worth only if it could serve the more fundamental cause of liberty: "the real design of the constitution."[16] The adherence to principle was what he meant by "constitutional."

In *Tyranny Unmasked* and in his other political treatises, Taylor rejected the argument that the majority of the American nation could impose its will upon any minority in order to achieve what was asserted to be in the general welfare. Since Taylor believed there was no American people, only a union of states, majority rule in Congress was irrelevant where it did not have the authority to act. The Constitution gave the federal government certain specified powers and it could not move beyond them. More to the point, Taylor would not bow to majority rule when it compromised principles of government. He thought governmental acts in violation of principle, even if sanctioned by a construction of the Constitution, were tyrannical. If advocated by a majority in Congress, it was a tyranny of the majority.

Taylor opposed those who advocated the expansion of national power and demanded banks and tariffs. Earlier, these included Hamil-

13. Taylor, *Construction Construed, and Constitutions Vindicated* (Richmond: Shepherd and Pollard, 1820), 22.

14. Ibid., 144.

15. Taylor, *Tyranny Unmasked*, 100.

16. Ibid., 102.

ton and the Federalists and later, the politicians of the Era of Good Feelings and 1820s who eventually became Whigs. As Taylor saw it, they sought to bring the British system to America, along with its national debt, political corruption, and Court party—which Taylor called the new "monied aristocracy."

Along with watching and trying to check nationalism and unlimited power, Taylor opposed the advocates of mercantilist economics. He best stated his perspective in 1818 in his grand agrarian treatise, *Arator*, in which he discussed a distinction between real and artificial wealth. Farmers could exist without government, and thus produced real wealth, but governments, new laws, and charters were needed to establish the professions of lawyers, judges, politicians, and bankers. These dependents produced artificial, or paper, wealth.

Taylor criticized financial gains realized at the expense of agriculture. Through taxation and tariffs, real landed wealth paid for the extravagance at Court. The Country grew poorer while the Court grew richer. For Taylor and the Old Republicans, independent farmers were fighting for liberty, opposing dependent, city-dwelling, immoral, and corrupt parasites who lived off the farmers' hard work.[17]

Having begun his career as a polemicist in 1794 by denouncing Hamiltonianism, Taylor, by 1822, when he published *Tyranny Unmasked*, believed little had changed. There was still a group of Northerners determined to use the federal government to bring about its economic goals. Its means were national banks, internal improvements, and tariffs—the last of which was the specific issue addressed in *Tyranny Unmasked*.

Taylor argued that tariffs used to build industry would raise prices, which would hurt farmers. Although developing domestic industry initially would increase demand for domestic food production, Taylor believed that agriculture eventually would decline as a result. By restricting the flow of imports, tariffs would also hurt international trade.

17. Taylor, *Arator, Being a Series of Agricultural Essays, Practical and Political* (1818; reprint, Indianapolis: Liberty Fund, 1977). See "The Rights of Agriculture," "Agriculture and the Militia," and the essays on "The Political State of Agriculture."

Further, he believed that the difference between the natural price and the artificial price caused by the tariff amounted to a tax. And he considered the federal government's taxing of agricultural regions in order to subsidize industry a violation of principle—and robbery.

Taylor has been portrayed as a pastoral, nostalgic dreamer, who fabricated a romantic, agrarian past that had never existed. He has been described as an idealist rather than a practical man, who, like other Anti-Federalists and Old Republicans, had never been in power and therefore, knew nothing of actually administering a government.[18]

Many of the Anti-Federalists and Old Republicans had known government first hand, though, having administered power at state and local levels. Drawn from the gentry in Southern states, their politics was influential in county courthouses and state legislatures. Their number included county justices of the peace, state legislators, governors, judges, and Congressmen—in Taylor's Virginia, such men as William Branch Giles, Patrick Henry, James Monroe, Edmund Pendleton, and Spencer Roane. Their experience had taught them to believe that governments did not have to be large and powerful. They held that county governments were good examples, being so small and weak that they offered little inducement for or reward from corruption. In contrast, they thought the more distant and more powerful a government, the greater chance of corruption. As Taylor stated repeatedly in his works, he would not trust written constitutions and checks and balances to prevent corruption. Great power should never be granted in the first place.[19]

Taylor's virtue was in the negative, in what he opposed. He devoted his life to protecting liberty and did not trust those who advocated the ideals of equality and freedom or who promised empire and prosperity. He took a strong stand against government expansion and corruption,

18. Most representative of this view is Robert E. Shalhope, *John Taylor of Caroline: Pastoral Republican* (Columbia: University of South Carolina Press, 1980).

19. Taylor, *News Views* and *An Inquiry into the Principles and Policy of the Government of the United States* (1814; reprint, New Haven: Yale University Press, 1950).

but he was likewise hostile to attempts to reform society through the use of government, from extending the suffrage to the abolition of slavery. In his polemics, he questioned the kind of society and economy desired in the American republic. In *Tyranny Unmasked*, he attacked the economics of mercantilism, preferring to continue with either agrarian republicanism or classical capitalism. If the national government compromised the Constitution, subverted state rights, and sacrificed individual rights and the interests of whole portions of the population, he wondered whether the form of a republic was retained without the substance.

In *Tyranny Unmasked*, Taylor was attacking a 15 January 1821 report of the Congressional Committee of Manufactures calling for tariffs to help expand industry. He also used this critique of the proposed tariff to discuss other threats to the republic posed by the friends of the tariff, to show the "real design of the protection duty, and all other exclusive privileges."[20]

While *Tyranny Unmasked* is not divided into chapters, it does have three clear sections. In the first section, Taylor makes a general attack upon the protective tariff policy and its advocates; in the second section, analyzed under nine headings, he summarizes his arguments against tariffs; and, in the third section, he takes up a general discussion of tyranny.

In the first section, he looks at tariffs from several perspectives, using analogies, examples from history, points of analysis, and counter arguments to reveal the ulterior motives behind his opponents' claims, which he portrays as sham and rhetoric. Taylor seeks to show that a coalition of political and economic interests used idealistic phrases such as the "general welfare" while intending to rob the country and extend its power and increase its wealth.

His style is polemical. His language, full of scorn and ridicule. He wished to counter politicians who said to their constituents: "We will gratify your avarice if you gratify our ambition." He feared what would

20. Taylor, *Tyranny Unmasked*, 55.

result if the "tribes of patrons and clients" would "unite their talents."[21] Taylor was greatly disturbed by the rhetorical mask used to cover the evils he saw being committed. His purpose was to reveal what was behind the mask: "Form is the shadow, but measures are the substance."[22]

Taylor saw certain measures of government leading to tyranny. At the heart of democratic politics a political science is developing that would teach the arts of deceiving the public. These arts "constitute the science of modern civilized tyranny."[23] Ideas such as "divine right" and "parliamentary supremacy" have been replaced by "general welfare" and "federal supremacy." Taylor writes that "tyranny is wonderfully ingenious in the art of inventing specious phrases to spread over its nefarious designs."[24]

In the second section, Taylor looks at the tariff's major consequences. A protective tariff would violate the Constitution, restrict the economy rather than expand it, and reduce the federal government's customs duties revenue because it would decrease the volume of imports. Tariff wars hurt international commerce. America had prospered through two centuries of foreign trade, but protective tariffs would seriously damage that trade. Government assistance for industry would hurt merchants, craftsmen, household manufactures, and—worst of all, for Taylor—farmers. Only the manufacturing interests—the owners of the factories and their financial backers—would gain.

A note of explanation is needed for Taylor's use in *Tyranny Unmasked* of the term "capitalists" to describe his opponents. When he began writing in the 1790s, he was more likely to use the phrase "monied aristocracy" to describe his enemies. Thirty years later, he believed the Constitution, Hamilton, Federalists, and Republican party moderation and compromise had allowed an aristocracy of wealth to rise in America. In America, instead of titled nobles, the lords were

21. Ibid., 49, 71.
22. Ibid., 9.
23. Ibid., 71.
24. Ibid., 78.

financiers. Instead of members of the House of Lords, they were the stockholders of the Bank of the United States. By the writing of *Tyranny Unmasked*, Taylor was using the more economic-sounding term, "capitalists," to refer to these aristocrats. But, he was not opposed to capitalism, and he often cited Adam Smith and capitalist economists in his works, including this one. Like Adam Smith, Taylor opposed government intervention in the economy and wanted a natural economy, a free market system. Taylor opposed those capitalists who were not satisfied with natural economics and who sought to benefit through government intervention. He described his opponents more precisely when he used such phrases as "manufacturing capitalists" or "protective-duty capitalists."

There was, however, a major aspect of capitalism that Taylor rejected. He would not condone the potential pluralism of the capitalist, liberal, or free market theory: an America consisting of competing interests. For Taylor, the only good interest was natural and productive, and, in America, where the vast majority were farmers, that was agriculture, which should remain predominant. He was an agrarian first and foremost; he was a capitalist as long as most capital was going into agriculture.[25] He believed there were fundamental principles in economics just as in politics. "Among these principles," he writes in *Tyranny Unmasked*, "the most important is, that land is the only, or at least the most permanent source of profit; and its successful cultivation the best encourager of all other occupations, and the best security for national prosperity."[26]

In the third section of *Tyranny Unmasked*, Taylor discusses tyranny, generally, and specifically the choice confronting Americans. What could preserve liberty? A balance of federal power could not do so, for the power of the parts combined could expand to overwhelming extent. The people as a whole could not serve as the main check because, despite the elections, politicians could still expand their power. And, certainly, the Supreme Court could not preserve liberty, for it was

---

25. Steven Watts, *The Republic Reborn: War and the Making of Liberal America, 1790–1820* (Baltimore: The Johns Hopkins University Press, 1987), pp. 16–28.

26. Taylor, *Tyranny Unmasked*, 157.

biased, being a party (as a part of the federal government) in any constitutional dispute between the federal and state governments. Assertive state rights were necessary to preserve liberty.

Taylor writes that Americans had to choose between federalism and a division of power or a consolidated national power; between small and weak government or large and powerful government; and between inexpensive government with low taxes or extravagant government with high taxes. Would America have a government that preserved the value of the labor of the productive members of society, he asks, or one that valued only the support of its "parasites and partisans"? Would the government preserve individual property or would it transfer property to a privileged aristocracy? Could a country have a clearer choice? Americans could pursue either of two kinds of politics and economics, one that maintained liberty and one that led to tyranny.

Taylor was more of a pamphleteer than a legislator, but, still, he represented constituents who supported state rights, local government, and the interests of the gentry. He matured while the American Patriots were taking their stand against the British and saw that pamphleteers helped rally Americans to the cause. He was a leading pamphleteer during the 1790s for the opposition that defeated the Federalists. He wrote his treatises against Federalists, nationalism, and the Marshall Court while Virginia renewed its interposition against the federal government. By 1820, he was at his height of popularity among his fellow Virginians and one of the chief architects of Virginia's state sovereignty doctrine.[27] Many Virginians would draw on his ideas as they defended state rights and countered nationalism. His ideas remained viable into the Jacksonian era and became part of the Southern state rights ideology. His critique of tariffs would be repeated by John C. Calhoun and the South Carolina nullifiers and by Southern Democrats to the Civil War.

The influence of Taylor's ideas should not be undervalued because

27. F. Thornton Miller, "John Marshall Versus Spencer Roane: A Reevaluation of *Martin* v. *Hunter's Lessee,*" *The Virginia Magazine of History and Biography* 96 (1988): 297–314.

they did not prevail in the end. As he wrote *Tyranny Unmasked,* he had good reason for hope. America did not have to use government subsidies to become industrialized. It is easily forgotten that another America existed prior to the Civil War. As Taylor had pointed out, America had had another choice. What Taylor feared was the America after 1860; the high protective tariffs, the vast industrial and urban expansion, and all the problems that confronted Americans during the late nineteenth century. He had alerted his constituency to the dangers he saw coming from industrialization and urbanization. Taylor had held up an alternative: America could have refused to become another Britain and, instead, have remained an agrarian republic.

Most of Taylor's world is gone. But, with the continued increase of the power of the federal government and the pursuit of policies that benefit specific constituencies, the principles set out in *Tyranny Unmasked* are as relevant today as they were in 1822. Taylor admonished us to watch government, to inform the people when it encroached upon liberty and rights, and, like him, to be ready to unmask the tyrant for the public to see.

A Note on the Text

The text used for this edition is the first edition of *Tyranny Unmasked,* published in Washington in 1822 by Davis and Force. I have silently corrected the few typographical errors. The footnotes are mine. The typography has been modernized completely, while the spelling has been modernized only slightly.

F. Thornton Miller
Southwest Missouri State University

SELECTED BIBLIOGRAPHY

Abernethy, Thomas Perkins. *The South in the New Nation, 1789–1819.* Baton Rouge: Louisiana State University Press, 1961.

Appleby, Joyce. *Capitalism and a New Social Order: The Republican Vision of the 1790s.* New York: New York University Press, 1984.

Banning, Lance. *The Jeffersonian Persuasion: Evolution of a Party Ideology.* Ithaca, NY: Cornell University Press, 1978.

Bradford, M. E. Introduction to *Arator, Being a Series of Agricultural Essays, Practical and Political,* by John Taylor. Petersburg, VA: Whitworth and Yancey, 1818. Reprint, edited by M. E. Bradford. Indianapolis: Liberty Fund, 1977.

Cunningham, Noble E, Jr. *The Jeffersonian Republicans: The Formation of Party Organization, 1789–1801.* Chapel Hill: University of North Carolina Press, 1957.

Dauer, Manning J., and Hammond, Hans. "John Taylor: Democrat or Aristocrat?" *The Journal of Politics* 6 (1944):381–403.

Ellis, Richard E. "The Persistence of Antifederalism after 1789." In *Beyond Confederation: Origins of the Constitution and American National Identity,* edited by Richard Beeman, Stephen Botein, and Edward C. Carter. Chapel Hill: University of North Carolina Press, 1987: 295–314.

Hill, C. William, Jr. *The Political Theory of John Taylor of Caroline.* Cranbury, NJ: Associated University Presses, Inc., 1977.

Howe, Daniel Walker. "Virtue and Commerce in Jeffersonian America." *Reviews in American History* 9 (1981):347–53.

Jordan, Daniel P. *Political Leadership in Jefferson's Virginia.* Charlottesville: University Press of Virginia, 1983.

Kenyon, Cecelia M. "Men of Little Faith: The Anti-Federalists on the Nature of Representative Government." *William and Mary Quarterly.* 3d ser., vol. 12 (1955):3–43.

Kirk, Russell. *John Randolph of Roanoke: A Study in American Politics.* 1951. Reprint. Indianapolis: Liberty Fund, 1978.

Macleod, Duncan. "The Political Economy of John Taylor of Caroline." *Journal of American Studies* 14 (1980):387–405.

Malone, Kathryn Ruth. "The Fate of Revolutionary Republicanism in Early National Virginia." *Journal of the Early Republic* 7 (1987):27–51.

Miller, F. Thornton. "John Marshall Versus Spencer Roane: A Reevaluation of *Martin* v. *Hunter's Lessee.*" *The Virginia Magazine of History and Biography* 96 (1988): 297–314.

――――. "The Richmond Junto: The Secret All-Powerful Club—Or Myth." *The Virginia Magazine of History and Biography* 99 (1991):63–80.

Mudge, Eugene T. *The Social Philosophy of John Taylor of Caroline: A Study in Jeffersonian Democracy.* New York: Columbia Press, 1939.

Murrin, John M. "The Great Inversion, Or Court Versus Country: A Comparison of the Revolution Settlements in England (1688–1721) and America (1776–1816)." In *Three British Revolutions: 1641, 1688, 1776,* edited by J. G. A. Pocock. Princeton: Princeton University Press, 1980.

Risjord, Norman K. *The Old Republicans: Southern Conservatism in the Age of Jefferson.* New York: Columbia University Press, 1965.

Shalhope, Robert E. *John Taylor of Caroline: Pastoral Republican.* Columbia: University of South Carolina Press, 1980.

Simms, Henry. *Life of John Taylor: The Story of a Brilliant Leader in the Early Virginia State Rights School.* Richmond: William Byrd Press, 1932.

Taylor, John. *Arator, Being a Series of Agricultural Essays, Practical and Political.* Petersburg, VA: Whitworth and Yancey, 1818. Reprint, edited by M. E. Bradford. Indianapolis: Liberty Fund, 1977.

――――. *An Argument Respecting the Constitutionality of the Carriage Tax.* Richmond: Augustine Davis, 1795.

――――. *Construction Construed, and Constitutions Vindicated.* Richmond: Shepherd and Pollard, 1820.

――――. *A Definition of Parties: Or the Political Effects of the Paper System Considered.* Philadelphia: Francis Bailey, 1794.

――――. *An Enquiry into the Principles and Tendency of Certain Public Measures.* Philadelphia: Thomas Dobson, 1794.

――――. *An Inquiry into the Principles and Policy of the Government of the United States.* 1814. Reprint. New Haven: Yale University Press, 1950.

———— . "Letters." In *John P. Branch Historical Papers of Randolph-Macon College*, edited by William E. Dodd, vol. 2 (1908):253–353.

———— . *New Views of the Constitution of the United States.* Washington: Way & Gideon, 1823.

———— . *A Pamphlet Containing a Series of Letters.* Richmond: E. C. Stanard, 1809.

Watts, Steven. *The Republic Reborn: War and the Making of Liberal America, 1790–1820.* Baltimore: The Johns Hopkins University Press, 1987.

PREFACE TO THE FIRST EDITION

Most political writers have concluded, that a republican govern-ment, over a very large territory, cannot exist; and as this opinion is sustained by alarming proofs, and weighty authorities, it is entitled to much respect, and serious consideration. All extensive territories in past times, and all in the present age, except those of the United States, have been, or are, subject to monarchies. As the Roman territory increased, republican principles were corrupted; and an absolute mon-archy was established long before the republican phraseology was abol-ished. Recently, the failure of a consolidated republican government in France, may probably have been accelerated or caused by the extent of her territory, and the additions she made to it. Shall we profit by so many examples and authorities, or rashly reject them? If they only furnish us with the probability, that a consolidated republic cannot long exist over a great territory, they forcibly admonish us to be very careful of our confederation of republics. By this form of government, a remedy is provided to meet the cloud of facts which have convinced political writers, that a consolidated republic over a vast country, was impracticable; by repeating, an attempt hitherto unsuccessful, we defy their weight, and deride their admonition. I believe that a loss of indepen-dent internal power by our confederated States, and an acquisition of supreme power by the Federal department, or by any branch of it, will substantially establish a consolidated republic over all the territories of the United States, though a federal phraseology might still remain; that this consolidation would introduce a monarchy; and that the monarchy, however limited, checked, or balanced, would finally become a complete tyranny. This opinion is urged as the reason for the title of the following treatise. If it is just, the title needs no apology; and a conviction that it is so, at least excuses what that conviction dictated.

From the materials for bringing into consideration this important subject, I have chiefly selected the report of a Committee of Congress upon the protecting-duty policy, for examination; as containing doctrines leading to the issue I deprecate, and likely to terminate in a tyrannical government. In justice, however, to the gentlemen who composed this Committee, and not merely from civility, it is right to say, that I do not believe they imagined their doctrines would have any such consequence. But as I differ from them in this opinion, there can be no good objection against submitting to public consideration, the reasons which have caused that difference.

In doing so, the idea of any compromise with the protecting-duty policy is renounced, because it appears to me to be contrary to the principles of our government; to those necessary for the preservation of civil liberty under any form of government; to true political economy; and to the prosperity of the United States. The evils of the protecting-duty policy, may undoubtedly be graduated by compromises, like those of every other species of tyranny; but the folly of letting in some tyranny to avoid more, has in all ages been fatal to liberty. A succession of wedges, though apparently small, finally splits the strongest timber. I have, therefore, adverted to other innovations, in order to show, that such wedges are sufficiently numerous, to induce the public to consider their effects.

The selection of the report on protecting duties for particular examination, gives to this treatise a controversial complexion, but I hope the reader will perceive, that such is only its superficial aspect; and that its true design is to examine general principles in relation to commerce, political economy, and a free government. The report contained many positions, which served as illustrations of general principles, and the application of principles to special cases, would cause them to be better understood. Many doctrines for this application are extracted from the report, because it afforded them more abundantly than any other state paper; but other political innovations are adverted to, for the purpose of exhibiting, in a connected view, the tendency of the combined assemblage.

Several objections against my undertaking this task presented themselves. The subject may be thought to have been exhausted by the admirable essays and speeches which have appeared. To avoid this objection, I have laboured to place the several questions treated of in new lights. But was not the undertaking too arduous for a head frosted over by almost seventy winters? Did it not require the animation of youth, and maturity combined, and the excitement of a hope to participate in the good it might produce? I confess that the experience of age is not a complete compensation for its coldness, but yet its independence of hope and fear, is some atonement for its want of spirit. The finest talents in the meridian of life, too often shine like the sun, upon the just and the unjust. But here the comparison fails. The rays of human genius are frequently sent forth to invigorate bad principles, that they may reflect wealth and power to those who shed them. Whereas old age, having passed beyond these temptations, is nearly independent of selfish motives, and is almost forced to be actuated by philosophical convictions. But may it not retain its prejudices? May not agricultural habits have inspired a partiality for the agricultural occupation, and obscured the importance of others? The reader must judge whether a partial preference, or an equal freedom among all occupations, is advocated in this treatise. This objection is, however, removed by recollecting, that the advocates of the protecting-duty policy, pretend that the encouragement of agriculture is their object. Both of us therefore having the same intention, it is no objection to me, that I am also its friend. The only question is, whether their arguments or mine will best advance the end, which both profess to have in view; to determine which, those on both sides ought to be considered. We are not rivals courting the same mistress; and only doctors, prescribing means for the recovery of her health, and the improvement of her beauty.

But the strongest objection remains; want of ability. Neither experience, nor integrity, nor independence of fear and hope, nor the indulgence of the reader, will remove it. Yet some extenuation of a presumption which is acknowledged, and an incapacity which is regretted, may be found in the considerations, that the treatise endeavours to suggest new views of the subjects which it contemplates, without venturing to repeat the arguments of abler writers; and that it may possibly have the effect of inducing those better qualified, to extend their inquiries. This is its chief hope, and its utmost arrogance. As to its style, it is dictated by a wish to be understood by every reader. The writer has not an ability to angle for fame with the bait of periods; nor a motive for consulting a temporary taste, by a dish of perfumes.

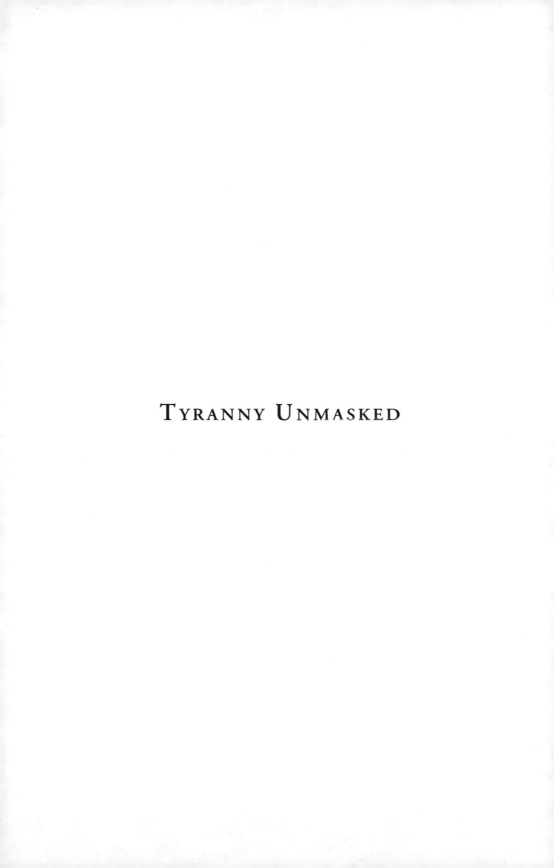

TYRANNY UNMASKED

❦

Unmasking the Protecting-Tariff Policy and Its Advocates from Many Perspectives

G ood maxims are often worshiped with pretended devotion, and clothed with the splendours of eloquence, when their subversion is meditated; like white heifers whose horns were tipped with gold, and adorned with ribbons, preparatory to their being sacrificed.

The report of the Committee of Manufactures dated the 15th day of January, 1821, commences with the usual zeal which precedes innovation, and with the common eulogy of principles intended to be violated. It is like a road smoothly paved at the beginning, but terminating in rocks and precipices. It embraces a great scope of information, condenses the arguments in favour of the advocated system, and is embellished by a style, only assailable by the simplicity of truth. It is the ultimate Thule upon which the disciples of the doctrine for restricting the liberty of property, have taken their stand; and if they can be dislodged from their last fortress, no other place of refuge will remain. If the general welfare is the object of this report, it courts an examination; and if ambition, avarice, or prejudice, lurks under a painted exterior, the same welfare demands their detection: for, though the Committee is dead, its ghost may haunt us hereafter.

The Committee state—

That at the end of thirty years our debt is increased $20,000,000; that our revenue is inadequate to our expenditure in a time of peace; that the national domain is impaired, and $20,000,000 of its proceeds expended; that $35,000,000 have been drawn from the people by internal taxation, and $341,000,000 by impost, and yet the public treasury is dependent on loans; that there is no national interest which is in a healthful thriving condition; that it is not a common occurrence in peace, that the people and the government should reciprocally call on each other to relieve their distresses; that the government has been too unwise to profit by experience, especially the experience of other nations; that its policy has been adopted for war and not for peace; that other nations shun our principles of political economy and profit; that the Cortes of Spain are establishing commercial restrictions; that history does not furnish another instance of a nation relying on the importation of goods as the main and almost exclusive source of revenue; that in every other nation agriculture, manufactures, and commerce, have been deemed intimately connected, each necessary to the growth and wealth of each other, but in ours there is said to exist an hostility between them; that the true economy of individuals is to earn more than they expend, yet this is said to be bad policy for a nation; that if the debts of the country were deducted from the value of property, the nation is poorer than in 1790; that our exports have not increased in proportion to our population; that the exportation of cotton has indeed prodigiously increased, but that to sixteen States it affords no profits, except by carrying and consumption; that it furnishes no foreign market for other productions; that the currency has been reduced in three years from $110,000,000 to $45,000,000; that no calamity has visited the country, and that in the last five years of exuberant plenty, our fat kine has become lean; that an overflowing treasury indicates national prosperity; that the causes of this distress cannot be in the people, and must be in the government; that revenue cannot be permanent whilst consumption is in a consumption; that there should be no system of restriction, but one of reciprocity; that this is a free trade; that this reciprocal system of restriction has aided our commerce; that year succeeds year and our troubles increase; that no other remedy for them has been offered but an extension of the restrictive system, which the Committee propose as a forlorn hope; that the means of consumption must be in the hands of our own people, and under the control of our own government; that the flood

4

of importations has deprived currency of its occupation; that there is more specie in the United States than at any former period, but it is not currency, because it is unemployed; that the importation of foreign goods was never so great, as when our embarrassments were produced; that the importer's ledger ought to settle the question; that in the cases of bankruptcy foreign creditors appear; that we have only the miserable and ruinous circulation of a currency for remittance to foreign nations; that they hold the coin and we hear it jingle; that the excess of exports over imports is the rate of profit; that we flourished in war and are depressed in peace, because manufactures then flourished and are now depressed; that there is an animating currency where they still flourish, and scarce any where they do not, except in the cotton-growing States; that the people are groaning under a restrictive system of bounties, premiums, privileges and monopolies imposed by foreign nations; that commerce is exporting not importing, and by reversing her employment she is expatriated; that they have no predilections for foreign opinions, and are less desirous to force facts to conform to reasoning, than to apply reasoning to facts; and that they trace the true principles of political economy to the conduct and the interest of the individuals who compose the nation.

Excluding rhetorical flourishes with which the report, inspired by a *furor dogmaticus*, or a zeal for truth abounds, I have literally extracted the plain assertions upon which its conclusion is founded. In examining the medley of truth, error, and inconsistencies, from which the Committee have drawn their inferences, the alternative is to use language sufficiently strong to express my convictions, and to convey my meaning without reserve; or smoothed like treachery towards the cause I am advocating. Wherever plain truth is considered as indecorous, or it is thought necessary to mingle adulation with reasoning, a nation has prepared its mind for the catastrophe of sycophancy; yet decency as well as firmness is a duty; and freedom of opinion may, I hope, be exercised, without violating the obligations of civility.

The leading facts from which the Committee have extracted their conclusion, are unquestionably true. In thirty years the people have paid in taxes $376,000,000; the public debt has increased $20,000,000, and the public lands have produced the same amount. The Federal treasury, having received $416,000,000 in thirty years, is bankrupt, and the people are distressed. The Committee have likened national to domestick economy, and the comparison is correct. A government, like an individual is embarrassed or ruined, by expenses beyond its income. It cannot export its patronage, its exclusive privileges, and its extravagance, to foreign nations, and bring back foreign cargoes of frugality and equal laws for home consumption. The Committee have reprobated the importation of foreign necessaries, but they have quite overlooked the effects of our having largely imported a catalogue of foreign political manufactures, which are the luxuries of governments, and infinitely more injurious to nations, than the luxuries which individuals import and consume. Let our governments surrender these dear foreign political luxuries, and we shall no longer feel the distress of buying cheap foreign manufactures.

Suppose an individual to have purchased an estate for one hundred millions—about the price of our independence; to have spent $376,000,000 of its profits in thirty years, to have sold and spent $20,000,000 worth of the land itself, to have added $20,000,000 to his debts, and finding his affairs very much embarrassed by this process, to have asked in his distress, the counsel of his friends. His agricultural friend advises him to diminish his expenses and to forbear to run in debt. His mercantile friend, to supply his tenants with necessaries at the cheapest rate, that they may be able to pay their rents; his factory-capitalist friend, to give him a bounty for making spinners and weavers of these tenants; and stockjobbing[1] friend, to continue his extravagances by the aid of borrowing. What would domestick economy, the honest referee of the question, chosen by the Committee, say to these counsels? Would she prefer the speculations of pecuniary craft upon the credulity of our landlord, to the sound common sense of tillage? Would she prefer the arithmetick of the stockjobber, to that of the merchant? Whence is the money to come according to the united advice of the stockjobber and speculator to pay usury to one and bounties to the other; and also to feed the landlord's extravagance, and discharge his debts? Some of his tenants who pay rents are to be transferred to factory-capitalists, who are to receive bounties and to pay no rents. His stockjobbers must have interest and premiums. His remaining tenants

---

1. "Stockjobber" and "stockjobbing" were derogatory terms used to refer to stockbrokers and financial speculation (other than land speculation).

will be rendered less able to pay their rents, by having to support these two combinations. He cannot draw money from foreign countries to sustain his extravagance, by manufactures, because theirs must be cheaper than his own for some centuries after he is dead. Would any landlord of common sense, who had considerably diminished his debts, and enjoyed great prosperity previously to his taking the factory-speculators and stockjobbers into his service, shut his eyes upon his own experience, and persevere in surrendering his own understanding to their counsels?

It is, in fact by too much proficiency in the art of political spinning and weaving, and not by too little patronage of capitalists, that our prosperity has been lost. By spinning legislative into judicial powers; by spinning federal into local powers; and by spinning exclusive privileges out of representations created for securing equal rights, the oppressive results stated by the Committee have been produced. We can spin out debates about economy, so as to make economy itself an instrument of waste. We can weave legislative and judicial powers into one web, to exhaust time, and increase the income of the workmen. We can weave law and judgment into more durable stuff than constitutions. Our parties have not been deficient in shooting the political shuttle for weaving republican threads, into a web compounded of extravagance, patronage, heavy taxation, exclusive privileges and consolidation. They are weaving a co-ordinate, into a sovereign and absolute power. They have woven the people out of four hundred and sixteen millions in thirty years. Considering that Washington's administration worked well with three or four millions, that Adams' worked ill with ten, that Jefferson's worked admirably with six; and when this revenue was increased by commerce, accounted for the surplus by paying a large portion of the public debt, and a part of the purchase money of Louisiana; a republican party must work by very different rules, which requires twenty-five millions in time of peace for carrying on its trade. The true manufacturing system proposed by the Committee, is to extend this species of trade. It offers more money to avarice, and even urges the enormous expense already endured, as an argument for aggravating the distresses it has already produced. But the estimate of the Committee, high as it is, excludes the great sums of money out of which the people are worked by unnecessary State expenditures, and by the machinery of banking and protecting duties. These items in-cluded, and at least the enormous annual draft of sixty millions is now taken from them in the existing appreciated money. Compare this deduction from the profits of labour, with the deductions in the times of Washington, Adams, and Jefferson, and consider how it happens that both the people and the treasury are famished. Can it have resulted from any other cause, but some new political system, by which the old one has been overturned? The remedy proposed for these wonderful and seemingly inconsistent misfortunes, is no less wonderful than the misfortunes themselves. They have been caused, say the Committee, by the want of wisdom in the government, and they propose to mend the workmanship of political jacks by mechanical jinnies; and to finish the web for conveying the nation to suitors for money, instead of imitating the conduct of the wise Penelope.

Let us, say the Committee, persevere in the wise imitations by our foolish government, of other nations, by which they have acquired; hear reader!—by which these envied other nations have acquired—wealth and happiness. The prosperity of European nations, is reiterated to provoke our envy, and urged as an argument to convince our reason. Yet it is only a palpable evasion, and a delusive bait. The delusion lies in substituting the word "nations" for "governments," and the bait, in varnishing over the miseries of European nations, with the wealth of privileged classes, in order to hide the hook intended to be swallowed. "The interest of nations!" What government except our own is so constituted, as to enable a nation to pursue its own interest? If there be any such, it is time for us to adopt it, admitting the truth of the Committee's assertion, that our government has not been guided by the national interest. If no European nations are able to compel their governments to pursue the national interest, it is a naked sophistry to assume, that they have done, what they could not do. The fact is, that all the European governments are so constituted, as to be completely able to sacrifice the national interest to their own. Have we forgotten human nature? When did such an absolute power chasten governments of avarice, and convert their administrators into patriots? We ought to have had the phenomena pointed out to us, before we were desired to believe, that a political miracle had been worked in Europe, sufficient to induce us to resign our faith.

Look steadfastly at these supposed martyrs to patriotism; these self-denying political mummeries; these immolaters of avarice and ambition upon the altar of national interest. The admired government of England is compounded of a noble order; of an unequal place-hunting and place-holding representation, ready to sell their votes bought of rotten boroughs; and of an hereditary George. The government of Spain, said by the Committee to be particularly worthy of our imitation, is compounded of an equally infected representation, and an hereditary Ferdinand. That of France is of the same complexion. Ethics informs us that human nature is guided by self-interest. History proclaims in every page that governments exhibit conclusive proofs of this truth. Is it probable, that in the management of commerce (the best fund for their self-gratifications) the European governments have forgotten themselves, and remembered only the interest of the nation? If not, an inference from what is false, must be defeated by an inference from what is true, and the argument becomes a syllogism. Governments able to do so, uniformly sacrifice the national interest to their own; the European governments possess this ability; therefore they have regulated commerce with a view to advance their own interest, and not the interest of the nation. The recommended imitation is of course perfidious in exhibiting to our view European nations, actuated by national interest, instead of European governments, actuated by an insatiable lust of power and money; and in suggesting that the recommended measures are imitations of the measures of wise nations instead of oppressive governments. If we pursue these measures, whatever may be the western motives, the eastern consequences must be produced. Form is the shadow, but measures are the substance of governments; and by copying the measures of the English government, we adopt its substance. There is none which has co-extensively fostered avarice at the expense of the people, or managed commerce both foreign and domestick more successfully for this end. The Committee endeavour to allure us into this English mode of acquiring happiness, by a splendid picture of the English government; and that government can only compel the people to be as happy as the Committee propose to make us, by a great mercenary army. This wise nation must either be very foolish in compelling the government to force them to be happy by the sword, or this patriotick government must be very tyrannical, in saddling the people with a heavy unnecessary expense. The English nation, besides being awed by an army, is bribed to approve of the measures which constitute the system of their government, by the annual contributions of sixty millions of people in Asia, of vast continental and insular possessions in America, of a large territory in Africa, and of money-yielding possessions in Europe. But rich tributes from the four quarters of the globe, cannot prevent a frightful degree of pauperism, nor reimburse the people for the distresses inflicted upon them by commercial restrictions. The reason is, that these are so contrived as to destroy all the good which commerce could have produced for the mass of the people, by making it merely an instrument for taxing them, and for intercepting all the wealth and tribute it brings in, to convey both into the pockets of the government, and of the exclusively privileged allies it has created. But admitting the tributes of the English territories to be palliations of their system for regulating commerce, why should we be induced to believe their drug sweet without any such saccharine ingredients, when the English people themselves evidently abhor it. They flee to their own fleeced colonies, and even to the United States, less blessed, or less cursed, by commercial restrictions and exclusive privileges, to escape from this policy; the effect of which is, that the labours of above sixty millions of tributaries cannot enable twelve millions of Englishmen, inhabiting the finest island in the world, and unequalled in industry, perseverance, and ingenuity, to subsist comfortably.

Reasoning deduced from mismatching things to be compared, must be eminently erroneous. We ought to chasten the argument by a parallel between things of a similar nature; by comparing governments with governments, and nations with nations. An absence of similitude precludes the possibility of imitation. A free nation is not like an European government, nor an European government like a free nation. The wealth and splendour of a government, is seldom or never the wealth and splendour of a nation. Even our government cannot be likened to the British government, because it has not the foreign possessions, the tributes of which enable the British government to persevere in its system of extravagance, bounties, exclusive privileges, and oppressive taxation. The British nation would yet rebel against this system of their government if they could do so successfully; we may prevent the introduction of the same system into this country without rebellion, if we will. If the Committee are to be understood literally, as advising an imitation of the British nation, they counsel us to abandon a system which that nation would overturn except for mercenary armies. If they speak figuratively, and mean the government when they use the term "nation," they recommend an imitation of the British government by our government. The example of the British government is undoubtedly the best which has ever appeared for extracting money from the people; and commercial restrictions, both upon foreign and domestick commerce, are its most effectual means for accomplishing this object. No equal mode of enriching the party of government, and impoverishing the party of people, has ever been discovered. By classing the objects to be compared correctly, and confronting things of the same nature with each other, we get rid of the confusion produced by mismatching them; and discern that the Committee, as advocates on the side of government, reason soundly in recommending an imitation of the system adopted by the British government; because it must be admitted that no other example can be adduced, by which a government can extract as much money from the people. It would certainly exalt our government up to the British standard, and as certainly humiliate our people far below the British people, because we do not possess the foreign auxiliaries, by which they are hardly able to exist under the system recommended for our imitation.

But the Committee have endeavoured to forestall this argument by asserting "that an overflowing treasury" (the end they have in view) "indicates national prosperity." This is the chorus of all the songs uttered by those who receive such overflowings. But what painter has drawn Liberty as a mogul almost suffocated with money and jewels; or with an overflowing treasury in her lap, and scattering money and exclusive privileges with her hands? Would not a Sciolist have been ashamed of such a picture, and a Reynolds or a West have viewed it with contempt? Upon this egregious political heresy the committee have founded their system. It is a species of political irrigation which exsiccates a nation to overflow a government and exclusive privileges. Louis the fourteenth, when he bribed Charles the second and other princes, had an overflowing treasury; yet the English, with a treasury insufficient to supply the extravagancies of Charles, were happier than the French. The richest treasury in Europe was at that time united with the most miserable people, instead of being an indication of their happiness and prosperity. The Swiss Cantons are remarkable for the poverty of their treasuries, and the happiness of their people. The severity of their climate and sterility of their soil, are both compensated by the frugality of their governments; and two great natural evils are more than countervailed by one political blessing. If a poor country is made happy by this cardinal political virtue, what would be its effects in a rich one? The Committee are fond of comparisons. Let them compare the situation of Switzerland; a rugged country under a severe climate; with that of their neighbours the French and Italians, favoured with fine soils and genial latitudes. All writers unite in declaring that the happiness of the Swiss far exceeds theirs. It exists under governments aristocratical or democratical, because of the absence of those paraphernalia by which rich treasuries are surrounded. Does this comparison prove that we ought to abandon the principles by which a barren country is converted into a paradise, and adopt those by which the finest countries in the world are converted into purgatories for purging men, not of their sins, but of their money? An overflowing treasury in imperial Rome, impoverished the provinces, fed an aristocracy, corrupted the empire, and enslaved the fairest portion of the earth. That of the great Mogul, starved the people, enriched privileged orders, was a prize for Persia, and finally for England. Russia is a country of a soil and climate resembling Switzerland, associated with a rich treasury; and the government is a tyranny. The whole world proves that there is no fellowship between overflowing treasuries and the happiness of the people; and that there is an invariable concurrency between such treasuries and their oppression. They are the strongest evidence in a civilized nation of a tyrannical government. But need we travel abroad in search of this evidence? Have we not at home a proof that national distress grows so inevitably with the growth of treasuries, as to render even peace and plenty unable to withstand their blighting effects? Our short financial history faithfully recorded by the Committee, leads us from treasuries of republican frugality, to those of aristocratical opulence. If the great annual amount now drawn from the people by our governments and exclusive privileges, does not constitute an overflowing treasury, what sum of money will deserve that appellation? Have we experienced a concurrency between the happiness of the people and an overflowing treasury? The Committee have informed us that it does not exist in our case, and yet they advise us more ardently to pursue this heretical phantom. No, it is not a phantom: it is a real political Colossus, erected to overshadow and reduce to dwarfs, the comforts of the people, and the people themselves. Is not the confederation of European kings or governments, a treasonable plot against the happiness of nations? Is it not the essence of this plot to obtain overflowing treasuries, and to foster exclusive privileges, for the special purpose of sustaining the oppressions of governments? Would not our adoption of the same policy, be a tacit accession to this nefarious conspiracy? If our republican party, consumed by the rays of power, has died a natural death, may we not still hope that a new phenix will arise from its ashes, and again excite the admiration of the world by the beautiful plumage of frugality and equal laws, for increasing individual happiness; instead of towering above the people, in the European turban composed of exclusive privileges, extravagance, oppressive taxation, and an overflowing treasury.

The Committee say, "that in every other nation agriculture, manufactures and commerce, have been deemed intimately connected, but in ours there is said to exist an hostility between them." To remove an evil, we must previously discover how it has been produced. Enmities among men are produced by a clashing of interests, and the intention of republican governments is not to promote, but to prevent this clashing, by a just and equal distribution of civil or legal rights. If artificial enmities are superadded to natural, their true intention is defeated; and the very evil is aggravated, they are intended to correct. Such is the policy which has arrayed class against class in Europe, and marshaled all its nations into domestic combinations, envenomed against each other by an ardour to get or to keep the patronage of their governments. These patrons make their clients pay the enormous fees they covet. As no government can patronize one class but at the expense of others, partialities to its clients beget mutual fears, hopes, and hatreds, and bring grist to those who grind them for toll. Even brothers, whom nature makes friends, are converted into enemies by parental partialities. Will the partialities of a government between different classes promote the harmony and happiness of society? Is not their discord the universal consequence of the fraudulent power assumed by governments, of allotting to classes and individuals indigence or wealth, according to their own pleasure? Has not the English parliament been fatigued for centuries with eternal petitions, remonstrances, and lamentations from the artificial combinations it has created, or the natural classes it has favoured or oppressed, soliciting partialities, and deploring their pernicious effects? Does not the English press at this time, teem with complaints by the manufacturers, of the corn laws? What has produced our existing enmities? Are our agricultural, manu-facturing, and commercial enmities; our slave-holding and non slave-holding enmity; our banking and anti-banking enmity; our pension and bounty enmity; the enmity between frugality and extravagance; and our Federal and State enmities, natural or artificial? Do they not all proceed from an imitation of the European policy deduced from the claim of a sovereign or despotic power in governments to distribute exclusive privileges, local partialities and private property, by their own absolute will and supremacy? What then is the remedy for these crying evils? To remove or to increase their cause. The policy by which they are produced, caused for ages religious as well as civil enmities. A patronage of religious classes is yet attended in other countries with mutual hatred. Here, the removal of the cause, is proved to be the best remedy for the evil. If civil enmities, like religious, have every where attended legal partialities, the remedy is before our eyes. It is in vain to preach conciliation, if a policy, which inevitably begets division and hatred is adhered to. The justice of leaving wealth to be distributed by industry, is a sound sponsor for social harmony; whilst the injustice of compelling one class to work for another, as naturally excites rapacity and indignation, and is equally a sponsor for hostility.

The Committee inform us "that the true economy of individuals, is to earn more than they expend, yet this is said to be bad policy for a nation." The first assertion is universally known to be true; but the second is gratuitously and unfairly attributed to their adversaries, to discredit the very principle by which only the first assertion can be realized, namely, that industry should be free to save as well as to earn. Yet the two assertions combined are not devoid of edification. To get more than we spend is undoubtedly a thrifty maxim, applicable to governments and classes, as well as to nations and individuals. The Committee have illustrated its truth, by stating that the Federal government has received a very large sum of money, but that by expending more, it is reduced to the necessity of borrowing. True economy, say the Committee, consists in spending less than we get; and in lieu of this true economy, they recommend a project for making the treasury overflow by internal taxation. Yet overflowings of treasuries will increase public expenditures and taxation. Compare then the thrifty maxim applauded by the Committee, with their conclusion, and consider whether it will confirm or refute it. The government has spent more than it received; the maxim recommends an expenditure of less; and from these facts the Committee have extracted their policy for making the treasury richer, the expenditures of the government greater, the agricultural class which chiefly supplies these expenditures, poorer; and for enabling the capitalist class, which supplies none of these expenditures, to milk all other classes, which milk they sell, but never give to governments. Apply the maxim to classes. The Committee endeavour to persuade the agricultural class, that it is false as to that class, by asserting that it will be impoverished by buying cheap, and of course expending less; and that it will be enriched by buying dear, and of course expending more. There would be wonderful ingenuity in convincing both the spendthrift, and the receiver of the spoil, that the first lost nothing, and the second gained nothing. Yet the Committee have undertaken to perform both these exploits, by endeavouring to prove that the agricultural class, far from losing any thing, will be a gainer; and that the capitalist class, far from gaining any thing, must in the end sell cheaper than foreigners, and also buy dearer of the agricultural class. But, however strong the arguments of the Committee may be to prove both of these assertions, the capitalists obstinately persist in disbelieving them, and fatuitously contend for a bounty, designed only as a bait for the snare intended to overwhelm them with the double ruin of selling cheap and buying dear. The Committee have been more successful with the agricultural class than with these calculating gentlemen. A spendthrift is more convincible than one of your thrifty cautious people. If his character is compounded of vanity, ignorance, and generosity, he is exposed to flattery, cunning, and ambiguity; and the liberality of his mind is only frozen by the poverty resulting from his indiscretion. A portion of the agricultural class have credited the prophecy of a future cheapness of manufactures, and a future dearness of eatables, to be produced by violating the very maxim of thrift; whilst the capitalists unanimously disbelieve it, and eagerly prefer a bird in the hand. As to the mercantile, sea-faring, and professional classes, they have no products to carry to the visionary markets so alluring to some of the agriculturists; and being weak and defenceless, not even a prospective bonus is offered to them. The mechanical class, as I shall hereafter show, is treated still worse: only that class, strong enough to do itself justice, is complimented with being deceived. The temptation held out to the government and its satellites is proportioned to the power and perspicacity of this formidable class. More taxes, an overflowing treasury, and of course more power, to be immediately received, is offered to this class. The agricultural class is told—"you are rich, liberal, worthy, honest fellows, almost noblemen; assent to our project suggested by a great Italian artist, who either taught governments to oppress mankind, or mankind to detect the stratagems of ambition and avarice. Generous as you are, will you refuse to create a family of capitalists for the national good, by only paying double prices for your dainties and necessaries, when you will be reimbursed profusely by the pleasures of the imagination?" The argument addressed to the capitalists is short and solid. "You are to pay nothing for our project. It will double the price of your wares." And they vociferate for it. That addressed to the government is the strongest of all, "our project will beget an overflowing treasury." In this auction affair, the mercantile, mechanical, professional, and sea-faring classes are offered nothing at all, though they may remain in the vendue office, work as hard as they can, run about with errands, or make voyages in ballast.

The Committee endeavour to hide the effects of their policy to classes and individuals, by kneading up all of them into one mass called a nation; and assuming it for a truth, that the chymist *Self-Interest* cannot divide it into parts. Having created this imaginary one and indivisible being, more valuable and wonderful than the philosopher's stone, they conclude that its interest must also be one and indivisible. But as this being needs a head, without which the hands and feet would not know what to do, the Committee have made one for it, of the Federal government. The members of their political being, are supposed, like those of the human body, to have no brains; and the head of course can only know what is best for them. Could they have come up to the perfection of the model; could they have constructed a head, unable to hurt a member without hurting itself; to swell itself into a hydrocephalus, burdensome to the body; or to fatten some of its members by impoverishing others; the analogical argument might have been applicable to their imaginary political being. But until they can do this, a political head, able to advance its own power, to feed its own avarice, and to buy partizans with the property of individuals; will never resemble the heads which providence has been pleased to place on our shoulders. Why did God give brains to natural heads, if man could make a political head, better fitted to discern what will contribute to individual happiness? If a political head is better adapted for the attainment of this object, then the divine beneficence, instead of being the first of blessings, has only inflicted upon us the regret of having received a natural capacity to pursue our own good, which we are prevented from using by the interposition of political power. But, unfortunately for this policy, the artificial head must be composed of natural heads, which will retain the impressions with which they were born. They are impelled by the same self-love implanted in other heads, to pursue their own interest; and if they are invested with a power of controlling the capacity of other heads to do the same, they universally exert it for selfish ends. Slavery, either personal or political, consists only in the powers of some natural heads to dictate to others. Political liberty consists only in a government constituted to preserve, and not to defeat the natural capacity of providing for our own good. The States and the people, in constituting the Federal government, intended to reserve the use of their own heads. The States never designed to subject themselves to be partially taxed by the brains of other States; nor the people to surrender their own heads to the use of those which manage exclusive privileges.

The Committee contend that a transfer of the rights and capacities of natural heads to privileged heads, is the best mode of enforcing that true economy, by which only individuals can flourish. Individual saving is admitted to be the only true political economy. Nothing else can produce national wealth or capital, nor generally enrich individuals. A political economy which takes away individual savings by exclusive privileges, might have been exemplified, could Nero have killed his mother by the hands of mercenaries before he was born. The comparison between individual and national economy is no sooner used, and the assertion that saving constitutes the former, than the doctrine is proposed to be violated. How can an individual save by being obliged to buy dear and sell cheap? Thus compelled, he ceases to be a model for any species of national economy, unless its object is to buy dear, and sell cheap also. In one view only will the comparison apply to the project of the Committee. Individuals are compelled to buy dear of capitalists, and to sell cheap to foreign nations, in consequence of prohibiting exchanges; and thus individual and national economy are placed nearly on the same ground. The Committee however imagine, that the destruction of individual economy will beget national economy. This would be a rare anomaly indeed. But it is to be effected, say the Committee, by means of internal taxation, an overflowing treasury, and buying what we want at double prices, until we bribe capitalists to sell cheap and to buy agricultural products dear. The evils of going to war with the true principles of economy, are only proposed to last, until these speculations shall succeed; for the design is not to establish false principles of economy permanently, but only to use them until they shall beget true principles. It is only intended to extract national thrift from individual unthrift. But it is clear to my understanding, that this cannot be effected in any mode whatsoever; though it is quite easy to extract the thrift of exclusive privileges, from the unthrift of individuals.

A balance of trade is the chimerical price offered us for individual and national prosperity; those indissoluble twins, born only of individual industry. This balance itself is of the self-same parentage. In a competition for it between two nations, in one of which industry is invigorated by the freedom of buying as cheap, and selling as dear as she can; and, in the other, compelled to buy dear and to feed exclusive privileges; which competitor would gain the victory?

But it is supposed that practice in this case is at war with theory. The Committee say,

> that our exports have not increased in proportion to our population, cotton excepted, which affords little or no profit to sixteen States, and furnishes no market for other productions. That our currency has been reduced in three years from $110,000,000 to $45,000,000. That no calamity has visited the country, and yet in the last five years of exuberant plenty, our fat kine has become lean. And that the causes of this distress cannot be in the people, and must be in the government.

Neither theory nor practice disclosed these supposed symptoms of disagreement between the freedom of industry and national prosperity, for many years after we became independent; but now our exports, in proportion to population, have diminished, as taxes, exclusive privileges, and bounties have increased; or as the profits of industry applicable to its own use or consumption, have been curtailed; and yet the very causes of the deprecated consequences, are proposed to be aggravated. The first period of our political existence, was but little infected by taxation, exclusive privileges, and bounties, and the present has to struggle with a host of these machines. The first dispensed prosperity during many years of fluctuating fruitfulness; and the second, distress, during the last five years of exuberant plenty. Under the theory of leaving to industry as great a share of its profits as possible, practically enforced, the nation was prosperous; as this theory has been gradually violated, national distress has increased. But it is supposed that theory and practice, though they have travelled so many years together, have at length quarreled; and that the facts stated in the quotation are sufficient to prove it. On the contrary, these facts seem to me incontestably to establish the indissoluble connexions both between the freedom of industry and national prosperity; and also between national distress and protecting duties, bounties, exclusive privileges, and heavy taxation. Our former policy produced national happiness; the present produces national misery. Is it merely accidental that these two pair of yoke-fellows have drawn so exactly together? The Committee suppose that they have been mismatched, though they have worked in conjunction, and that industry will work better harnessed with more protecting duties, bounties, exclusive privileges, and taxes, than when she was not impeded by such trammels. But, aware of the consequence of a fair combat between speculation and fact, they expunge the existing protecting duties, bounties, exclusive privileges, and heavy taxes, from the history of our existing distress; and, as ingeniously, ascribe all the benefits produced by the freedom of industry to use its own earnings for many years, to occasional wars between foreign nations. Thus they contrive to strip the question, both of the prosperity attending the first policy, and also of the distress which followed the second. By this management, the system which produced our prosperity is artfully put out of view, and also that which has produced our distresses; and to prevent a comparison between them, by the unerring evidence of their respective effects, a comparison is drawn between war and peace, for the purpose of ascribing all the good effects of the first policy, to a war between foreign nations; and all the bad effects of that by which the first has been superseded, to the want of such a war. The result of this comparison, as admitted by the Committee, destroys their own argument. It is, that the existing policy, even when aided by peace and plenty, produces national distress. Our former policy is admitted to have been well calculated for producing national prosperity in time of war; our existing policy, for producing national distress in peace and plenty. One was then good for something, and the other worse than good for nothing, as it is not adapted for reaping advantages from foreign wars, and reaps distress from domestic peace and plenty. By getting rid, both of the merits of one and the vices of the other, and exhibiting both as virgin projects, which have hitherto produced no effects; since the effects of both are ascribed to foreign wars, or the absence of foreign wars; the Committee endeavour to free the question from the gripe of experience, and to bind it by the gossamer fibres of the imagination, and thus ingeniously avail themselves of our bias for the newly invented mode of construing constitutions; so pliant as to resist nothing, and yet so elastic, as to bound over all the restrictions of common sense. By such fanciful reasoning any facts, the freedom of industry, and local State rights, are all exposed to be manufactured into gratifications for avarice and ambition.

But the Committee would have disclosed still more ingenuity, had they suppressed more facts, and advanced fewer opinions. In also ascribing our distresses to a dimunition of bank currency, and urging it as an evidence of bad policy, they ought to have foreseen that the history of this fact was understood by the nation. We know that the plethora of bank currency was caused by the expenses of the last war, and by the influence of the banking bubble to awaken fraudulent speculations; and not by manufactures. Public expenditures and knavish designs united to produce it, and this plethora, urged by the Committee as a proof of national prosperity, was in fact one cause of national and individual distress. It tempted governments to launch into an ocean of extravagance, and individuals into an ocean of speculation, from a fraudulent hope of an increased depreciation. It produced a great number of bubbles, under the denomination of internal improvements, having the effect of enriching projectors and undertakers, and impoverishing the people. The bursting of the banking tumor left behind the sores of public extravagance, foolish public contracts, excessive taxation, and great private debts; all of which it had generated; and these are proposed to be cured, by letting them run on, and promoting a gangrene, by the new bubble of granting an enormous bounty to another set of undertakers, called capitalists.[2] The Committee say, "if the debts of the country were deducted from the value of property, the nation is poorer than in 1790." What has caused these debts? Banking, borrowing, taxing, and protecting duties. They united to increase expenses and mortgage property. Why have the Committee, in deploring our debts, concealed their origin?

During the revolutionary war, we experienced the effects of an abundant currency, united with exclusive internal manufactures. Necessity compelled us to push both to the utmost extent, and a general loathing of both experiments, induced us to resort to political frugality and a freedom of industry, and not to commercial restrictions, in search of a remedy for the national distress they had combined to produce. It was found in these principles, and was so sudden in its efficacy,

2. Taylor is referring to the vast expansion of banks and internal improvement projects during the Era of Good Feelings. The panic and depression that followed (called "the Panic of 1819") aggravated the distrust farmers felt toward banks. This was the economic context for the period during which Taylor penned his last three works, including *Tyranny Unmasked.*

that the public distresses speedily passed away like a dream. Another redundancy of paper currency, and another necessity to manufacture for ourselves, have combined to produce another state of national and individual distress, so severe as to render "our fat kine lean," but we do not resort to the policy which worked so well in peace and plenty, after the first event of the same character; and the distress continues for want of those remedies, then so successful. The Committee say, "that the causes of this distress cannot be in the people, and must be in the government." To remove the first distress, our governments used commerce, free industry, and frugality; and it was removed. Under the second, they adhere to commercial restrictions, exclusive privileges, and extravagance; and the distress continues. They admit the distress to have originated in the government and not in the people, "without either having been visited by any calamity"; but leave us to imagine the rare, if not the solitary, case in a time of peace and plenty, that it has not been caused by misdeeds, but by no deeds on the part of the government. It is utterly inconceivable how this taciturnity, this let-us-alone policy, could have so completely destroyed the usual effects of peace and plenty; but as the fact is, that our governments have been extremely loquacious in transferring its fruits from industry to idleness, there is no difficulty in discovering how they are lost. The system of commercial restrictions, bounties to bubbles, exclusive privileges, and excessive taxation, comprises the operative misdeeds which have caused the national distress, and solved the enigma, that plenty and distress are united. If the solution is true, the assertion of the Committee, so far as it supposes that the public distress has been produced by the neglect of deeds, is unfounded; and only correct in ascribing it, not to the people, but to the government.

In the same operating system, we find the cause of the decrease of our exports in proportion to population. Industry is discouraged, both by the internal spoliations inflicted upon it by governments, and also by impairing the resource of a free commerce for alleviating its losses. It is deprived of the enhanced prices produced by exchanges for imported products, and of its best customers by driving them into rival markets. It is made heartless by being subjected to the mercy of monopolists at home, and by being told that its chance for getting out of their clutch is only "a forlorn hope."

In order to discredit the national benefits arising from the great increase in the exportation of cotton, the Committee have unwarily developed their principles, and displayed their design. "Cotton," say they, "affords little or no profit to sixteen States, and furnishes no market to their productions." And what is the inference? That cotton agriculturists shall be made by law to furnish a profit to other States, and be forced to become a market for monopolies. Thus the object of making some States tributary to others is confessed; and the factory markets so dazzling to some agriculturists, turn out to be an agricultural market for capitalists, in which they will have the exclusive power of regulating prices, or weights and measures. As the protecting duty system is designed to make agricultural States profitable to capitalist factories, it must of course make all agricultural individuals, wherever situated, profitable also to them. How can this avowed object be reconciled with the pretence, that this system will be profitable to agriculturists? Can States and individuals both pay a tribute to factory monopolists, and also exact from them a greater tribute? Does not profit and loss require two parties? Thus the acknowledged intention of the protecting-duty system, is simply that of every legal fraud, however disguised, namely, to make some individuals profitable to others; and strictly accords with the tyrannical policy of making nations as profitable as possible to governments.

But the assertion of the Committee, "that cotton affords little or no profit to sixteen States, and furnishes no market for other productions," is so egregiously erroneous, that it could only have been hazarded to induce these sixteen States, to feel no sympathy for the cotton States. Supposing it to be true, it is the strongest argument imaginable, against the power and the justice of a legislation by these sixteen States, to settle a scale of internal profits to operate between the States. They constitute a majority in Congress; and are addressed by two arguments as little likely to make them legislate fairly and honestly, as can be imagined. One, that they derive no profit from the prosperity of the cotton States, whilst their industry is free; the other, that they may draw a profit from them by the factory monopoly. The assertion, however, is adverse to the known effect of the division of labour, to beget mutual markets. By creating additional skill and facility, it vastly increases necessaries, comforts, and luxuries; the exchange of which is the basis of political economy, and the sower of civilized societies. It would be superfluous to cite proofs of a fact, seen everywhere, except among savages. Will Alabama want nothing but cotton, should that State select this species of labour for its staple? Can she eat, drink, and ride her cotton? Can she manufacture it into tools, cheese, fish, rum, wine, sugar, and tea? Would it be beneficial to her to destroy the principle which produces perfection and success, by distracting her occupations? Do either the principles which recommend a division of labour, or soils, or climates, or habits, suggest the policy of making each State a jack of all trades? Is not Georgia a market for manufactures, and Rhode-Island a market for cotton, in consequence of the division of labour? If this division is highly beneficial to mankind throughout the civilized world, ought it to be impaired by making one species of labour tributary to another? In fact the profits arising from the extraordinary skill and industry of some States in raising cotton, are diffused through the States; but if such was not the case, it would not furnish an argument of more weight to justify the policy of making those States tributary to factories, than might be urged by sugar boilers to prove that the raisers of maple sugar ought to be tributary to them. The policy of making some divisions of labour tributary to others, after they have been adopted by States or individuals, is both fraudulent on account of the loss occasioned by a change of occupations; and also opens an endless field of contention and animosity.

The division of agricultural labours is visibly imposed by nature to diffuse and equalize her blessings. Seas and rivers transfuse them throughout the world, and the geography of the United States is particularly impressed with characters for that purpose. Look at the Mississippi and its waters. Do we not read in this spacious map "here are to be mutual markets?" Are not such markets already established? The cotton country purchases horses, meat, and flour of the upper States, and these receive returns in comforts which they cannot raise. Can it be for the interest of these upper States, composing I suppose a portion of the sixteen said to derive no profit from cotton, to tax the cotton agriculturists to enrich capitalist factories, and thereby impair the markets provided by nature for themselves? If the cotton States suffer a diminution of profit, it will correspondently diminish the market of the upper States; and the evil will in some degree reach every State embraced by the waters of the Mississippi, as a punishment for their having endeavoured to make a better scheme for themselves, than that formed by the Creator of the universe.

As the Mississippi States are markets for and profitable to each other, so are the Atlantick. In the latter, also, a division of labour begets mutual markets, and mutual benefits resulting from that happy principle. South-Carolina and Georgia are markets for northern corn, flour, and manufactures; and the northern States are markets for rice and cotton. The eastern States are markets for the live stock of the western. It has been more beneficial to them to raise cotton, tobacco, and bread stuff, than live stock; but as these occupations are rendered less profitable by commercial restrictions and factory monopolies, the loss will re-act upon the western States, by diminishing the capital applicable to this species of internal commerce, and compelling the eastern to raise articles, which they would otherwise buy. The division of labour, if left free, invigorates industry, increases skill, and diffuses general benefits. No State can be benefited by impairing this principle. A monopoly established to transfer the profits of labour from south to north, is a precedent for transferring such profits from the upper to the lower States on the Mississippi. In both cases the monopoly would be bestowed on rich capitalists, and be paid by poor industry. But it would not be so generally injurious to the whole Union, as the Atlantick monopoly at this time, because the effects of the latter spread far wider.

"That free local occupations dictated by climates and soils, destroy markets and mutual profits"—said by capitalists to be both false and true, for a purpose not impenetrable; is the assertion, by which we are desired to be convinced of the wisdom and justice of giving an enormous bounty to these rich gentlemen. The free exchanges of local products with foreign nations, will not produce mutual profit or benefit to the exchangers of property, and therefore the principle, in that case, is false; but the free exchanges of local products between united States will produce mutual profit or benefit, and therefore the principle is true. But it is perfectly obvious that the profit or benefit, in both cases, arises from exclusive local facilities in the production of articles to be exchanged, and therefore that the principle must be true in both cases or in neither. It is admitted to be true in the latter by the profession of the protecting policy, that it intends ultimately to restore the principle of free exchanges, and only to destroy its effects at present. As to foreign nations it endeavours to get over the truth, as to the effects of free exchanges, by the fact, that they have by their laws obstructed the free exchanges by which this happy principle is able to diffuse the most mutual profit or benefit; and yet it proposes to create greater obstructions of the same character, by domestick laws, more capable of execution, liable to fewer checks, and operating more oppressively. Let us suppose that sixteen States shall be convinced by the Committee, that they derive no benefit or profit from the cotton States, and that they possess the power of getting from them as much of both as they please. What can be a greater degree of tyranny to the cotton States? Will it not cost them more to feed the avarice of sixteen States, than that of an individual tyrant? Has the tyranny of republics over provinces or districts, which they could make subservient to their own avarice, been uniformly more or less than the tyranny of single despots? Did not the tyranny of republican Rome, in pilfering the provinces, drive the people into the arms of a military chief. With equal truth or falsehood it may also be said, that sixteen States derive no profit or benefit from raising tobacco or rice, or from prosecuting the fishery by other States, and this majority in Congress have also the power of making these, and many other local employments, subservient to their avarice. Thus a general hostility would be created among all the local divisions of labour; and their capacity to diffuse mutual profit and comfort, would be defeated. But if this policy is wise and just, as applicable to each natural division of labour, because hardly one covers a majority of the people, it is still more forcible when applied to the artificial divisions of labour. These are more personal and local, than the former. They do not supply objects of consumption more necessary nor more universal than their comrades. Each of the artificial occupations embrace only a minority in every State. Supposing that cotton planters and other cultivators of local products, ought by law to be made profitable to a majority of States, ought not the capitalists to be made profitable to a majority of the people according to the same principle? Is it not infinitely more grossly violated by making these cotton planters profitable to an inconsiderable number of capitalists, than it would be by leaving them at liberty to make the most of their product by a freedom of exchange. Capitalists are undoubtedly more local, and will be guided by an interest more exclusive, than that national interest subservient to the natural divisions of labour. How then can the general good be advanced by sacrificing the interest of this vast majority to the purpose of enriching a very small minority; by inflicting a deep wound upon all the natural divisions of labour, for the purpose of bestowing a monopoly, operating upon and impoverishing the whole of them, to create a local and exclusive class of capitalists? Such a policy is equally unfavourable to the invigorating and perfecting principle of a division of labour, whether that division is natural or artificial; and if its violation will produce evil in one case, it must do so in the other. But a trespass upon the right of free exchange, belonging to natural divisions of labour, is more pernicious to the common good, than a trespass upon the same right belonging to artificial divisions of labour, because it makes more victims. The question is, Which will produce most general good? The enjoyment of this right by all divisions of labour, natural or artificial; or the subjection of all the rest to the avarice of one, the capitalists, if theirs may be considered as a laborious occupation. Recollect, reader, that republics can be avaricious, and then seriously consider the doctrine, that sixteen of these republics have a right, under the federal constitution, to make a few other republics subservient to their own profit. What power can be more tyrannical? Where are its limits? Under it, will any minority of States be free republics, or provinces dependent on a combination of sixteen.

Let us advert to the nature of currency, in order to discern, how it is subservient to the mutual benefits diffused by a division of labour, and how it is made to destroy these benefits. It possesses two generick capacities; those of exchanging, and transferring, property. Under the first is comprised the intercourse between individuals; under the second, all payments made without receiving an equivalent in property, invariably computed in exchanges. If an individual sells his land to another, though he receives currency, he receives in fact an equivalent for his land in other property which the currency represents. But, when an individual pays money or currency to a government or to exclusive privileges, that portion of his property which the currency represents, is transferred without his receiving any equivalent in other property, and is to him an actual loss. In such payments for the support of a free government, he obtains an equivalent in social security, but not in property; and even these expenditures, though highly beneficial to him, constitute a loss of property, sustained for the preservation of the residue. But when such payments are extorted to feed either an oppressive government or exclusive privileges, they degenerate into actual tyranny, and individuals receive no equivalent either in property or in liberty. Government has been called an evil, because it requires a transfer of property; but it only becomes a tyranny by aggravating this evil without necessity.

As its degeneracy advances, more currency is required for the purpose of transferring more property from one individual to another, because in this operation it acts only periodically; annually, only for the most part in the case of governments, between the gainer and the loser of property; but more frequently, in the cases of the property, it transfers to exclusive privileges, so as to aggravate the deprivation. One portion of currency is employed in exercising its capacity of transferring property, and another in exercising its capacity of exchanging it. But as the latter portion passes with infinitely more rapidity from hand to hand in performing its occupation than the former, there is no need of an exuberant quantity of currency to fulfil this salutary end; nor can this pernicious exuberance long exist, because it must be limited by the extent of exchanges; by which the value of currency in circulation will either be raised by appreciation, or brought down by depreciation, to a level with the demand for carrying on exchanges, so as to correct the evils both of a deficiency or redundancy. Far different is the character of money or currency employed for the purpose of transferring property. Its quantity must be increased, as this occupation is increased; nor is it liable to the salutary restriction interwoven with its capacity of exchanging property, because these artificial transfers of it are subject to no limitation, so long as the people have any thing to lose. It is true that these occupations, though perfectly distinct, appear to run into each other, because currency, like Araspes the Persian, has two souls.

Its capacity to exchange property is its good soul, and its capacity to transfer property, its bad one. When its good soul prevails, it dispenses justice; under the influence of its bad one, it becomes a violator of each man's spouse, private property. Will Congress be less magnanimous than a Cyrus? Will it encourage the adulterous or the chaste soul of currency?

Even the money paid to the officers of government is a transfer of property, either transitory or permanent. So much as is used by the receiver for his current subsistence, is transitory as to himself; but the payer receives no equivalent in other property; and so much as augments the wealth of the receiver, is as permanently transferred as property can be. If a robber seizes the money of an individual, the loser receives but a poor equivalent for his loss, because the robber throws it into circulation, either in procuring subsistence, or by purchasing an estate. In like manner money paid to officers of government and to exclusive privileges is a transfer of property, having the same effects. In the case of exclusive privileges the similitude is exact, but not in the case of the officers of government, so far as exactions for their compensation are necessary for social order, of which the security of property constitutes an essential article. In this case also the similitude becomes exact, whenever these exactions exceed the legitimate object of sustaining a free government, and are gradually introducing an oppressive one. In fact, out of this distinction between the good and evil capacities of money, flow most or all of the phrases used to convey an idea, either of a good or a tyrannical government.

It is the identical distinction which constitutes the contrast between our own and the European governments, and if it is lost, I should be glad to learn what will be the real value of a mere theoretical remnant. The distress of England at this juncture is at least equal to ours. It provokes a much greater degree of national disquietude. The distress of Ireland far exceeds ours. This foreign distress has not found a remedy in manufactures and exclusive privileges. To obtain it by the same policy, we must therefore push it further than the English have done. As the cause of the evils under which England and Ireland are groaning, cannot lie in a want of the advocated policy, it is only to be found in its existence. It undoubtedly lies in the encouragement given by the government to the bad soul of money. Its wicked capacity of transferring property is patronized by a multitude of laws, for enriching the officers of government, privileged combinations, projectors, pensioners, and sinecures, beyond the limits prescribed by social considerations. Thus the effects of the good soul of money are nearly suffocated, and the predominance of its bad soul dispenses the mischiefs to be expected from an evil spirit.

If we cannot ascertain the extent in which we have cultivated the capacity of currency to transfer property, because it is impossible to discover how much has been transferred by its depreciation, we can yet compute it with considerable accuracy, so far as this capacity is exercised by taxation, State and Federal, by dividends paid to bankers, and by bounties paid to capitalists. These united cannot amount to less than sixty millions of dollars annually, and as this enormous sum of money transfers every year the property it represents, we need not wander any further in search of a cause for the public distress. As it represents and transfers twice, or perhaps thrice, as much property as it did a few years past, the distress which has awakened the compassion of the Committee, was unavoidable; but they propose to alleviate it by pushing still further the policy of transferring property. They say we have but forty-five millions of currency. If such be the fact, what must be the consequences of laws compelling these forty-five millions to transfer, annually, sixty millions worth of property, and also to perform the whole business of facilitating exchanges. The first duty being imperative, in its present magnitude, must chiefly employ the supposed quantity of currency, and leave but little of it to be employed in the second; so that the great increase in the efficacy of money or currency to transfer property, unites with the insufficiency of the amount applicable to facilitating exchanges, brought about by the enormous sum absorbed in its pernicious employment, to produce the present state of things.

A permanent increase of currency can only be effected by employment for it in exchanging or transferring property, but its increase for one or the other object, produces very different consequences to a nation. When currency is increased by a demand for it to facilitate exchanges, it indicates national prosperity; but when it is increased for the purpose of transferring property, it is an infallible proof of fraud and oppression. The operations of currency in exchanging and transferring property are so interwoven, that it is easy to delude the people into an opinion, that the former and not the latter design is at the bottom of its legal augmentation; and debtors are bribed by a hope of depreciation, to mortgage the remnant of their property, with themselves and their posterity, to the property-transferring policy. When currency is increased, as in the case of banking, for the primary object of transferring property, a temporary depreciation ensues, which robs once by this means, and again by appreciation. Upon either alternation, however frequently they occur, injustice is perpetrated. But the effect of either between individuals is moderate and shortlived, because the demand of currency to be employed in exchanges will regulate its value; and in making such exchanges it will be computed by its representative relation to property. An increase of currency, for the purpose of transferring property, contains no such internal remedy against the evils of excess. Governments and exclusive privileges increase their exactions at least comparatively, and usually take care that their compensations shall exceed a temporary depreciation. When it ceases, or appreciation happens, the transfer of property from the people to themselves, commenced by increasing currency under the pretext of facilitating exchanges, is aggravated without any new law; and the numerical acquisitions are doubled or trebled in value, merely by saying nothing. When wheat was worth two dollars a bushel, sixty millions of dollars would transfer property equal to thirty millions of bushels of wheat; but when wheat is reduced to one third of that price, the same sixty millions transfers property equal to one hundred and eighty millions of bushels. Is this chasm so wide and deep, that the national distress cannot be discerned in its bottom?

The disciples of the capacity of currency for transferring property, are more ardent and skilful than those who are contented with its utility in exchanging it, because the cultivation of that capacity is their trade, in which they become perfect by practice; and because mankind have ever thought it very pleasant to get rich without industry. Hence a school appears in every country for teaching nations that taxation, stocks, and exclusive privileges, are the best guardians of their prosperity. This school is perpetually lecturing us in the newspapers and in pamphlets, with a success demonstrated in the present state of things, obtained by confounding the very different capacities of money to transfer and to exchange property; and by considering its abundance, whether created for either purpose, as equally an evidence of national prosperity. Thus it has deluded us into the error of coveting the abundance, without considering in which of its capacities it will operate. Yet in every instance, when a plentiful paper currency has been created for the purpose of transferring property, or has produced that effect, though created from considerations both honest and patriotick, evils in no degree dubious have been identified with it. The abundance of paper currency in England, far from being a dispenser of individual happiness, is a severe oppressor, because it is chiefly employed in transferring property. The abundance of our revolutionary currency, though created by patriotism, produced great distress, in its effect of transferring property. The late abundance of our bank currency caused great distress by transferring property. In all these cases we see clearly, that national distress uniformly occurs in proportion as property has been transferred. Yet the Committee propose to remove the existing national distress, proceeding from the enormous amount of property now annually transferred, by transferring still more property to capitalists, by producing an artificial demand for more currency to work in its transferring character, by increasing taxation, and by diminishing the business of its exchanging character, in excluding the importation of foreign commodities to a great extent. Suppose the importation of foreign commodities should be quite prohibited, that our revenue should be doubled, that our bounties, exclusive privileges, and public expenses should be also doubled, and that our currency should be increased up to a complete sufficiency for transferring an hundred and twenty millions worth of property annually; would this policy be an index of national prosperity, or recover the happiness of individuals?

I cannot discern upon what principle the Committee have founded their computation as to the amount of our currency, nor even what they mean by the term; and yet accuracy in both respects is indispensable, before we can draw any correct conclusion from this amount. If they mean by the term "currency," bank paper only, it is hardly possible that they could have obtained credible returns of its amount from all these institutions, unsubjected to compulsion, and influenced to secrecy by the strongest motives; and it would be equally incredible, that only forty-five millions of currency could perform the business of transferring annually sixty millions of property, and also of discharging so much of the business of facilitating exchanges, as our commercial restrictions have left for it. If they understand by the term "currency," bank paper, metallick money, funded stock, and incorporated stock, all of which possess the capacities both of transferring and exchanging property, their computation is widely erroneous. If these capacities constitute currency, that of the United States is enormously redundant at this time, for the employment of exchanging property. It consists of funded stock for old debts and new loans, of the stock of the whole family of banks, of the stock of many other corporations, of all the specie in the country, and of all the bank notes in circulation. If at some antecedent juncture a larger amount of bank notes was in circulation, it was not associated with any thing like so large an amount of stock and specie as at present. We ought to estimate every species of circulating currency capable of transferring or exchanging property, to procure a sound foundation for an argument extracted from that source; and as these stocks possess such qualities, and are transferable for such purposes, our computation would be erroneous, should they be excluded. In the case of banks, their stock or shares constitute a portion of the circulating medium, as well as their notes; and perhaps we should not deviate far from the truth, by doubling their stock, to come at the total of banking currency, made up of the items of stock and notes.

These items would, undoubtedly, far exceed one hundred millions of currency; funded stock, State and Federal, considerably exceeds another hundred millions; and the metallick currency in the country may be, probably, estimated at thirty millions. Our astonishment excited by the idea that we have only forty-five millions of currency, to transfer annually sixty millions of property, and also to perform the whole business of exchanges, now ceases; and we also discover, that an abundance of currency, far from being an evidence of national prosperity, may be the identical cause of national distress. Two hundred of our existing two hundred and thirty millions of currency, have been created or are calculated for the very purpose of transferring property;

and, though this capital also performs some share of the business of exchanging it, yet this association of the good capacity of currency with its bad one, alleged as a proof of merit, is only a cloak of fraud. Under the pretext of facilitating exchanges, the bad capacity of currency has obtained the profits of labour to a ruinous amount. The metallick currency is incarcerated, to create a necessity for a transferring currency; and extravagance and borrowing is used to increase its quantity, to carry our lands and goods to capitalists. The more of these which are intended to be transferred, the more of the transferring currency becomes necessary to facilitate the conveyance; and it has at length grown up into a monster which eats faster than five successive years of uncommon fruitfulness could furnish food; and so impoverishing, that we must either direct against him the thunderbolt of common sense, or submit to his ravages in despair. If it was true, that this monster had diminished down to the weight of forty-five millions, there might be some hope of his becoming extinct; but, as the fact is that he has already exceeded that size four- or five-fold, it behooves those whose fruits he eats to look about them, when it is proposed to make him grow still larger.

As an argument for replenishing his larder by another cut-and-come-again carcass, the Committee assert, "that we flourished in war and are depressed in peace, because manufactures then flourished and are now depressed; that there is an animating currency where they still flourish, and scarce any where they do not, except in the cotton-growing States." Manufactures then, it seems, do actually flourish somewhere in the United States, their depression notwithstanding, so wonderfully as to reflect around their orbits an animating pecuniary halo, no where discernible around any agricultural sphere, that of cotton excepted. It seems strange that wealth should attend factories in spite of oppression, and that poverty should lay hold of agriculture, though fortified by commercial restrictions. An impartial judge, from these two facts asserted by the Committee, must conclude that agriculture had already given too much of her estate to her children in some fit of morbid fondness, and that one of them must think her in her dotage, who can tell her gravely "I am rich, you are poor, therefore make me richer." Is not this the language of an ungrateful favourite,

who thinks his beneficent parent an old fool, and fit only to work or
starve. But it seems that one species of agriculture still presumes to vie
with the factories in getting money. As this is the great merit by which
the Committee sustain the claim of the factories to further bounties,
one would think that the same merit ought to have attracted the same
philanthropy to the cotton planters, because they also gain and circulate
an animating currency where they flourish. But no; this solitary agricultural interloper in the trade of growing rich, is treated as a culprit, for
doing that which acquires for a factory the character of patriotism. It
yields no profit to sixteen States, and therefore it deserves no bounty
like the factories, for making money. But this is not all. It is to be
treated as all monopolists treat those who have the presumption to
interfere with their privileges. The profits of raising cotton, far from
recommending them as objects of bounty, are considered as a trespass
upon the capitalists' privilege of exclusive accumulation; and even the
prosperity of this last item of successful agriculture, is to be assailed for
the benefit of our enormous pecuniary monopoly, because it is so local
as to yield no profit to sixteen States. It is impossible to find a more
lasting argument for transferring the profits of agriculture to capitalists,
than that they are local. Even factories may be transplanted from place
to place. Capitalists can follow their speculations. Travelling pedlars
are ambulatory. And poor agriculture, being immoveably local, ought
to be made subservient to the avarice of these pedestrians, under the
notion that cotton planters can do no good to sixteen States. But
cannot the cotton travel as well as the cloth made out of it? Cannot
the money earned by cotton and tobacco planters make its escape from
them? Whence came the enormous capitals accumulated in a few large
northern towns, if it is true, that local agricultural profits do not
promote the general prosperity?

These assertions of the Committee, however, require a graver consideration, and are calculated to bring matters to light, of which they
were either not aware, or did not perceive the force. It is freely admitted
that currency is infinitely more plentiful in several States where factories
flourish, than in those without them. It is even admitted that there is
a local redundancy of it in a few hands, so very considerable at this
juncture of its general scarcity, that it is seeking for borrowers; and that

governments and individuals can obtain loans at a lower interest and premium than at any former period. If the factories produced this redundancy, they are already, almost suffocated with wealth, drawn to them by the property-transferring policy; and it cannot contribute to the general interest that a body of capitalists, already so rich that they know not how to employ their capitals, should, by an addition to this redundant capital, be bribed to use their influence for encouraging the extravagance of government, to obtain employment for their capitals by repeated loans. It is very important to consider how the enormous and local accumulation of redundant capital has been produced; because, if the diffusion of currency will dispense more national prosperity than its monopoly, the instrumentality of the factories towards effecting the latter cannot be a merit with the nation, however grateful it may be to their owners. Let us, therefore, take a glance at the process by which this has been gradually effected, that we may at least know by what road we have travelled to get where we are, and be able to determine, with our eyes open, whether we will proceed in the same track.

The local redundancy of money, confined to a few persons, and factories, was originally produced, and has been subsequently increased, by using currency more to transfer, than to exchange property. This policy commenced with our first funding system. The sudden appreciation of revolutionary certificates above twenty-fold beyond the value at which they were bought, was a transfer of property by law, of about one hundred millions from the public to a few fortunate speculators. The local residence of Congress, the local expenditures of the war, and the local ingenuity of those who formed the funding project, had amassed these certificates in the north, and their conversion into national debt, not by the scale of value like the paper money, but numerically, suddenly created a great property-transferring capital or currency. In this acquisition, the majority in no State participated; it was bestowed on the initiated few, skilled in the secrets of legislation, and able to manage its stratagems for their own emolument. The effects of a transferring currency being thus tasted by a capitalist junto,[3] and

---

3. "Junto" was generally a derogatory term used to describe a corrupt elite in control of a local or state or the federal government.

its wealth having invested it with legislative power, it of course adverted to banking as another item of the property-transferring policy. This second mode of transferring property settled in those districts where the first had provided a capital to give it efficacy. Thus the certificate capital was made to transfer property both by interest and dividends. The new project was imitated throughout the Union, most calamitously in States unprovided with the transferring capital created by the funding system; and whilst the people in those States wherein this capital resided, lost only the regular transfers of property caused by the banking and funding systems, those States wherein capital only existed partially or not at all, sustained a vast additional loss, by an unavoidable succession of frauds and bankruptcies. Every individual of all the States not enriched by this second deluge of property-transferring currency, contributed to the wealth of the few, who were so; but the western States which held a very small share of the artificial certificate capital, suffered most, and so sorely, that some of them have been searching for a remedy with great assiduity. Ohio struck at the root of the evil by endeavouring to repel the machine for transferring property from the people to capitalists, but she is told that this is both a wise and a constitutional operation, and that she must for ever submit to it. She has only an election it is said, between transferring the property of the people to the stockholders of the bank of the United States, or to stockholders of her own creation; but for want of the resident capital created by the funding system, and as she has no means of raising up an internal capitalist sect, she cannot avail herself of this poor right of election, and must remain tributary to the existing transferring capital, residing without the State. The late war was a third source for increasing the amount of property-transferring capital or currency. The loans, premiums, and expenditures, or the permanent profit made by the war, chiefly settled, where the existing property-transferring capital or currency chiefly resided; and became a great auxiliary to this monopolizing policy. The little war with France had previously given it some impulse. But the capitalists sect, not content with these several modes for transferring property from the great body of the people of every State to itself, and whetted by previous success, has ingeniously introduced two others for effecting this object. They still roll along this policy, although its accumulation, like that of a snow-ball, has already uncovered the humble herbage to many a pinching frost. By encouraging the extravagance of governments as a basis for loans, and by protecting-duty bounties, they have at length established the European system, by which employment for their redundant capital may be provided without limitation, and property may be transferred without end. The surplus beyond the prices which would be fixed by a freedom in exchanging property, gained by the owners of factories, transfers property without any equivalent, and goes in company with the other enumerated means, to the accumulation of a property-transferring capital, and not to the increase of a property-exchanging currency. It is an accumulation of the same character with that which creates capitalists in London, and pauperism in Britain; and transfers self-government from a nation to a combination between the governing and capitalist sects. The principle of this policy in all its modifications, consists in using currency or capital by legal contrivances, to effect the end of transferring property without an equivalent. If the assertion of the Committee, "that the local factories have created an animating currency around themselves," is true, it is an unanswerable argument against transferring to them more currency to be extracted from a suffering public by protecting duties. But the fact is, that our local and personal redundancies of money are not caused by the wares manufactured at these factories, but by the several enumerated modes for accumulating property-transferring capitals, among which the bounties given to factory owners is one of great effect. It is not accidental, but unavoidable, that these factories should fall into the hands of the capitalist sect, because old contrivances for transferring property both suggest and absorb new contrivances for the same end; and it is as evidently a mistake to imagine, that the factories have created a local redundancy of currency, which in truth created them, as that new loans caused old loans. This redundancy is notoriously caused by a current of wealth constantly flowing from all states, districts, and individuals, towards the places at which the attracting transferring capital resides; and by such currents individuals are fraudulently enriched, and the people fraudulently enslaved. Whether the animating currency said to reside near to factories arises from the lucrative nature of their employments, or whether it arises from the property-transferring policy, there seems to be no reason, either for giving bounties to factories which have been able to create an animating currency for themselves, or adding to the accumulation of capitals already partially created by laws, at the expense of the great body of the nation, languishing for want of an attracting capital, or an animating currency.

The Committee say, "that we flourished in war, and are depressed in peace, because manufactures then flourished, and are now depressed"—depressed by drawing around them an animating currency. They had before asserted that the policy of the government was adapted for war and not for peace. However doubtful it may be what species of war they mean by the last assertion, it is obvious that the quotation refers to our own war with England. "We flourished in that war." Who are We? Not the people of the States generally. They were loaded with taxes, deprived of commerce, and involved in debt. Those who really flourished by the war, can only be embraced by the assertion, and with these the Committee identify themselves. The families which flourished during the war, were the contracting and capitalist families; the latter by loans and premiums, and by selling the wares of their factories at a profit of fifty or an hundred per centum. Had the great family of the people flourished, they would not have hailed peace with transport. But we flourished in war, and are depressed in peace, say the Committee. And what is the remedy which we propose as a remedy for this depression? To revive in peace the property-transferring policy which operated so delightfully in war, *that we may still flourish* as we did then. Thus the Committee have made out their assertion "that the government was adapted for war and not for peace." It is a consequence of war to transfer property, and this has been hitherto considered as one of its evils. No, say the Committee, it is a blessing: we flourished by it during the war, and therefore this effect of war ought to be still enforced in peace, that we may still flourish. The congruity of the policy of our government in war with the interest of these We, was an unavoidable national calamity, and when peace enables it to avoid this evil of war, the Committee in supposing that our government is not adapted for peace, only mean that they do not push the transferring policy quite as far as it was carried in war. The capitalist family very modestly come forward and say, "We got more property transferred to us in war than in peace, and demand that the difference should be made up to us by protecting duties." Upon the same principle they ought to require the government to waste and to borrow.

The Committee having previously eulogized an overflowing treasury (the chief feeder of the grand European policy of using currency to transfer property) observe, "that revenue cannot be permanent whilst consumption is in a consumption, and that the means of consumption must be in the hands of our own people, and under the control of our own government." Consumption is in a consumption! A pun may be true as well as pretty, but we ought not to lose sight of its moral, in contemplating its smartness. Is this hectick natural or artificial? Have the people lost their appetites, or the power of gratifying them? How can they be gratified, except by exchanging the fruits of their own labours for the fruits of the labours of others? Has not currency superseded barter, and become the medium of such exchanges? If instead of being used for this purpose, by which consumption is both encouraged and supplied, it is used to accumulate wealth for capitalists, or any other separate interest ennobled or hierarchical, must not the consumptions of the people be diminished? Suppose a law should pass for compelling the rest of a community to barter with a few capitalists hogs for hogs, or cattle for cattle, but forcing them to give two hogs, or two cows, for one. In this barter, the injustice would be seen by every one in his senses, because the case would be stripped of the obscurity produced by hiding the very same thing with the vizor of a transferring capital or currency. Compulsory exchanges of two measures of labour for one, between our capitalists or factory owners and the rest of the community, is the same case. The nation is not made richer by such exchanges of cattle and hogs, but their consumption is diminished, because those who give two hogs or cows for one, must eat less; and those who receive the two are not thereby enabled to eat double, and must of course accumulate stock instead of increasing consumptions. Such fraudulent accumulations, in fact, make nations poorer by converting the profits of labour, the only fund for sustaining consumptions, into a dead capital. They are like the iron chest of misers, which locks up, and robs money of its utility in promoting exchanges and consumptions. The annual sum, whatever may be its amount, transferred from industry to officers of government, to privileged corporations, and to receivers of bounties, beyond the expense of their individual subsistence, is transferred from the business of promoting consumption, to that of promoting accumulation. A robber might plead that he consumes some portion of what he seizes. A furious democracy, which invades private property, and scatters it among a multitude, might, with far more force, urge the plea of encouraging consumptions, than our property-transferring policy. Is there any moral difference between effecting a transfer of property by violence, or by fictitious currencies or legal privileges, except that one must be transitory and the other may be permanent. It is curious to observe that mobs and aristocracies aim at the same object by the different instruments of force and fraud, and that though brothers in principle, they are converted into deadly foes by their contest for pillage.

As the policy of transferring property has increased, the diminution of consumptions has followed. I remember when fifty times as many families drank wholesome liquors as now do, and when it was quite common to give good wine to the poor as a medicine. Many, then able to practise a charity, often extending to the preservation of life, now need the same charity themselves; but it is almost abolished by the restrictive system. In the time of one of the Edwards, a law was made in England prohibiting the common people from eating the best meats, and confining them to the most ordinary. As they were brought down to the food next to dry bread, we are nearly reduced to the drink next to common water. Do such privations increase consumptions? Pardon me ye whiskey drinkers! I do not mean to deprive you of an enjoyment as delicious when compared with water, as neck beef is when compared with cold bread, but only to assert that there is something tyrannical in "using a control of consumptions" to deprive you of the liberty of comparing whiskey with wine. But, say the Committee, "the means of consumption must be in the hands of our own people, and under the control of our own government." Never have I seen two more hostile positions coupled together. Of what value to the people are the means of consumption, if the government can control their use? One is almost a perfect idea of liberty, and the other of despotism. Can any power be more tyrannical than one which prescribes to its slaves what they shall eat, drink, or wear? Yes. A power to transfer from industry that portion of its profits by which the most agreeable gratifications can only be purchased, to the augmentation of another's capital. Before the last union, the means of consumption, and the liberty of applying those means, resided in the people of the States. Without the liberty of application, the possession of the means of consumption is entirely nugatory. Did the reservation to the States, or to the people, exclude a right essential to liberty? Certain rights were intended to be retained or surrendered to the Federal government; but it is now said to be so difficult to draw a line between these two classes of rights, that it is best to obliterate it entirely, by an unlimited power in Congress to control all our consumptions; and in virtue of this power to enable Congress to transfer our property to exclusive privileges. Is not this a cat, not of nine tails only, but of nine thousand, by which individuals and whole States, may be as well lashed as the maddest despotism can desire? And for what reason are we to bear this severe discipline? Truly, because it is inflicted by a government of our choice. But are high-minded Americans yet to learn, or can they be made to forget that every species of government, uncontrolled by constitutional checks, will become a despotism, and reduce their boasted liberties down to the standard of the rights of man (pardon me reader for using an obsolete phrase) as they exist in Europe.

Governments have universally exercised a despotic control of consumptions, sometimes from humane, but chiefly from fraudulent motives. Laws for limiting the prices of consumable articles, unattended by the desire of transferring property are of the former description; and laws for controlling consumptions, with the covert intention of transferring property, of the latter. But whether the motive by which such laws have been dictated has been good or bad, their effects have been uniformly tyrannical or pernicious. They have even sometimes created the famines they intended to prevent. The whole code of these laws is a commentary upon the policy of subjecting consumptions to the absolute control of governments, however constituted. When these laws design to provide the multitude with bread, they starve them; when they pretend to supply the multitude with money, they impoverish them.

Let us look at a few of our own transferring laws. The bounties bestowed by the General and State governments upon supposed revolutionary officers and soldiers, may probably embrace ten thousand persons, and transfer property to the amount of three millions of dollars annually. This sum alone suffices to inflict upon us the additional transferring necessity of making loans. The bounties bestowed by the exclusive privilege of banking may embrace fewer persons, and transfer annually four times as much property. The manufacturers are said to amount, with their families, to half a million of persons. If the bounty supposed to be bestowed upon this number by controlling consumptions, should be equal to the pittance necessary to relieve an old soldier, it would be enormous; if it is only five millions, annually, it would yield only ten dollars to each person, a sum insufficient to influence their industry to any sensible extent. But the fact being that the bounty goes into the pockets of the officers of the supposed five hundred thousand manufacturers, it infuses only into them a corresponding portion of excitement. A capitalist would laugh at his share of the bounty, if he only received an equal share with his workmen. He would despise the pension of even a war-worn general. He pants for the rewards of a Wellington. Contemplate then an army of five hundred thousand manufacturers, commanded by fifty or an hundred capitalist generals, dividing the bounty arising from controlling consumptions among themselves, and you will see the controlling system as it operates. The military pension list dwindles into a feather compared with it. That dies daily; this daily grows. Russia has given to us a model of this policy. A hundred square miles of land, with all the people upon it, is sometimes given to a nobleman by the government, to enable him to work some mine for the public good. His privilege only operates over this limited space, and only enables him to control the consumptions of a few thousand people to enrich himself. The Federal government, far more bountiful than an imperial despot, extends the principle of controlling consumptions over millions of square miles and millions of people, for the public good also; but the noble capitalist is, undesignedly to be sure, enriched by it. The wages of the Russian boor, being barely necessary for his subsistence, instead of increasing, diminish his consumptions; he must regulate them by his scanty stock, and not by free industry. The profits of his master are applied to accumulation. Thus also our control over consumptions will neither increase consumptions nor the revenue. Should the army of five hundred thousand manufacturers each, unexpectedly, acquire some pittance of the bounty, it would only be the means of their consuming that which those who pay it would have otherwise consumed; but whatever portion of the bounty goes to enrich the generals of this army, correspondently diminishes both consumptions and revenue.

Suppose that comfort and pleasure should both be excluded as ends of consumption, and revenue should be allowed to constitute all their value. A wise politician, though governed by this sole motive, would not have his head as well as his heart indurated, so as to diminish the enjoyments of his fellow creatures, merely to defeat his own object. As wants are the basis of consumption, he would discern at once, that obstacles to their gratification would diminish its capacity to produce revenue; and that fruition united with industry, was one of the best resources for taxation. Industry, unattended by fruition, soon flags. The comparison between the civilized and the savage man would demonstrate to him, that the multiplication of wants and enjoyments, and not their dimunition, was the ally of national wealth and an ability to pay taxes; and therefore if he only extends his views to common defence and national welfare, he will not exceed that nice limit to which revenue may be carried, without diminishing those gratifications which beget or invigorate the ability to pay. How, then, has it happened that a truth so obvious should have been so frequently violated by proscriptions to human wants, and controlling consumptions? It has entirely arisen from using the power of controlling consumptions to transfer property to exclusive privileges. When fair and honest revenue for genuine public purposes is the object of a government, it will compute how much tax the consumption will bear, without killing the want or gratification which is to pay it; but when the object is to transfer property from the public to exclusive privileges, by controlling consumptions, the computation is, not how much the revenue for public purposes may lose, but how much the exclusive privileges may gain. This latter design is obliged to admit that it will cripple revenue to-day, but then it promises to set its dislocated joints in future. It also exclaims, "that revenue cannot be permanent whilst consumption is in a consumption," whilst it is innoculating revenue with a fatal hectick, by investing the government with the power of controlling consumptions, for the purpose of enriching an exclusive privilege.

The tyranny of a power to control human gratifications; its peculiar capacity, if exercised by the Federal government, for begetting the most oppressive partialities, and destroying the rights reserved to the people or to the States; and its evident hostility to the object of revenue; suggested to the Committee a necessity for rebutting such formidable objections, by a verbal vindication of the freedom they are stabbing with a political poniard, deadly to a creature compounded of wants and sustained by consumptions. They say, "that there should be no system of restriction, but one of reciprocity. That this is a free trade. That this reciprocal system of restriction has aided our commerce. That year succeeds year, and our troubles increase." In Russia, formerly, many articles of commerce were monopolized by the emperor; at present he contents himself with a monopoly of salt, brandy, saltpetre, and gunpowder; articles internally produced. As his monopolies were diminished, commerce flourished, and the prosperity of the country increased. He yet, however, extracts a very great revenue from the four articles of monopoly retained. Our protecting-duty monopoly, less moderate than the imperial, extends to an infinite number of articles, capable of producing a much larger income, than the four with which an absolute monarch is contented. But this income is given to capitalists, instead of being applied to public use like the Russian, and exhibits the pure policy unmingled with an extenuation, which has not been able to defend the Russian from the charge of despotism. In Russia, the government gets the whole profit of the monopoly; here the government cannot even divide the spoil with the capitalists.

Supposing it to be true, "that restriction united with reciprocity begets a free trade," as the Committee assert, must not the principle be as applicable to domestick as to foreign commerce? The former affects private property, individual happiness, and national prosperity, more deeply than the latter. If a violation of reciprocity between the United States and foreign nations may impoverish or enrich one of the parties, may not a violation of the same principle, as applicable to States or to particular interests, impoverish or enrich one of the parties also? Will not a restriction upon domestick commerce enrich factory owners, and correspondently impoverish those from whom this wealth is obtained? Between nations, it is said, that one restriction may balance or compensate for another; and upon this ground only, such restrictions are justified. Between States and domestick interests, the same policy must be justified upon the same ground, or be destitute of defence. Now, where is this compensating reciprocity to be found, in the regulation of domestick commerce by the protecting-duty restrictions, without which, in the opinion of the Committee, a free trade cannot exist? Is there any equivalent, reciprocal, domestic monopoly, bestowed upon the agricultural, commercial, or any other interest, except the banking? Yes, it is replied; we give you an invisible inoperative monopoly to compensate you for our visible and active one. Only learn to weigh smoke, and you will discover a fine paper system of reciprocity, in laws for prohibiting the importation of bread stuff, cotton, tobacco, or fish. To make this system completely reciprocal, upon paper, it only remains to prohibit the importation of land.

But let us no further imagine that complete retributive justice may be accomplished. That monopolies can be so nicely balanced, as that the loss inflicted by one, will be reimbursed by the profit acquired from another; and that the system will eventuate in leaving private property exactly where it found it, without transferring a cent from States to capitalists, or from one individual to another. In short, that a perfect system of domestick reciprocity and compensation may be established by commercial domestick restrictions, and its equal and fair execution effected, so as to produce a domestick free trade by these reciprocal restrictions. What will the nation gain by it? All the States, all interests and all individuals, would only stand in the same relative situation, which they previously occupied, with a single exception, namely, the general loss incurred by a successful execution of the system itself, according to its fairest profession. There is no political system so expensive, and requiring so many public officers, as that of regulating domestic commerce by restrictions, monopolies and reciprocities, because it abounds with temptations to violate a multitude of laws; and because such violations are considered as self-defence by the sufferers, though they are called frauds by the monopolists. The total of this expense is an enormous sinecure, if the system honestly leaves property where it found it, as is promised by the doctrine of reciprocity and compensation; and is therefore a dead loss and a living oppression to the people. If this doctrine lies when it promises not to transfer private property, it is a swindler; if it speaks the truth when it promises to prevent this fraud by reciprocity and compensation, its whole effect is to expose nations to the torments and expense of being watched and controlled in all their dealings and gratifications, by an army of public officers.

But suppose that this new idea of applying the doctrine of balances to private property, should turn out to be as fallacious as the old one of applying it to political power; and that some one monopoly should be able to absorb property, by its exclusive privileges, as the king of England absorbs power by his prerogatives, like the capitalists of the same country. Do the acquisitions of property now making by pensions, banking, borrowing, extravagance, and protecting duties, forbid such an apprehension? Where are the reciprocities and compensations for these transfers of property to be found? They are in fact always promised, but never found under any system of restriction and monopoly, applied to commerce, foreign or domestick; and such systems universally inflict upon nations the two misfortunes of having the property of individuals transferred to other individuals without an equivalent, and of being saddled with a heavy and lasting expense necessary to enforce the injustice.

A system of adjusting by law the numerous balances of property, is a machine infinitely more complicated, than the system of political balances. Ours is already so much disordered, as to have called forth the utmost talents of project-menders. Various schemes for patching it up have been tried and failed. The inference is, that all legal machines for transferring property are incurably vicious, and that industry and talents are better regulators of it. Their introduction by funding and banking caused some dissatisfaction, but the pretexts were specious, and the oppression was at first light. As they have been multiplied, the oppression becomes heavier, and the dissatisfaction increases. But the Committee say, "that a reciprocal system of restriction has aided our commerce." How? Why, they add "that year succeeds year and our troubles increase." Palpable contradictions are not arguments. Year succeeds year, and commercial restrictions are multiplied. What kind of aid is that by which our troubles are increased? But let us search for a reconciliation of assertions apparently so hostile. It cannot be our foreign commerce which has been aided by a system of reciprocal restriction, for the Committee have told us "that our exports have not increased in proportion to our population." And this is admitted to be growing worse as restrictions are multiplied. Our domestick must, therefore, be the commerce, aided by our restrictive system; and it is certainly true that protecting duties have operated more feelingly upon this, than upon our foreign commerce. The chief existing species of domestick commerce has been undoubtedly vastly extended, and the capitalists think aided by the system of transferring property, or as the Committee are pleased to call it, of reciprocal restriction; and our troubles have also increased in concomitancy with it. The system pretended to be levelled against foreigners, has only hit ourselves. How can this have happened except by its internal operation in transferring property, and accumulating capitals at the public expense? This, say the project-menders, has been caused by the oversight of not giving to industry some countervails, to balance the avails extorted from her to enrich privileges and capitalists; and therefore to establish a restrictive, reciprocal, free trade between agriculture and factories, it is necessary to get together colonies of mechanicks by bribes to capitalists, numerous enough to consume the fruits of the earth. When this is effected, the two classes will be employed in a delightful game of shuttlecock, that is, in passing a bag of money to and fro between themselves, without its producing the fraudulent transfers of property, which have only increased our troubles for want of this just reciprocation.

Thus the apparent contradiction is removed, and we are driven to consider, whether reciprocal restrictions can constitute, or were ever intended to constitute, a free trade, foreign or domestick. If these restrictions amount to prohibitions, yet if they are reciprocal, according to the position of the Committee, the trade is free. It would be exactly the case of a pacifick war, in which two nations should make laws that neither should attack the other, but that each should shed at home a reciprocal portion of its own blood. Let the agricultural and capitalist interests stand for these two nations. As protecting duties draw much of the blood or money of one, an equal portion of blood or money ought to be drawn from the other, to make a free trade or a peaceable war, by means of reciprocity. Neither can be effected, if the blood or money drawn from the veins or pockets of the one, should be infused into the veins or pockets of the other. That would only be the experiment of exchanging youth for decrepitude, by surrendering a vital principle. Rare as it has been to persuade or compel individuals to submit to this species of free trade, the operation has been frequently performed upon separate interests in all civilized countries, under some pretext of reciprocity. The pretext for it in the case under consideration, is less specious than any I have met with. Invigorate us now with your blood, say the capitalists to the agriculturists, and you shall bleed us in your turn, after both you and ourselves are dead. This is the proposed restricted-reciprocal free trade.

Chaptal, a French financier, has said "that it is impossible to reconcile hostile interests, and that the legislator must balance the censure he receives from one party, by the approbation of another." This honest confession denies the practicability of effecting just pecuniary balances by legislative favours or exclusive privileges, as contended for by the avaricious and ambitious schools, and avows the true principle of the policy to consist in suppressing the dissatisfaction of the injured, by the aid of the favoured class. The universal policy of these schools is to bribe each other with money or power extorted from nations, and to unite this power and money in self-defence. Such is the restricted, reciprocal, free domestick trade established in England; and exactly the same coalition which sustains fraudulent transfers of property there, is rapidly growing up here. The only reciprocity produced by the policy, is between the corrupters and corrupted, each party in the trade alternately acting in each character. We will gratify your avarice if you will gratify our ambition; or we will gratify your ambition if you will gratify our avarice—comprises all the negotiations and all the reciprocity between statesmen and exclusive privileges. This coalition has already become so formidable in the United States, that it openly and earnestly pleads its own cause, without faltering from beholding the mischiefs it has already caused. It remains to be seen whether it can delude the Americans by the same arts with which it has deluded the English.

All monopolies and exclusive privileges have succeeded by using the same argument urged by the Committee. It is invariably condensed in the single word "reciprocity." These stratagems say, "give us your money or your rights, and we will give you something more valuable. We will give you heaven for dirty acres or filthy lucre. We will give you protection for manors and feudal powers. And now, we will give you a restricted, reciprocal, domestick, free trade, for a profit of fifty or an hundred per centum upon most of your consumptions." To these arguments, they never fail to add their own verdict, that such reciprocities will advance the national welfare. But are they impartial judges? We have a notion that the only proper judge in giving away his own property, is the man himself; and that each person ought to make his own will. If it is a just notion, the capitalists ought to have no vote in transferring to themselves a vast tax upon the consumptions of every body else. If a man should combine with a government to take away another's property, the tyranny of the act would not be obliterated by the power of an accomplice. Had the man who foolishly killed the goose that laid the golden eggs, spared her life, and only persuaded her that she did not lay such eggs at all whilst he was daily taking them away, it would have been a case fitting both the capitalist and agricultural interest. The facts are stated to be "that agriculture has ceased to lay golden eggs; that factories will lay them in abundance; and that, when laid, the capitalists will give them to the agriculturists." I shall not presume to say which of the parties would represent the goose.

The Committee have ingeniously endeavoured to divert our attention from a bad principle at home, to the same bad principle abroad. They say "the people are groaning under a restrictive system of bounties, premiums, privileges, and monopolies, imposed by foreign nations." If these devourers of property, even at a great distance, are so dreadful, as to make us groan, they will certainly make us roar like the European nations, when well fixed among us. Why do they make us groan though so far off? Because, as the Committee contend, they are stratagems for transferring wealth from one nation to another. Is their ability to prowl for property across an ocean, a proof that they will graze like lambs at home? How comes it, that fostered by our own laws, unobstructed by distance, unchecked by competition, and unresisted by retaliation, they will suddenly lose their very nature, and cease to transfer property fraudulently; whilst they make one nation tributary to another, in spite of the resistance opposed to their voracity by the sufferers? If it is the innate principle and design of foreign bounties, premiums, privileges, and monopolies, to transfer wealth from one nation to another, must it not also be the innate principle and design of domestick bounties, premiums, privileges, and monopolies, to transfer wealth from one domestick interest to another? In fact, this latter is the vital principle of the whole family of mercenary stratagems, and the political only imitates the military tactician in calling off the attention of his adversary from the true point of attack, by feigning a false one.

It is improbable that one nation can do any material or permanent injury to another, by its bounties, premiums, privileges, and monopolies; but quite certain that governments can injure, oppress, and enslave nations by these instruments. Should one nation even succeed in getting a little money from another by these tricks, it certainly loses a great mass of liberty at home; and a nation which should lose this money but retain its liberty, would be happier than one which should get the money but lose its liberty. But the free nation will speedily prove too hard even in the contest for wealth, with a nation which may be groaning as we are, or roaring like the English and Irish, under a system of bounties, premiums, privileges, and monopolies. Bounties and premiums given by the supposed cunning nation, upon their exportations, would frequently be received by the importing free nation. Privileges and monopolies would transfer property from productive labour to capitalists, and diminish industry; and would moreover produce a system of smuggling and expense, which would also foster the commerce of the free nation. It is as impossible to prevent it, as it was for Canute to stop the waves of the ocean; and if all the nations in the world should plunge yet deeper into the system of bounties, premiums, privileges, and monopolies, I believe that it would nurture the commerce of the United States, provided the imitation of this oppressive system was expunged from our statute book, and it was made really free. The invigoration of industry by its freedom, would inevitably work down the industry cheated by stratagems for transferring property, and heavily laden with taxation, just as a well fed and well paid army, will beat an army half starved.

The idea of what is called "a balance of trade" has furnished the authors of all the stratagems for transferring property internally by restrictions, privileges, and monopolies, with ammunition for this formidable political artillery, which has been so successfully used against the liberty and happiness of mankind. Accordingly the Committee observe "that commerce is exporting, not importing, and by reversing her employment she is expatriated," meaning thereby, that unless a country exports more than it imports, so as to have a pecuniary balance in its favour, it has a bad commerce or none. It is impossible to suppose, as the words imply, that exportation alone constitutes commerce, or that such a commerce could even exist. No selection of a basis upon which to erect a system of premiums, bounties, privileges, and monopolies, could have rivalled in dexterity this of a balance of trade. Its intricacy leaves it at liberty to assert whatever it pleases; and the total ignorance of the mass of every nation as to such assertions, invests the initiated few, if there are any such, with the advantage of making the most of the impenetrable secret, to advance their own designs. When an agriculturist murmurs at our system of bounties, premiums, privileges, and monopolies, he is told that the balance of trade is against us, and that it is necessary to pilfer him by this system to get it in our favour, because otherwise the nation cannot be wealthy. The argument is beyond his reach; he has no reply; he submits; but the Committee say he groans. If the happiness of nations really depends upon a pecuniary balance of trade, with other nations, several surprising consequences follow. A great blunder in the structure and scheme of this world must have been committed, as few, or at most not above half mankind, can acquire this enviable balance; so that one half the world must be in poverty and trouble. The situation of all inland people must be peculiarly miserable. They can never lose or gain much money by this balance; yet they must be made subject to domestick stratagems for transferring property by bounties, premiums, privileges, monopolies, and an expensive government, in order to obtain an enigma. Domestick commerce must be converted from an instrument for fair exchanges, into an engine for foul transfers of property, under pretence of realizing a dream. All mankind have hitherto mistaken the chief cause of their troubles. They have not been caused by forms of government, sustained by bounties, privileges, monopolies, and oppressive taxation, no, they have been caused by not having a balance of trade in their favour. If the idea is not nearly or quite a delusion, invented for fraudulent purposes, even supposing it to contain some truth, yet a nation which sells its liberty to exclusive privileges for the sake of a balance of trade, ought to ascertain how much money it will get, for the commodity it is disposing of and how long they will keep it, lest the bargain should turn out to be a bad speculation.

The speculation is merely a barter of liberty for privileges, monopolies, and heavy taxation. It does not propose to bring us more land, or more articles of consumption, in exchange for it. The minimum of necessaries, conveniences, and luxuries, is considered as the maximum of the supposed blessing. To be a good thing, the balance must be paid in money. The advocates of this balance of trade and exclusive-privilege doctrine, use our avarice to make us forget what money is. It is the representative or emblem of consumable property only, between nations. It is kept in fusion by circumstances beyond the control of any one nation. It is as hard to hold as quicksilver. If it is held, it is good for nothing. It is a bird of passage, and when it cannot find food in one country, it flees to another. If we purchase this fugitive at the expense of establishing privileges, monopolies, and heavy taxation, the necromancer, Commerce, waves its wand, and presto, it is gone; but the Tyranny incurred to obtain it, hangs upon our necks for ever. Let us not give a valuable estate, of which we have been so proud, for a slave who will infallibly run way. Suppose a balance of trade should bring us ten millions annually in hard money, and even that we could retain it for ever. Should we be a cent the richer for it? Would it not depreciate like local paper money, the moment it exceeded the demand for employment? If we could find the undiscovered secret of prohibiting its exportation, and deprive it of its emigrating character, the accumulation of specie by a constant pecuniary balance of trade, would only produce the same effects as an accumulation of local paper money by the operation of the press, and only invest us with the blessings of depreciation. We should grow numerically richer, as a miser would by converting dollars into cents. If we cannot discover this worthless secret, restrictions, exclusive privileges, and monopolies cannot keep the money they promise to bring. If they should really extract money from foreign nations, instead of transferring property at home, the money cannot be retained, but the property transferred can. The residence of money is regulated by a power beyond the reach of legislation itself. It will go from the place where it abounds, to the place where it is scarce. As the emblem of commodities, it will search for the cheapest. If restrictions, exclusive privileges, and monopolies could bring in so much money, as to destroy the equilibrium of its value between ourselves and other commercial nations, they would have done their utmost; but the acquisition would be transitory, because the equilibrium would be restored, like the level of water after it has been disturbed by a storm. The influence of exclusive privileges, commercial restrictions, and monopolies upon other countries soon ceases; but it remains as to separate interests at home. If these stratagems could have both gotten and retained wealth from other countries, it would have somewhere been seen both enormous and permanent; for though they pretend to be too conscientious to transfer the wealth of their fellow citizens to themselves, they have no scruples about transferring that of other countries to their own. The bargain therefore made by a nation, which establishes commercial restrictions, exclusive privileges, and monopolies, to obtain a balance of trade, is only a permanent subjection to an oppressive policy, for the sake of a pecuniary acquisition, which will probably be never obtained, and if obtained, cannot be permanent. The oppression may grow into unlimited tyranny; but the acquisition can never grow into unlimited wealth. The exclusive privileges and monopolies can never prevent the departure of money, but they may prevent the recovery of the principles surrendered to obtain its temporary appearance.

If the nature of money is correctly stated, the idea of governing its value by commercial restrictions, exclusive privileges, and monopolies, is more chimerical, than that of governing the local value of paper money by tender laws; and as its value is not regulated by these jugglers, but by the universal laws of commerce, it is evident that all their tricks for making money travel and settle where they please, are fallacious.

To conceal their inability to effect any such thing, the whole protecting-duty, restricting, monopolizing or balance-of-trade family, have used paper money as a mask for their legerdemain. If it was true that protecting duties would bring to us a balance of trade in specie, what necessity could there be for the banking exclusive privilege, or paper money? This consideration is a test and detection of the real design of the protecting duty, and all other exclusive privileges. If the protecting-duty monopoly would secure for us a pecuniary balance of trade, a surplus banking monopoly of currency would be worse than useless, as serving to banish the money which the sister monopoly boasts of bringing in. It is curious to see the United States equally zealous for two monopolies, one to bring in money, the other for sending it away. Both have loudly boasted of their capacity to enrich the nation, and both have been very patiently tried. The results are, first, that the nation is distressed; secondly, that our governments have been made extravagant by confiding in these promises and are reduced to borrowing; thirdly, that exuberant personal capitalists have been created; and fourthly, that the two monopolies have generated a third, that of supplying the government with these loans. If the capitalists would give up two of these monopolies provided they might retain one, it might bear some distant analogy to their doctrine of reciprocity and compensation, as it would be a considerable retribution in a thief who had stolen three horses to return two of them; but to demand another horse because he had already gotten three, would almost stagger an adept in that species of property-transferring occupation. But reciprocity, compensation or restoration, constitute no part of the exclusive-privilege policy; one privilege or monopoly begets another; the two a third, as we have already experienced; and the more there are, the more they breed.

The supreme power of commerce has defeated laws for compelling local paper money to fulfil its promises of reciprocity and compensation; and therefore no laws can compel exclusive privileges and monopolies, which carry on their operations by the instrumentality of currency, to use it according to the principles of reciprocity and compensation, and not to use it for transferring property to themselves. The supremacy of the universal law of commerce, is demonstrated in the fate of every species of paper money. Foster it by privileges or defend it by tender laws, it is exposed to fluctuation, depreciation and death. A balance of trade in specie is subject to the same laws. It must flow out after having run in, or it will generate a putrid miasm. The Committee propose to produce an influx of specie by restrictions upon commerce; but if the project should succeed, the money would be useless, and might be pernicious without a reflux. This pecuniary balance must go out again in search of something. Not of a cargo of money in return for a cargo of money, but of moveable consumable property. Which would be the most economical mode of managing commerce for the purpose of obtaining a profit or a balance in our favour; to send out a cargo of wares to bring back a cargo of money, and then to send out a cargo of money to bring back a cargo of wares; or to bring back a cargo of wares for a cargo of wares? The first is a kind of exporting commerce recommended by the Committee, to come at a balance of trade.

Money, far from being the regulator of the balance of trade, has its own value regulated by the price of commodities; and the price of commodities being regulated by plenty or scarcity, by superfluity and want, by fashion and folly, by climates and soils, by durability and decay, and by a thousand other circumstances, which are continually fluctuating, the wit of man is unable to find the Proteus, or pecuniary balance of trade; or if it could be found, to hold the perpetual metamorphosis. This never-ceasing fluctuation is the basis of commerce, the invigorator of industry, and the equalizer of comforts. It is also the appraiser of money, and bills of exchange are used to execute its valuations. As money itself has no fixed value, the exchange of this emblem of commodities rises or falls, as the value of the substances it represents locally fluctuates. The shadow will go in spite of laws, wherever it can acquire most substance. A balance of money may be against a nation, and yet a balance of trade in its favour. If a nation gains more of this substance than it loses by commerce, its prosperity and comforts will be increased, although it should lose more of the shadow than it gains. The balance of the shadow of commodities, has for near two centuries been in favour of Spain, by reason of the money she has drawn from her provinces; but the balance of trade has always been substantially against her. Even commodities themselves cannot furnish any certain rule for ascertaining the balance of trade, because the value of labour by which they are produced, is unsettled. The cultivation of a poor soil, must give more labour in exchange for other labour to supply his wants, than the cultivator of a rich soil. Seasons and healthiness will constantly affect the value of labour. A balance of trade in commodities is however greatly preferable to a balance in money. It possesses the most valuable quality of money; that of being able to go abroad in search of other commodities needed by a nation. The only commercial value of money is its capacity to obtain from other nations articles for consumption, and commodities are articles for consumption. They constitute a fund for taxation. Money itself is in a very small degree an article of consumption, nor is it susceptible of taxation, on account of its invisibility, except through the medium of its purchases.

How then can a balance of trade be ascertained? Not by money, because its value fluctuates. Not by labour or commodities, because scarcity, rarity, taste, sterility, fertility, seasons, and endless circumstances, render both scales utterly unsteady. Not by corn, because the value of that also is governed by demand, and influenced by most of the circumstances which influence the value of other commodities. As neither of these scales are sufficient for ascertaining a balance of trade; as such a balance, if obtained in money, could not be lasting, on account of the acuteness of money in search of its equilibrium; as a balance in commodities must be consumed or re-exported to procure other articles of consumption; and as even corn is subject to these laws, it follows that a balance of trade, estimated by either of these scales, is either an idea wholly chimerical, or exposed to perpetual fluctuations. But if we change terms, and rejecting this equivocal and fluctuating idea of a balance of trade, consider whether commerce has contributed to the wealth and prosperity of the United States, or has been the cause of the distress they are now enduring, the evidence will at once strike us as more intelligible, and the conclusion as more certain. Agricultural improvements, building houses and raising up cities, manufacturing improvements and ship building, are among the strongest proofs of a permanent increase of national wealth and prosperity. In these and other acquisitions the United States have been unrivalled by any nation ancient or modern. If our commerce has produced these effects, what reason is there for subjecting it to the regimen of exclusive privileges contrived for transferring property internally? With what exultation have we seen a free commerce delineating our wide-spreading canvass with all the representations of national prosperity! With what anguish do we behold commercial restrictions wrenching the pencil from this successful artist, and obliterating the work! Our commerce, both before and since the revolution, increased the national prosperity, with undeviating progress, and we are exchanging its solid benefits for restrictions, bounties, exclusive privileges, and monopolies, recommended by recondite and intricate speculations about the balance of trade.

The proposition itself "that commerce is exporting and not importing" urged by the Committee to justify this change of policy, would in my view contain more truth, if it were reversed. I should think that the most gainful commerce which imported more than it exported. If two dollars are exported and only one imported, is it a gainful commerce? The case is the same if such a commerce is carried on in commodities, or in their representative, money. If two measures of labour are exported in any form, and only one imported, a loss ensues. If one is paid for in money, so as to equalize the exports and imports, that money is only the representative of the labour it leaves behind, and must be sent back for it; or remitted to some other place upon a similar errand. If a nation can pay for its imports, the greater they are the more it will flourish, as a superiority in gratifications is the highest degree of human prosperity; as these gratifications re-create themselves by exciting industry; and as this industry obtains its gratifications by things which would be of no use to it, unless they are so employed. If a nation cannot pay for its imports, the trusting nation will be the loser, and the importing nation the gainer. But no importing trade could continue with an inability to make payment. It would inevitably stop of itself. Does not this fact explode all the theories about the balance of trade? Does it not prove that commerce must contain some reciprocal compensating ingredients, or cease, according to its own laws, to exist.

The Committee have endeavoured to overturn all these ideas by the following assertions. They say

> that the flood of importations has deprived currency of its occupation. There is more specie in the United States than at any former period,

but it is not currency because it is unemployed. The importation of foreign goods was never so great as when our embarrassments were produced. The importer's ledger ought to settle the question. In cases of bankruptcy foreign creditors appear. We have only the miserable and ruinous circulation of a currency for remittance to foreign nations. They hold the coin and we hear it jingle. The excess of exports over imports is the rate of profit.

Dictums of impartial judges are the lowest species of authority, and those of lawyers pleading for clients are of no authority at all. Both are often inconsistent with truth, contrary to sound principles, and liable to answers by which they are easily refuted. The report of the Committee abounds with this kind of authority, uttered with a confidence often inspired by a destitution of better arguments. Let us see if this family of dictums can bear an examination.

"The flood of importations has deprived currency of its occupation." So then, the flood of paper money has been no cause of our troubles; on the contrary this flood of commodities has deprived the flood of bank paper of its occupation, and thereby caused the national distress. Had the exchange of property been the occupation of paper money, the greater the importation of exchangeable commodities, the more this occupation would have been increased. But if the chief occupation of bank paper is to transfer property, and this flood of importations has really diminished that occupation, the regret expressed by the Committee on the occasion, is only an indication of their preference for the transferring policy. It is hardly conceivable how the introduction of more exchangeable articles, could have deprived currency of its occupation in exchanging property, except, that as cheapness is a consequence of plenty, less currency suffices to exchange more commodities, than when the price of these commodities is enhanced by an artificial scarcity. In this view, the scarcity of manufactures produced by the protecting-duty system, undoubtedly increases the occupation of bank currency in transferring property. If this flood of importations had consisted, not of things represented by money, but of the representative itself, would not the universal law of commerce have operated upon an exuberance of money? The quantity of money being increased, and the stock of commodities diminished, from which money derives its occupation of facilitating exchanges, both the causes which generate a depreciation of money would have existed. Scarcity or plenty affect the value of money, precisely as they affect the value of commodities. There is however a great difference to us between the depreciation of each. The depreciation of foreign commodities produced by exuberant importations is a loss to foreign nations, and a gain to us; but the depreciation of money, which would also be produced by exuberant importations of that article, would be a gain to foreign nations, by enhancing the prices of their commodities, and a loss to ourselves, until an equilibrium was produced. A depreciation of money is not an accumulation of national wealth, and therefore a nation may both abound in currency, and also become poor and wretched. This is, invariably, effected by the system for increasing currency, combined with regulations by which its occupation of exchanging property is contracted, and that of transferring it, is extended. The supreme law of commerce governs currencies both local and universal. We have fully experienced its uncontrollable power. A redundancy of paper money enabled individuals to acquire more currency, nominally, but its cheapness or depreciation made most of them substantially poorer. Nations are individuals in respect to universal currency. A redundancy, if they keep it, does not enrich them, because its value is reduced by depreciation. A specie balance of trade in favour of Spain for two centuries, attended by a domestick system of exclusive privileges, exhibited a rich class, and a poor miserable people. Her exuberance of money and its consequent cheapness, served only to invigorate foreign industry. If we could, by the tricks of exclusive privileges, import annually the product of the mines of Mexico and Peru, we should be enriched like Spain. It would bribe industry (the only true and lasting source of national wealth) to become idle; and excite fraud to become industrious. If industry is the only true and lasting source of national wealth, the idea of burdening it with exclusive privileges; of taxing the great mass of it to obtain a balance of trade by giving these taxes to one or a few of its objects; must be chimerical. If the favoured products should become redundant by the tribute they receive from the others, this redundancy would produce depreciation, and terminate, not in a retribution for the expense they had cost, but in a positive loss. A redundancy contains the seeds of calamity unless it is dissipated. Whilst Spain clung to the idea of enriching herself by a redundancy of money, Holland, but a splinter of the enormous Spanish monarchy, pursued a policy precisely the reverse. A flood of importations in money and a flood of importations in commodities, side by side, engaged in war and in commerce; and tried both the prowess and profitableness of the adverse systems. Rich mines and every physical advantage were on the side of Spain. A free trade, but few people, and a small slip of half-drowned country, on the side of Holland. A free trade turned the scale, and bestowed a double victory on the dwarf. Is not this fair trial more weighty towards ascertaining truth, than a complexity of facts and speculations, so useful to monopolies and exclusive privileges, but so inimical to plain honesty and common justice? It proves that a balance of trade in imported commodities, excites industry by increasing enjoyments, and by furnishing a surplus for re-exportation; and that it augments wonderfully both national wealth and strength. The abundance of commodities invited by a freedom of commerce, enables the re-exporting merchant to make up cargoes fitted for their destination, more speedily and cheaply, than in ports stripped of variety by commercial restrictions; and to undersell competition by a vast economy of time and expense.

The Committee proceed to say "there is more specie in the United States than at any former period, but it is not currency, because it is unemployed." We have then already obtained a redundancy of specie, and the policy it has suggested to the Committee, is to increase it by exporting more than we import; and to diminish its business of facilitating exchanges, by prohibiting the importation of commodities. If the existing redundancy is a useless surplus, would not its augmentation, if it can be augmented by a domestick monopoly, produce another useless surplus? If with a surplus of currency beyond our wants, national distress has appeared, it is demonstrated that the remedy for national distress is not deposited in a surplus of currency; and the speculations in reference to a pecuniary balance of trade, having such a surplus for such an end in contemplation, are of course exploded. The proposed monopoly system also says, that we possess a great surplus of agricultural commodities, which, though not entirely unemployed, like the surplus of money, is yet by abundance considerably diminished in value; and in its patriotick enthusiasm, it has humanely prohibited the importation of more tobacco and other articles, lest this agricultural surplus should become quite useless. The same reason was still stronger for prohibiting the importation of more money, because we have already a useless surplus of it. Instead of candidly acknowledging that a surplus or redundancy either of money or agricultural products must be governed by the same commercial laws, the Committee press into view the latter disguised in the garb of a calamity, and seize upon the prevalent love of money to make us believe that a redundancy of money is a blessing, and to hide, with this delusion, the evils brought upon mankind by monopolies and exclusive privileges. Their doctrine is this. "Continue and increase commercial restrictions, and tax agricultural products because they are of very little value, to increase a surplus of specie, already of no value at all for want of employment." It would be a better policy to bring in more flour, cotton, and tobacco, as these commodities might have been of some use, instead of laying in the vaults of a bank, like a dead nabob in his funeral robes. But how did this useless surplus of specie get into the United States, if the balance of trade in that commodity is against us, and why is it not employed as currency? The answer to the first question cannot be very conclusive; we cannot unravel the labyrinths in which money travels; custom-house computations are uniformly erroneous; the prices at which commodities actually sell, can never be ascertained; whether this useless surplus of money has been brought here by our own commodities, or by the re-exportation of foreign goods, or by the sale of bank and debt stock to foreigners, we cannot tell; we know, however, that it has not come gratuitously. But the answer to the second question is more satisfactory. The imported specie is useless as currency, because we have more bank currency than we can find employment for, and because the expulsion of foreign commodities to a considerable amount, has correspondently diminished the use of money for facilitating exchanges. If the dead specie surplus, said by the Committee to exist, has been produced by the sales of stock, commerce will inevitably seize and scatter the accumulation, unless we should be saved by a beneficial bankruptcy of all our banks. The capitalists look with dismay at this possibility, because it will break to pieces the master wheel of the property-transferring machine; and therefore they strive by prohibitions and restrictions to deprive the nation of a free trade which would bring in comforts and wealth for individuals, lest it should seize the specie deposits of banks, and destroy a fiction for transferring property. Their object is to regulate commerce for the attainment of two ends; one, to prevent it from assailing bank deposits; the other for preventing it from supplying individuals with necessaries, and investing capitalists with a privilege of doing so at double price. Thus it happens that they advise us to destroy the best and most enriching species of commerce, that of exchanges, and to sell our products for specie, though they tell us that this specie cannot find employment. By destroying our commerce, they hope to save their banks; by prohibiting importations, they will certainly increase their capitals. And thus the banking and manufacturing capitalists are united by a common interest, the magnitude of which is sufficient to awaken the great talents they possess, and to excite all the industry and perseverance they have shown. If the expedient of protecting duties is able to keep the specie deposit in the banks, and prevent their currency for transferring property from blowing up, it would be able to supply the nation with a currency chastely devoted to the end of exchanging property, and render it unnecessary that a currency for making property tributary to capitalists, should any longer exist.

We are startled to hear from the advocates of the protecting-duty system such positions as these.

> Money is so scarce, as to cause general distress, and to impede both agricultural and manufacturing improvements. It is so scarce, as to disable the people from paying taxes, and to force the government to borrow. It is so scarce that debtors are unable to pay their debts. Money is so plenty, that a great sum of specie is useless for want of employment. It is so plenty, that capitalists know not what to do with their abundance. It is so plenty, that loans are obtained by government at a lower rate than ever was known before, and individuals who can secure re-payment, can borrow below the legal interest.

But a little reflection will convince us that these apparent contradictions are all true. By adverting to the legal arrangement of the community into monopolists and contributors to monopolies, they may be reconciled. With the contributors money is scarce; its scarcity has caused general distress, because the contributors constitute by far the greatest portion of the community; its scarcity bears hard both upon agriculturists and mechanics, because both belong to the class of contributors; its scarcity disables the people from paying taxes, because they also belong to the contributing class; and disables debtors from paying their debts, because by incurring these debts they have not been able to escape from the contributing to the receiving class. Now let us turn our eyes from that side of the canvass, on which about ten thousand of us, out of ten thousand and one, are depicted, to the little smiling fat group which complains of a redundancy of money. Alas! say these gentlemen, money is so plenty, that we have a large sum of specie which is not currency for want of employment. Capital is so abundant as to stifle enterprise and speculation. It is so abundant, that when loans are called for, capitalists jump over each other's heads in a contest of underbidding. It is so abundant that they rejoice in the public calamity of borrowing. It is so abundant that they buy stocks at enhanced prices.

Our surprize vanishes upon discovering facts, at a glance so irreconcilable, to be true; but it returns with tenfold force, and rises up to amazement, upon being told, that the omnium of these facts, proves the wisdom and justice of increasing both this scarcity and this plenty of money, by a new bonus to capitalists. As extravagance, exclusive privileges, and monopolies have already involved the great bulk of the nation in distress, scattered poverty, disabled the people from paying taxes, and sorely afflicted debtors; and as they have already created a superabundance of capitalists who know not what to do with their wealth; a remedy for the mischief, and not its aggravation, seems unavoidably to present itself. When the fat-sow monopoly, confesses that she has swilled wealth, until her corpulency had become distressing, it would be like murder to pour more down her throat, and run the risk of bursting her. What should we think of a physician who should propose to make the nose larger than the whole body, by converting the aliment of the other members to its growth? Would he be a bad model of the politicians who have bloated up a capitalist interest to a pecuniary plethora, by starving down the other members of the body politick, to a pecuniary famine? Can a republican party have been this quack? Will a republican party increase the political nose, until its necessary amputation may endanger the life of the patient?

The Committee use many expedients to draw off our attention from this political caricature; this sport for capitalists and death for the rest of the nation; and by huddling assertion upon assertion, leave us to imagine that there must be some nostrum in the multitude of medicaments, able to reduce the monstrous nose to a natural size, or at least sufficient for the present to hide it. They sometimes endeavour to make us fall in love with the huge nose, by telling us that when it is made still larger, all the other members may feed upon it; and that though it starves them now, yet it will afford them a delicious repast, like the tail of a cape sheep, so soon as it has grown to a sufficient size to fatten all the rest. At other times, they ascribe the leanness of the other members, not to the excessive fattening of the nose, but to certain conjurations of necromancers three thousand miles off, able to impoverish all the members, except this fortunate nose. But the Committee have neither told us, how it has happened that British machinations have been able to starve all our social interests, except the capitalist; nor how this one interest has fattened up to excessive corpulency, in spite of these machinations. Have the British been giving bounties to this interest, whilst they were endeavouring to impoverish all others? Let it then apply to its benefactors, and say, "you have wisely made us enormously rich at your own expense, and therefore you will act still wiser, by making us still richer." How would the British regard such an argument, though attended with an assurance, that a compliance with it would at some future day increase their wealth and prosperity? If the great wealth of the capitalists were not extracted from the British, let them say from whom it was extracted, and address the same argument to the prodigal donors. Should it be of domestick origin, it must of course result, that not British, but domestick machinations have created an enormously rich unproductive class, and thereby inflicted upon productive classes a very considerable degree of distress.

In pursuance of the policy of diverting our attention from the phenomena of exuberant capitals and a general distress, the Committee have thrown out other lures. "The importation of foreign goods was never so great as when our embarrassments were produced." In the whole report of the Committee there is no hint that a legal accumulation of capitals in a few hands, has had the least influence in producing the national distress. A pecuniary inquiry, if its object was truth, could not have overlooked the largest pecuniary item, having a more extensive influence upon our pecuniary situation, than all others united. Whilst the advocates of exclusive privileges pretend to so much skill in calculation, and have been prodigal of figures, it is marvellous that they, and more marvellous that a Committee of the legislature, raised to find out the causes of our distress, should have been so covetous of both, as to have passed over with the most cautious silence, our enormous legal or artificial accumulations of capital. But a fair accountant will confront this item, in searching for the causes of our distress, with that of an importation of foreign goods. Suppose we change the assertion and say "the importation of foreign exclusive privileges, monopolies, and modes for accumulating capitals in a few hands, was never so great as when our distresses were produced." We are then left at liberty to consider which of these contemporaries contributed most towards producing our distresses. There was certainly a new procreative power disclosed by an importation of foreign goods, if that produced them; and it is even miraculous, that an importation of property, at least equivalent in value to its emblem, money, should suddenly have reduced us to distress, after we had flourished many years under such importations, less restricted, and often larger in proportion to population. But there is nothing either new or miraculous in the capacity of a system of extravagance, exclusive privileges, and monopolies, to produce national distress. How could it happen that exchanges of property with foreigners should ruin us, but that transfers of property to capitalists should do us no harm? In one case we receive an equivalent estimated by ourselves; in the other, we receive no equivalent at all. Is sudden ruin from a great importation of property more likely to ensue, than ultimate ruin from our progressive policy of transferring property from industry to capitalists? The original funding system, subsequent loans, a flood of bank currency, the bankruptcy of some banks, and the refusal or inability of all to pay their debts, the extravagance of our governments, loans, pensions, and the great increase of protecting duties, in many cases amounting to a prohibition, are so many instruments for cutting off every species of property from industry, to enrich capitalists, as the Abyssinian fattens himself with steaks cut from living cows; and this transferring property now assures us, that the pain and anguish at length produced by its operations, were occasioned by an importation of foreign goods. As such an importation was unavoidably contemporary with the catastrophe of the property-transferring policy, it gave the Committee an opportunity of exclaiming, Aha! we have detected the thief who has stolen our domestick property. Foreign property has done the deed, and reduced us to distress. We have, against this mode of stealing, the resources of eating, drinking, wearing, exporting and selling the thief himself; but we cannot eat, drink, wear, export or sell our capitalist, our pension, our banking, or any of our exclusive interests.

But "the importer's ledger ought to settle the question, and in the cases of bankruptcy foreign creditors appear." The doctrine of the balance of trade not being sufficiently intricate and dark for the purposes of exclusive privileges and monopolies, they are driven by fear, and by the want of arguments more suitable for examination, to appeal to a perfect camera obscura, hoping that it may afford some gleam sufficient to turn objects upside down. What a tenure is this for our liberty and property? Both ought to be determined by importers' ledgers in the opinion of the Committee, which ledgers are to decide whether exclusive privileges and monopolies are their friends or foes. Did the Committee really intend that the nation should examine and settle up these ledgers, to be able to estimate the evidence they might afford; or that our liberty and property should depend upon their own intuitive or inspired conviction, that there is decisive evidence hidden in these ledgers in favour of monopolies and exclusive privileges? Instead of endeavouring to extricate this evidence from its numerous dungeons, it may be wiser for the nation to open a ledger between itself and the several modes for transferring its property to capitalists. The items are few and notorious; and the balance between the nation and monopolies and exclusive privileges may be discovered with infinitely more facility, than a security for our liberty and property in importers' ledgers. The following might be the form of an account:

Capitalists and exclusive privileges to the nation, Dr.
To property transferred by banking, loaning, pensions and protecting duties—annually about $30,000,000

Credit, 00,000,000

Here is a plain loss to the nation of six hundred millions of dollars in twenty years. Can the importers' ledgers possibly contain any thing to prove both that it ought to be continued and even increased? But the estimate is too low, because the property-transferring policy ought to be charged with so much of the extravagance of our governments as it has caused. This item is somewhat harder to estimate than the others, because it is blended with the blessings of government; but the others return no compensation to the people either physical or moral. They both take away property and aggravate moral evils.

I have laboured in vain to discover, what bearing the appearance of foreign creditors to claim some dividend, in our cases of bankruptcy, can have upon the subject. Credit, like currency, is governed by the common law of commerce, and both are liable to be counterfeited. If we could give to foreigners our bad bank money for goods or specie, it would not be a bad trade. In giving them bankrupts for goods or specie, the trade is the same. But in the trade of bankruptcies loss and gain is reciprocal, and it would be as difficult to find how the balance stands, as to discover and hold the long-sought and yet unfound balance of trade, or the conclusive evidence said to reside in the importers' ledgers. A free nation would never submit to a plain system for transferring property; and, as it was therefore necessary to make the protecting-duty item of this system, as obscure as possible, I do not know that the Committee could have found better arguments in its favour, than a balance of trade, importers' ledgers, and casual bankruptcies.

"We have only the miserable and ruinous circulation of a currency for remittance to foreign nations. They hold the coin and we hear it

jingle." The contradiction in these very short assertions is palpable.
How can we make remittances in coin which foreign nations hold? It
is palpable also compared with the assertion "that there is more specie
in the United States than at any former period, but it is unemployed."
How is all this? Foreign nations hold the coin, yet we hear it jingle.
We hold more coin than at any former period, more than we can
employ, yet we remit it to foreign nations. Was a pretty antithesis a
temptation not to be resisted? Did a jingle of words cause the Committee to be content with a jingle of facts? Instead of our having a currency
for remittance to foreign nations, we abound in a currency which will
not answer that purpose; which cannot leave us; which is not subject
to the honest common law of universal commerce; and which sticks to
us for better or worse, as a bad wife sometimes does to her husband,
long after he wishes she was dead. We have, in fact, but little of that
kind of currency in circulation, which serves for remittance. It is true
that we have heard the jingling of this kind of currency in the newspapers, and the Committee have rung the same bell, but our ears are thus
regaled, merely for the purpose of keeping up the credit of that kind
of currency, not liable to be remitted to foreign nations, and so happily
employed at home in transferring property and creating capitalists and
paupers. A free commerce would bring the musical kind of currency
into our pockets, and diminish the bad effects of the transferring
currency, by exposing it to the wholesome discipline by which commerce regulates the value of specie. To evade this discipline, the Committee propose to impose further restrictions upon commerce, lest it
should lay hold of the specie deposits of banks, and destroy the credit
by which they are enabled to transfer so much property. This is
necessary to keep up the exhilarating jingling, which dispenses dividends of transferred property, and will also acquire an additional
monopoly under the pretext of supplying us with manufactures, as its
predecessor succeeded under that of supplying us with money. If
remitting specie, to acquire what specie represents was an evil, free
commerce would certainly remove it, but the property-transferring
policy is fraught with the essence of modern tyranny, and admits of no
remedy except that which puts an end to the power of doing mischief.

"The excess of exports over imports is the rate of profit." However impossible it may be to ascertain this excess (since every calculation is deranged as soon as it is made by the perpetual fluctuations of commerce) it is not hard to discover the sophistry of the position itself. Both exports and imports are property, of which money is the emblem. Suppose trade was carried on by importing and exporting the emblem only of the things it represents. Where would be the misfortune of importing regularly more money than we exported? It would lie only in its exuberance, depreciation, and inutility, arising from the inhibition to exchange it for foreign commodities. If there is any difference between trading in the emblem, or in the substance itself, it is in favour of the latter, because a surplus of the emblem would be less useful than a surplus of the substance. The latter affords more comforts, excites more industry, and employs more shipping. The substance is also as re-exportable as the shadow. A trade in the substance may be permanent; in the shadow it cannot long exist, on account of the equalizing power of commerce, and the depreciating nature of money. Being only an instrument of exchanges, its office cannot be impaired or destroyed, without impairing or destroying commerce itself. A permanent surplus of money, beyond its instrumentality for facilitating exchanges, cannot be gotten and held if commerce exists, because when its plenty makes it less valuable than in other countries, the exuberance will be drawn off to the countries where its scarcity has made it more valuable. In like manner a permanent surplus of the commodities represented by money, cannot long exist, because the same power which acts upon the emblem, will act upon the things represented by it. In this view the importation of more money or more commodities than we export, is equivalent. Commerce acts in the same way on either surplus by re-exportations, and profit results from the greater degree of mercantile skill and industry inspired by liberty. The question therefore is whether it is better to leave the regulation both of imports and exports, either of money or the commodities which it represents to the common law of commerce, which other nations may occasionally disorder but cannot repeal, and which must continue to act powerfully in concert with individual interest, in spite of fraudulent interpolations; or to resign their regulation to two monopolies—to banks, as to the regulation of currency; and to protecting-duty capitalists, as to the regulation of the price of commodities. The coalition between commerce and individual interests by perpetually labouring to diffuse comforts, wealth, and happiness, invigorates industry. The labours of the combination between their privileged rivals are devoted to a monopoly of comforts, wealth, and happiness, discourage industry, and generate pauperism.

But, say the Committee, "no other remedy for our troubles has been offered, but an extension of the restrictive system, which they propose as a forlorn hope." Among the assertions hazarded in the report this is the boldest. Does not this controversy propose a remedy? Do the advocates of this remedy acknowledge it to be a forlorn hope? Has public opinion remained torpid longer than the dormouse, or is it entranced by the musick of exclusive privileges? On the contrary, is it not distinctly groaning under the whips and scorn of the various modes of transferring private property by legislative acts? It is one of the greatest misfortunes to mankind, that the justice which can only be rendered to nations by frugality in governments, has never been able to find a shield which could not be pierced by the arrows of wit, cunning, and ridicule. The tribes of patrons and clients, unite their talents to caricature every proposition suggested by benevolence to nations, and the Committee with contempt assert, that no remedy for our troubles, except their own forlorn hope, has been offered. Such arts constitute the science of modern civilized tyranny, and are therefore universally opposed to advocates for frugality, and its offspring, civil liberty. Even at the head spring of hope, in legislative bodies themselves, the refreshing water of frugality, is already muddied by those impurities which a blind confidence will for ever generate. Are legislative wages to be increased? Arguments abound: are they to be reduced? None can be found in favour of the frugality by which the public confidence was won. Speeches and professions are made; delays are practised to feed the public hopes with unfruition; and when these hopes are tired out and blunted, some member whose local influence is secure, strengthens his legislative influence by defeating the proposition. He addresses an internal sympathy; he easily appeases an external opposition; and he welds to himself all who can be persuaded that they deserve the salaries they exact. Among the artifices practised to smother frugality even in the womb, is that of mingling legislative wages with moderate salaries, in order to make good objections against diminution in one case, obstacles to reform in the other. The most plausible argument in defence of high legislative wages, is, that money buys talents; but it also buys corruption, fraud, ambition, avarice, and legislative patronage. Sound policy ought to take her stand between two extremes; one, a rate of wages so low as to expel talents; the other, a rate so high as to awaken vices. We may discover the golden mean by comparing facts. When the rate of wages was lower than at present, the abuses of extending unconscionably legislative sessions; of trying private suits without any judicial powers to ascertain truth, under the pretext of their being instituted in the guise of petitions; of patronising individuals at the public expense; of creating a horde of pensioners; and of corrupting election by flattery, deceit, and a waste of public money; were infinitely less abundant. To determine whether the nation has obtained an accession of talents, integrity, and patriotism, by an increase of legislative wages, former legislatures must be compared with the present. Will the former Federal and State legislatures be thrown into the back ground by this comparison? Under which policy, that of moderate or high legislative wages, did the nation enjoy most prosperity? Which has nourished most extensively the oppressive policy of transferring property? What power can be more tyrannical than this, or more extensively excite those arts by which election itself, our last hope (may it not be forlorn) is corrupted, and converted into an instrument for avarice and ambition? What do high wages beget but parties and pay, zeal and adulation, fraud and usurpation? An elective government thus poisoned, communicates the infection to the people, and is itself the cause of the spreading malady. Will its health be restored by the poison? Will its integrity be increased by bribes to become vicious? Was the situation of New-York, arising from an enormous legislative patronage, through the medium of a dependent and party council, no evidence of the consequences to be expected from such a policy. If it pollutes a State government, will Congress be purified by an absolute power over property, and by patronizing itself with high wages and protracted sessions? Our distresses answer the question with melancholy veracity. Must not legislatures pull the mote out of their own eyes, before they can introduce a general system of frugality? No policy can be worse than that of bribing representatives by high wages, to entail lasting evils upon their country; and therefore an inquiry how far we are falling into it, cannot be superfluous.

As the remedy for over-grown power, constantly proposed, is more power to suppress the disorders it produces; so the remedy for exclusive privileges, as constantly proposed, is more exclusive privileges, under pretence of removing the oppressions they have caused. With some inaccuracy the Committee have called an extension of the restrictive system, "a forlorn hope," as it is by no means so to capitalists, whatever it may be to the rest of the nation. It will certainly produce both sweet and bitter fruits in great abundance, and we are only to discern how they will be distributed.

The rival remedy for our troubles, so insignificant in the eyes of the Committee as to be wholly suppressed, although it has been often enforced by a multitude of able writers, and some patriotick statesmen; and although it was the basis of two federal administrations, which diffused more happiness and prosperity than can be otherwise obtained; is reducible to a few principles, which may be comprised in a few words. Return to frugality; restore a free trade; abolish exclusive privileges; retract unjust pensions; surrender legislative patronage; surrender, also, legislative judicial power; and vindicate the inviolability of property, even against legislatures, except for genuine national welfare. Not that spurious and thievish species of welfare, which usurps forbidden powers and steals private property, but the true kind, honest enough to discern a distinction between devoting rights and property to the infernal deities, ambition and avarice, or leaving both to the real owners.

The Committee have closed their proem by a protestation "that they have no predilection for foreign opinions, and are less desirous to force facts to conform to reasoning, than to apply reasoning to facts; and therefore trace the principles of political economy to the conduct and to the interest of the individuals who compose the nation." Such protestations are the children of either innocence or guilt. If the Committee were conscious that their opinions bore no resemblance to a foreign policy, where was the necessity for a protestation, that they had no predilection for foreign opinions? If they were conscious that foreign opinions and practices had really suggested the policy they have so ardently recommended, how could they protest that they had no predilection for them? They should have boldly asserted that the British policy was the best in the world. In this controversy protestations have abounded. The Committee have protested that no remedy for our troubles has been offered, except their forlorn hope of extending the restrictions upon commerce. Farmers' friends and merchants' friends, having slept very quietly without showing the least sympathy either for farmers or merchants, are now bred in abundance by the plastic power of love, either for the long-forgotten farmers and merchants, or for bounties and exclusive privileges. So very affectionate are these new friends, that some of them who know nothing of farming or commerce, zealous to correct the errors of those instructed by experience, give them long calculations and laboured directions, even at the risk of being very ridiculous. What gratitude is due to such heroic adventurers, merely from motives of disinterested friendship! But lest such conspicuous merit should be overlooked, protestations of patriotism accompany those of affection for farmers and merchants. Our protesters are for ever declaring, that they hate foreign opinions, that they abhor the British policy, that they love our own free principles above all others, and that public good is their sole object, without the least mental reservation of a local nature, or in favour of capitalists. If the farmers should undertake to instruct these protesters how to manage exclusive privileges, and augment artificial capitals, it would excite their gratitude or derision. I know not a better emblem of protestations, than hiding freckles by paint; and as it is extremely important to discover the foreign freckles with which we are disfiguring our fair republican countenance, I shall endeavour to wash off a little of the paint of protestation that they may be seen.

Suppose the Committee had recommended monarchy, but protested at the same time, that they had no predilection for this foreign opinion. Would the protestation have rendered monarchy not only harmless but nutricious to our republican principles? A policy for transferring property by exclusive privileges, pensions, bounties, monopolies and extravagance, constitutes the essence of the British monopoly, and is sustained by a conspiracy between the government and those who are enriched by it, for fleecing the people. This policy is the most efficacious system of tyranny, practicable over civilized nations. It is able to subject the rights of man, if men have any rights, to ambition and avarice. It can as easily deprive nations of the right of self-government as it can rob individuals of their property. It can make revolutions re-organizers of the very abuses they overturn, and merely a wheel for turning up or down combinations equally oppressive. What is the difference between recommending the form or the substance of the European monarchies? Would it not be better, like the Lacedemonians, to adopt the form of monarchy without its substance, than to adopt its substance without its form? It is said by the holy alliance, that both the form and substance of all monarchies, however corrupt or oppressive, ought to be maintained, because they are established. By an alliance, not less holy, between our abuses, it is contended that these also ought to be maintained, because they are established. In both cases reformation is forbidden upon the same ground. England conceals the crimes of her policy by an impartial execution of her laws, but when the judicial ermine is stripped from her legislation, though it proceeds from a government called representative, the strict execution of her partial laws, are visibly an extension of the oppressions and frauds they are calculated to perpetuate. The execution of laws contrived for transferring property, only brings men to suffer the torture of a legal rack.

The British parliament, some years past, resolved, "that the influence of the crown had increased, was increasing, and ought to be diminished." Is it not at least as true here, that the influence of exclusive privileges and extravagance in our governments, has increased, is increasing, and ought also to be diminished? Which is most oppressive, the influence of one man, or the influence of a combination between several thousand men, to rule and plunder a nation? Which can be most easily overturned, a single-headed or a many-headed tyrant? In England, the instrumentality of royal influence in extending the policy of transferring property, was the evil which the parliament believed required diminution: but such was the force of this influence, that the parliamentary conviction has never been able to check it. Here the instrumentality of capitalist influence, has been able hitherto to suppress the national conviction that it ought to be diminished. Does its strength and success prove the wisdom of making it stronger, that it may become, like royal influence, irresistible even by the legislature? In England, the nature of the government requires some regal influence, and therefore the parliament only resolved, that it ought to be diminished: here, the principles of the government forbid any fictitious capitalist influence, and therefore it ought to be abolished. In England the abolition of regal influence would be a revolution; here the establishment of a privileged influence, would also be a revolution. I blush to behold a love for the principles of limited monarchy, inducing a British parliament to speak truth; and look with sorrowful disappointment for a similar proof of affection for our constitutional principles from republican legislatures. Instead of resolving that the several modes for creating a moneyed aristocracy, have increased, are increasing, and ought to be abolished, or even diminished; and not content with a tacit approbation of this revolutionizing policy, they have laboured actively for its introduction. The Committee protest that they have no predilection for it. They only propose to drive it, not away, but towards its oppressive English completion.

The machine for this end is worked by "fictitious capital," which turns out the same effects, by whatever wheels it is kept in motion. But the machine itself is not a fiction. It is a political loom driven by the steam of avarice, manufacturing tapestry for some and dowlas for others. Governments shoot the shuttle to weave golden garlands for themselves; and if the distribution of the two manufactures is complained of, they assert their patriotism by protestations, and their confederates exclaim, "a government of our own choice, like kings, can do no wrong." Though the capitals of exclusive privileges are no fictions, but woeful realities to those from whom they are drawn, let us use the terms, real and fictitious, to illustrate a necessary distinction. Fraudulent and honest, or forged and genuine, would have been better phrases, but I conform to common parlance. The thrift and comforts conferred by real capital, are general; by fictitious, partial and local; one is free, the other forced; but the generick difference lies in the chief quality of each; real capital being an accommodation in exchanging property, and fictitious an instrument for transferring it. The artifice of blending the characters of these two kinds of capital, like an attempt to conceal the infamy of a thief by showing him in good company, has deluded mankind by a superficial resemblance, to overlook the essential quality and primary design of fictitious capital. Even writers of high reputation have arranged credits between individuals, under the head of fictitious capital; such as bonds, notes, and bills of exchange; but they ought not to be placed there, unless they are forgeries. If they are genuine, they are honest exchangers of property, being merely an evidence, that for property delivered, other property, or its value, is to be returned. These papers are neither local, nor their acceptance compulsory, like paper money. Their credit arises from the property of individuals subject to their redemption, and is exposed to the decisions of free will. Whereas the credit of every species of fictitious capital, arises from delusion, and is more or less compulsory. Here we discern an impropriety in applying the term "confidence" indiscriminately to these two kinds of capital. Applied to the genuine species, including bonds, bills, and notes, it implies a belief, that the debtor possesses sufficient property to redeem his obligation; applied to the fictitious species, it implies a belief that the government will sustain its own fiction or forgery. A confidence in power, sustains fictitious capital. A necessity, caused by the laws for the introduction of fictitious capital, unites with power to give it currency, though we know it to be a vehicle for conveying our property into the pockets of others. An exclusion of real capital, an increase of fictitious, and an aggravation of taxation, unite to create this necessity. But this necessity is not confidence, though called so by those who inflict it, to transfer the odium from their own fraud, to the folly of a community; and to hide the compulsion under a veil like free will. Whenever the circulation of fictitious currency or capital is obstructed, governments, conscious that this property-transferring machine works for the conspiracy by which it is fabricated, protect their associates; not because they possess, but because they do not possess the public confidence. This legal interposition to enforce a system for transferring property, is ingeniously said by the Committee, "to trace the true principles of political economy to the conduct and interest of the individuals who compose the nation." The most eminent political writers have united in an opinion, that to govern too much is an error, and even tyrannical. How can government be pushed further, than into the very mouths of individuals? What other power can despotism need, after it has obtained a complete control over all the physical interests of the individuals who compose a nation? It boasts in the United States, that it leaves the mind free. The criminal extended on the rack still retains the freedom of his mind. Though confined in a dungeon upon bread and water, he may be of what religion he pleases. So bodies, impoverished, and sometimes starved by being encircled with the magical chains of exclusive privileges, may boast under the hardship of deprivations, that their minds are still free; that they can adore, though they cannot enjoy, those republican principles, which teach that governments ought to be instituted to secure the right of providing for our own wants, according to our own will, and not according to the will of the government; because such a power in the government, however it may leave the mind speculatively free, is a real despotism over both mind and body, since they are indissoluble except by death.

Tyranny is wonderfully ingenious in the art of inventing specious phrases to spread over its nefarious designs. "Divine right, kings can do no wrong, parliamentary supremacy, the holy alliance," are instances of it in Europe. "Common defence, general welfare, federal supremacy and political economy," are impressed into the same service here. When the delusion of one phrase is past, another is adopted to work out the same ends as its predecessor. Political economy is represented as a complicated system of deprivations and compensations, or of getting and giving back money. In the multitude of transactions implied by this notion of political economy, will none of it stick to the fingers through which it passes? Will the privileged bands of brokers get nothing by this economical traffick? Will the officers necessary to enforce this species of political economy, require no salaries? An economy exposed to endless frauds, and incomputable expenses. The pretence "that though it inflicts deprivations, it bestows compensations," is one of those gross impositions upon the credulity of mankind, believed upon no better grounds than the stories of ghosts and apparitions. In the history of the world, there is no instance of a political economy bottomed upon exclusive privileges, having made any compensation for the deprivations it inflicts. The Committee have likened it to household economy. What should we say of the household economist, who should keep a train of idle servants, surrender to them all his keys, entrust them with all his money, and buy of them all his necessaries at double prices? Would not his system of economy be the same with that of a nation, which creates a train of idle capitalists by exclusive privileges, surrenders to them all the keys of individual interest, intrusts them with its currency, and buys of them its necessaries at double prices? The similitude fails according to the Committee, because we choose our governments. But the individual also chooses his servants. Let us try it in another aspect. Suppose a train of servants, agents, or representatives; call them what you will, should offer their services to a wealthy individual, upon condition that they should have the power of prescribing to him in all his wants, of prohibiting some of his comforts, and of enhancing the price of others; would he believe that the proposal was made to advance either his wealth, liberty, or happiness? Again: Suppose our household economist had employed a train of servants, but upon the suggestion of another train desirous of getting into their places, that they were deranging his affairs, he should displace them and employ the friendly informers. If the new servants should embarrass his affairs more than the old did, would he say to them, "well done, ye good and faithful servants?" In all these views, household economy is no bad mirror for reflecting that species of political economy, managed by successive parties, as an engine for transferring property.

The Committee have untirely overlooked by far the most important branch of political economy, namely, the economy which teaches nations not to expend the principles which secure their liberty, in search of money. If we waste this treasure, under the idea that we shall thereby increase our treasure of currency, capital, or money, we should imitate the man who bestows the best part of his estate upon a swindler, because he promises to improve the residue. A waste of our republican principles certainly involves a waste of our money. Have the monopolies, extravagance, and exclusive privileges of European governments, saved the money of the people? No, but it is said, that the loss, both of liberty and money, caused by the political economy which minutely regulates the interest of individuals in Europe, proceeds from the badness of the governments, and that ours, being a good one, it can guard abuses against abuse, and make tyrannical principles the saviours of civil liberty. This very unpromising experiment, to make a blessing of actual tyranny by theoretical liberty, has never yet succeeded any where else, and the picture drawn by the Committee of the distress to which it has already conducted the United States, is a strong indication of the improbability of its success here. The endeavour to guard abuses against abuse, seems to be utterly hopeless, from our own experience. Specie payments was the guard against the abuse of banking, but the guard sleeps whenever the abuse requires it. The protecting-duty abuse, and the abuse of exclusive privileges, are guarded against abuse by our good theoretical governments, exactly as they are by the bad theoretical European governments. They are extended. The abuses of extravagance and borrowing, can grow under our governments, as fast as under those of Europe. In fact, the introduction of abuses, is an infallible prophet of their continuance. The nation which imagines that a government which introduces, will not foster them, or that a good government can by provisions convert fraud into honesty, relies upon a moral impossibility for the preservation of its liberty.

It is confessed, that the predilection of the Committee for foreign opinions or abuses, only extends to some of the modes for transferring property, by monopolies and exclusive privileges, without expressing an approbation of all. They have not approved of the regal, hierarchial, and sinecure modes, nor have they directly recommended chartered companies to carry on particular branches of foreign commerce. It may, however, be inferred from their approbation of a law charter to capitalists, conveying an exclusive privilege for carrying on many branches of domestick commerce, that they would have no objection to its own brothers and usual associates. But whatever modes of monopoly and exclusive privileges for transferring property they may love, and whatever modes they may hate, they have strenuously recommended one, which has become obsolete in England. Monopolies of domestick commerce, like our restrictions upon the importation of tobacco, have been tried and deserted in that country, and we are only dressing ourselves in our father's old clothes.

Chaptal[4] observes, "that the advantages which England derives from a system excluding competition in the markets, are, in preserving

4. Jean Antoine Chaptal (1756–1832), French chemist and, under Napoleon, minister of the interior and director of commerce and manufactures; author of *On French Industry* (2 vols., 1819).

the workmanship which supports her population; and in being able to tax every thing that goes immediately into internal consumption." The superiority of our workmanship has not awakened a jealousy of its being copied by other nations. Our population is supported by agriculture, and this motive for imitating the English policy, could not be urged by the Committee. Its remaining advantage of taxing every thing which we consume, though it would not have advanced their object to make the most of that argument, is yet prospectively eulogised by a pleasant view of the English excise system, which, like the second curse inflicted upon the Egyptians, feeds upon mankind. Through a dark avenue of intimations, cautiously planted here and there in the report, and fearfully suggesting the deficiency of revenue resulting from the restrictive system, we clearly discern the English excise system, or the policy of taxing all internal consumptions. But out-stripping their model, the Committee propose to pay this excise twice over, though the English writhe under the agony of paying it only once. To get internal commodities for taxation, we are first to pay an enormous excise to capitalists, and when we come to consumption, another excise is to be paid to government, to supply the loss in the customs, produced by the first tax. Thus we shall be doubly exposed to this dark, expensive, vexatious, and oppressive mode of taxation. Whereas commercial restrictions in England do not enhance the prices of home consumptions to give an excise to capitalists, as their manufactures are cheaper than any they could import; and this cheapness has suggested to some other nations, like ourselves, prohibitions and restrictions upon English competition. As England undersells other nations, they cannot undersell her: wherefore she only pays an excise to her government, and the exclusion of foreign competition bestows no bounty or excise upon her capitalists. Their exclusive charter to manufacture certain articles is now a dead letter, but ours is a more enormous tax, than could be inflicted by conferring on a mercantile company, an exclusive privilege of carrying on any one branch of foreign commerce, because it embraces internal necessaries to a far greater extent, which are less capable of being renounced than foreign importations. Our sweeping domestick monopoly is exactly of the same character with that established by several despotick English kings, by grants or charters to individuals.

The Committee may therefore speak correctly, when they say, that they have no predilection for foreign opinions. In this view of the subject, they propose to introduce a species of monopoly which the English do not retain; and to discourage a species of industry, which the English have endowed with a monopoly. Not the manufacturing capitalists, but the landlords are enriched by a monopoly. Their exclusion of foreign manufactures does not enhance the price of domestick; but the exclusion of foreign corn does enhance the price of bread, and constitutes a tax or excise paid by its consumers; having the effect of a bounty to landlords by raising rents. But though the Committee deviate from the English policy, in their selection of the interest to be patronized, by sacrificing the land-owners to the capitalists, instead of sacrificing the consumers of bread to the landlords, they adhere to the principle of their corn laws.

The exclamations with regard to the English are curious. In that country the whole tribe of abusers are vociferating, "Oh! how happy we are." The sufferers from these abuses are groaning, "Oh! how miserable we are!" Here, monopolies, exclusive privileges, and extravagance, hold up the English happiness for our imitation, and our patriots represent English misery as highly to be deprecated. Is it not curious that the same foreign policy should furnish two comparisons; one to prove that we are a weak and miserable nation; the other that we are the wisest and happiest in the world?

The before-mentioned foreign political economist, Chaptal, regarded by capitalists as such an apostle of their creed (a creed for making themselves great pecuniary dignitaries) that they have translated, condensed, and published his doctrines, observes,

I grant it would have been wiser for each nation to confine its ambition to cultivating and perfecting that kind of labour, for which nature has particularly designed it; but all wish to obtain all kinds, and hence have arisen those principles of an interest badly understood, which isolates and reduces them to their own individual resources. I well know that the laws of nature are fixed, and that sooner or later every nation will resort to that species of industry she has marked out for it; but the evil is done, and the deviation of this departure from true principles will be much more considerable than is generally supposed. A nation which receives its manufactured articles from abroad, cultivates with care the productions of its soil to exchange them in return; this culture would be naturally more neglected, when the exportation is lessened by the refusal to admit foreign manufactures in exchange. We are not ignorant, besides how difficult it is to contract, and to resolve to sacrifice capitals, and annihilate manufacturing establishments when a nation has once engaged in a false route; her hasty change from it cannot be expected, unless by the will of the government, and the nation's recollection of its own interest.

This is a fair statement of the question, by a monarchical economist. Excluding those arguments resulting from the difference between a monarchical and republican form of government, he yet allows the exclusive-privilege system to be a false route. He admits it to be only defensible when it has been established, and asserts that every nation will return to that species of industry marked out by the laws of nature. The United States are at the crisis when they must determine whether they will persevere in this false route, or retrace their steps whilst they can. If we persevere, the difficulty of retraction will increase as it becomes more indispensable. The government will be implored in the names of good faith, of humanity, of honour, and of other virtues, impressed by self interest into a mercenary service, to sustain every abuse, monopoly, exclusive privilege, and extravagance, for transferring property, which it may have fatuitously established; and as its administrators always get a share of the spoil, they will be excessively charitable. The mammoth would have continued his ravages for ever, if his having been created, was a good reason for his perpetual existence. The wolf must be suffered to prowl without interruption after prey, because he exists. The sheep should even be forced into his jaws. In this doctrine lies the secret by which political devourers of the earnings of industry have been fed and multiplied. It is the cement of the holy alliance between frauds, abuses, and oppressions of every complexion, and of every degree of malignity to human happiness. The cruelty of restoring their own to the people, and of preferring the happiness of a multitude to the luxury of a few, causes the crocodile power, to shed affected tears of compassion, and is used for alluring unwary victims to their ruin. Chaptal uses England as a scare-crow to frighten France, not out of, but into the policy, which he says is a violation of the laws of nature.

The Committee use England and other nations to frighten us into the same policy. And thus the folly is rolled from nation to nation, and generates abuses and tyranny in all its progress.

This doctrine of imitating errors has already conducted us to a crisis at which we must once more decide whether we will be a free nation. Freedom is not constituted solely by having a government of our own. Under this idea most nations would be free. We fought in the revolutionary war against exclusive privileges and oppressive monopolies. Will a monopoly which can tax internal consumptions to a vast extent, be less avaricious or less oppressive, than the similar monopoly of which the article of tea was designed to be the entering wedge? What a spectacle for the Deity do we exhibit? We beseech him to deliver us out of a gulf of distress, and plunge ourselves deeper and deeper into it. Are bad political principles infectious like the plague, and can our constitutions afford us only a quarantine against them of forty years, after which we are to use no precautions against their liberty-killing effect, in imitation of the apathy with which the Turks behold that body-killing pestilence?

Such is that species of political economy which pursues the money, the food, and the clothing of individuals. Like money, political economy has two souls. It can increase individual happiness by diffusing comforts, or it can destroy it, by accumulating capitals for a few. A species of political economy having the latter effect, is only another species of paper currency for transferring property and comforts. If no tyranny can be more complete and more tormenting, than one which dictates to individuals in all their comforts and enjoyments; which prohibits some and enhances the price of others to enrich capitalists; the argument that we ought to establish this tyrannical species of political economy, because other nations have done so, is precisely of the same value, as the argument for introducing monarchy, aristocracy, or any other species of oppression, because other nations have established them. If we are under the necessity of adopting bad principles, because other nations do not, or rather cannot adopt good principles, the progress of civil liberty is at an end. Must we go back to their bad political principles, because they are unable to proceed forward towards our good political principles? Why then, liberty must be abolished by tyranny; and honest political economy, the ally of the former, must be supplanted by fraudulent political economy, the most powerful ally of the latter. The mind has full evidence in the experience of nations, upon which to decide between the species of political economy which breeds monopolies, enriches capitalists, and deprives the people of comforts; and that which leaves to individuals the free use of their earnings, undiminished by any legal transfers, the contributions excepted, necessary to sustain a free and frugal government.

The whole benefit supposed by the Committee to lie in the spurious kind of political economy, is to result from an exchange of the balance of liberty and comforts which we ought to possess under our constitutions, for a balance of trade with foreign nations. To advance this speculation, a moneyed aristocracy, already created, is to be made so strong as to place in our mouths a great number of padlocks, lest we should consume our earnings, instead of giving them to this aristocracy, that it may secure the coveted balance. The pecuniary balance in foreign trade thus obtained, would either be transitory or settle upon a pecuniary aristocracy, which would absorb the powers of government. But the balance of liberty and comforts surrendered to obtain it, as well as the pecuniary balance between a moneyed aristocracy and the people, is lost for ever. It is constantly repeated (an old story in Europe) that the capitalists will produce a home market, and compensate all other interests by purchasing their labours with their own money. If the argument is a good one, there can be no such thing as a pecuniary tyranny. Aristocracies of all sorts are not pecuniary frauds, because they eat. Hierarchies, bishops, and monks, are blessings, as they eat also. All the European monopolies, exclusive privileges, and sinecures, being composed of men, far from being oppressive or tyrannical, are only political economy, because they afford markets for those from whom the money is extorted, by which their products are purchased. It is the very argument which has been used time out of mind by all those governments whose maxims we scorn, and whose oppressions we condemn.

There are features in the species of political economy proposed by

85

the Committee, very much resembling those which we have sometimes seen in stay-laws,[5] as they are called, but far more fraudulent. It proposes to meddle more deeply with the contracts of individuals, and to control far more extensively the freedom of will. These stay-laws have often enacted, that the property offered by individuals, shall be valued by disinterested appraisers, and that the creditor shall receive it at this valuation. By depriving the creditor of this right to judge for himself, he is frequently defrauded, and always compelled to take things badly constructed, which he does not want, or which he could obtain cheaper, had he retained the right of laying out his money according to his own judgment. The system of economy advocated by the Committee enables the capitalists to value their own goods, and compels the purchasers by prohibitions and restrictions, just as they were compelled by war, to purchase them at the valuation of the sellers, although except for this compulsion, they might have been gotten cheaper. The stay-laws are only defended as temporary expedients, and only borne because they are soon to expire. Our new system of political economy is proposed as a permanent policy. The stay-laws pretend to the benevolent intention of benefiting the poor, and relieving the distressed. Our system of compulsory political economy proposes to give bounties to the rich at the expense of the poor, to be exacted by their own consciences in the valuation of their own wares. The stay-laws are honest in theory, but fraudulent in operation. The compulsory system of political economy is foul in theory, and less fair in its operation between capitalists and consumers, than stay-laws between debtor and creditor. The stay-laws are a species of political economy, contrived to effect a transfer of property between individuals, without the free will which constitutes fair exchanges. The compulsory political economy of protecting duties, effects a transfer of property between a combination of capitalists and the rest of the nation, in which the freedom of will is all on one side. The valuation under the stay-laws may sometimes be in favour of the

5. Stay-laws were passed by legislatures generally to postpone trials or the execution of judgments in debt cases. Advocates claimed that they were only temporary relief measures, passed during agriculturally depressed times. Critics contended that the prodebtor legislation compromised the ability of creditors to recover debts.

creditor. Under the compulsory system of political economy, it can never be in favour of the nation. The creditor, by a stay-law valuation, gets something for his demand. All that the capitalist gets by his own valuation, beyond the price at which the purchaser could have gotten the commodity, except for the compulsion bearing upon him, is a total loss to the purchaser, and an entire acquisition to the capitalist of so much of the purchaser's property. Such a system of political economy must obviously be more ruinous to all interests except the capitalists, than the stay-law economy is to creditors.

The principles of political economy, as advocated by the Committee, terminate in two conclusions; one, that of producing a pecuniary balance of foreign trade; the other, that this balance will be gained by manufactures. By the first, the honest species of internal political economy, must be destroyed; by the second, the efficacy of agricultural products in regulating the balance of foreign commerce, is wholly overlooked. However equivocal the term "manufactures" may be, yet, as the Committee have used it to distinguish between the different products of human labour, I shall adhere to it for the purpose of enquiring, whether those products to which they have exclusively applied it, are in fact more efficacious in acquiring a balance of trade, than those to which they deny such a power.

In ancient times, the products of agricultural industry greatly preponderated, and constituted nearly all the objects of commerce; in modern, though this preponderance is considerably diminished by the improvements in manufacturing, it must still be confessed, that they retain a considerable superiority in value. Tea, a single agricultural product, obtains for a great empire, a balance of trade in money. Spices do the same for Holland. Liquors, sugar, and coffee, are staples which bestow wealth on other countries. Cotton, tobacco, grain, meat, live stock, rice, fish, tar, pitch, turpentine, potash, timber, and other articles, are the means of the United States for procuring a balance of trade. Chaptal thinks, "that it would be wiser for a nation to cultivate and perfect that kind of labour for which nature designed it, than to seek for wealth by prohibitions and restrictions upon commerce." The Committee are for forcing nature out of her course, by discouraging the long list of occupations which she patronizes, and fostering one at their expense, upon which she must frown for ages. According to their doctrine, China ought to diminish the cultivation of tea, and other countries that of spices, sugar, and coffee. The United States also, ought to diminish the cultivation of the entire mass of articles, which bring them all the money and commodities they get by commerce, for the purpose of encouraging an occupation, by which they gain nothing from foreign nations. Their scheme is to diminish the whole mass of our exports, in order to increase a species of labour which furnishes but few; and they call it "political economy." As its hopefulness depends more on the degree of favour it may expect from the laws of nature, than on the power of legislation to defeat those laws, we ought maturely to consider what these laws now decree, how long it will take us to make them null and void, and what will be the expense of a legislative war with them.

The laws of nature operate upon a great variety of circumstances in respect to commerce, both moral and physical. Among these, extent of country and the number of inhabitants, are of irresistible force. The relation of these two circumstances to each other, determines her mandate on the subject we are discussing. We discover that relation by considering the difference between population and populousness. The population may be considerable, and yet a country may not be populous, comparatively with its extent. Such is our case. Whatever may be the actual census of the United States, yet a superabundance of uncultivated land, will long prevent them from being populous. To determine correctly how nature legislates in such a case, we must be governed by the character she has given to man. The first objects of his solicitude are, a home, independence, and leisure. Where land is good, cheap, and plenty, he will certainly estimate the prospect of acquiring these objects, either by becoming the owner of a farm, or a day labourer for hire. He will compare the beneficence of the Deity with the beneficence of a capitalist; and consider whether it is better to work himself for another, than to have the best labourer in the world, the earth itself, to work for him. He sees this good mother ready to supply him spontaneously with meat, butter, milk, honey, and many other comforts, not earned by labouring at the anvil, or toiling at the shuttle, for the live long day; and to repay bountifully his moderate exertions; and he will never be deprived of these blessings for which his heart pants, except by the tyranny of force, or the influence of bounties, equivalent to his sacrifices. As coercion cannot be used, he can only be assailed by bribes; but these will be intercepted by his master, because he cannot rival foreign nations, except by reducing the wages of his workmen to a level with theirs. In the interval, the cheapness of land must enhance the wages of mechanicks, and if the bounty should also get into the pockets of the workmen, it will accelerate their ability of acquiring the domicil for which their hearts languish. Have not the laws of nature decided, which is the best substratum for commercial rivalry and competition, cheapness or dearness? Shall we build up a competition with foreign nations upon the cheapness of our land, or upon the dearness of our manufactures, both destined to live for centuries, and slowly to disappear together? I cannot discern the impolicy of erecting our commercial competitions upon the cheapness of land, so long as it remains; and transplanting them to the cheapness of manufactures, whenever that shall occur in a natural course.

In addition, however, to the considerations arising from the present plenty of land and relative scarcity of people, we ought to take into view the permanent difference between maritime and inland countries. As the latter can never become considerable manufacturers for exportation, it would be as preposterous and unjust to impose the manufacturing occupation upon them, as to compel maritime countries to be agricultural. What must be the bounties which would enable our inland people to rival the English and other maritime nations, with our manufactures, in foreign nations? If they were sufficient to effect that object, with respect to our inland people, would they not be so superabundant to our maritime people, as to enable them to undersell and suppress their interiour competitors. The protecting-duty bounty would therefore be chiefly or entirely received by a slip of maritime country, inferiour to our inland country in extent and population; whilst the latter would be equally subjected to an excise system of taxation, without partaking of the bounty.

The political economy of procuring a balance of trade in our favour, by manufactures, can only be effected by their exportation, and until the object is thus accomplished, we must diminish the value and quantity of all exportable commodities, and subject all our consumptions to a double excise, or all our lands to a direct tax. Chaptal justly observes "that a nation which receives its manufactured articles from abroad, cultivates with care the productions of its soil to exchange for them in return; this culture would naturally be more neglected, when the exportation is lessened by the refusal to admit foreign manufactures in exchange." The project of the Committee is to lessen the exportation of the productions of the soil by refusing to admit foreign manufactures in exchange for them, to cause their culture to be neglected by this effectual obstacle to their sale, to put a stop to the only means we have for drawing money, property, or capital from foreign nations, and to enable the class of capitalists to draw money, property, or capital from all other classes, by giving it an excise upon consumptions. This is a species of political economy which Chaptal seems to have overlooked.

The different modes in which governments have managed the machine called political economy, would suffice to fill volumes. In Russia, an empress declared from the throne "that the removal of agriculturists to towns, in order to follow manufacturing employments, greatly checked population, prevented the cultivation of large tracts of country, and impeded the prosperity of the empire to a great extent." Here it is contended "that the removal of agriculturists to towns and villages in order to follow manufacturing employments will advance the prosperity of the United States," although it will also check population, and prevent the cultivation of a larger and better extent of country. But the nobility of Russia, having a power of exacting from their boors an unlimited capitation tax called an obrok, obstructed the wise and benevolent designs of the empress, because they could extort a higher obrok from them by means of a manufacturing monopoly, than by agriculture. Here the capitalists, like the Russian nobility, are endeavouring to get agriculturists into factories, because they will be thereby enabled to draw more money from their labours than they could otherwise do. But they have outstripped the dull Russian nobility in acuteness, by obtaining an obrok to be levied upon those who will not go into their factories, by the protecting duties. What are poor mortals! The Russian obrok for enriching an ennobled class is universally admitted to be a grievous species of slavery; our obroks for enriching a privileged class of capitalists, is eulogized as an admirable species of political economy.

In England, the capitalists perceive that the importation of raw materials, duty free, will enable them to draw an higher obrok from their factory slaves. Here, the capitalists have discovered, that by diminishing the value of agricultural products, they can draw an obrok both from factory and agricultural workmen. And both of these contrivances are called political economy.

Russia, as I gather from its eulogist, Tooke, having a four-fold population beyond the United States, exports only one fourth as much in value. Her exports, like ours, are agricultural. By this exportation she is said to gain a small pecuniary balance of trade. Here it is supposed that a four-fold exportation of agricultural products by one fourth of people, must lose it. But it will be vehemently asserted by the protecting-duty policy, that Russia gains her annual trifling pecuniary balance by commercial prohibitions upon importations. The fact is doubtful; as even an indisposition for expensive consumptions owing to the uncivilized state of the great mass of its people, and other causes, may very deeply affect it. But let it be admitted. Her exportations are sixteen-fold less than ours in proportion to population, and her duties only amount to three millions of dollars annually. To discover whether a small pecuniary balance of trade, thus procured, is a wise policy, we must compute the cost. First, the smallness of the agricultural exports, must be ascribed, as Chaptal observes, to the refusal of admitting foreign manufactures in exchange, and demonstrates that agriculture must be reduced to a very bad state. Secondly, the smallness of the importations demonstrates that forty millions of people can derive a very inconsiderable portion of comfort from other climates. And, thirdly, the prohibitions and restrictions upon commerce having rendered the customs wholly inadequate to the expenses of the government, a frightful catalogue of excises, obroks, and internal taxes of every description, has been created to supply the deficiency. The balance of trade in money is trifling compared with the oppressions arising from resorting to these resources, which it causes. These oppressions are permanent; and though Russia may get this small balance by inflicting them, she cannot prevent it from leaking out continually, so that she is obliged to resort to vast emissions of depreciating paper money. Besides, the commercial prohibitions and restrictions have reduced the price of agricultural products so low, as to inflict annually a pecuniary loss upon that one occupation, infinitely exceeding in amount the inconsiderable and fleeting pecuniary gain from a balance in trade. This part of the Russian policy, is the political economy recommended by the Committee. Even Russia is still obliged to take back many of her raw materials in a manufactured form, such as iron, furs, and wool, because the laws of nature have hitherto decided that she shall not be an exporting manufacturing country.

Athens, Carthage, and Holland, being deficient in commodities, both agricultural and manufactured, resorted to a free trade, and availed themselves of their maritime situations to excite industry by the utmost latitude both as to exports and imports. These examples of political economy have been admired by all the world. They raised three small barren districts to wealth and power. One was raised out of the sea. What then would be the consequence if we should unite the policy by which they flourished, to the advantage of possessing an extensive and fertile country, producing many indigenous commodities; when these little districts found it so efficient without such powerful auxiliaries?

Russia had no money when she had no trade. If a small trade will procure some money, a great trade will procure more. As we have no mines, the Committee propose to get money by diminishing trade. Suppose we had enough to facilitate domestick exchanges; ought trade to be therefore diminished? If so, the same reason would dictate its entire abolition. What will the money then be? As valuable and not more so than local paper money answering the end of facilitating local exchanges. Why is it true that money is every thing? Because it may be expended in obtaining comforts from foreign nations. Metallick money, locked up by commercial restrictions, is nothing in reference to other nations, beyond local paper money. Nations are individuals in relation to each other, and in locking up money, would act as wisely as an individual who should keep his money in a chest during his whole life. This is the political economy, for the sake of which we are advised to subject ourselves to the taxation of internal monopolies and exclusive privileges.

It is urged that governments ought to supervise the affairs of individuals, and that in order to promote their prosperity, they should give bounties to domestick obstacles, to be paid by domestick facilities, in order to enable these obstacles to undersell foreign facilities. By this policy the impracticability of equalizing climates, soils, situations, habits, and arts, is undertaken: and that, which, to a benevolent mind is still more beautiful, it will rob the ocean of its terrors, so soon as it is effected by all nations; and it may thenceforth roar and rage without swallowing up any more victims. The rival policy advises governments either to encourage the natural facilities of a nation, or at least to suffer them to produce as great a surplus as they can, to be exchanged for the facilities of other nations. If one of these systems of political economy is in its senses, the other must be run mad. No! It is not mad: It is an acute artifice practised by governments, under pretence of supervising the affairs of individuals, to enrich themselves, and their instruments of oppression.

The effects of bounties upon either imports or exports, are often very far from promoting the wealth or happiness of the nation which pays them. The consuming or exporting nation frequently receives these bounties from the paying nation, as in the cases of the bounties paid by England on the exportation of Irish linen, or the importation of corn. If the system of political economy recommended by the Committee, in the long, long run, should so completely succeed, as to enable the capitalists to become exporters of manufactures, the bounties preceding that distant epoch will have been paid to them, that foreign nations may receive those which shall succeed it. Drawbacks of duties, on the contrary, are allowed to be highly beneficial to commerce. These are special acts of freedom. Ought not the advantages resulting from them to suggest at least a drawback of all duties beyond the demands of revenue, as likely to have a similar effect upon commerce? It would be a general freedom.

There remains an argument if founded in fact, sufficient to overturn the whole theory of the Committee: and it seems perfectly plain to me, that the fact sustains the argument. The Committee say "that they have applied reasoning to facts, and traced the true principles of political economy to the conduct and the interest of the individuals who compose the nation." Let us adopt this correct principle, and consider whether the Committee have applied it so as to effect or defeat their object of procuring a balance of trade in our favour, from foreign nations. They contend, as is certainly true, that national political economy must have its source in the individuals who compose the nation, and therefore they go in search of it to "the conduct and interest of these individuals." Unless these individuals have a surplus of income beyond their expenses, the nation cannot acquire a balance of trade in its favour, because a national surplus, like a river, can only be formed by the streamlets of individual surpluses. If these rills are diverted into other channels, the river becomes dry. Suppose the income of an individual to be one thousand dollars, and his expenses eight hundred, two hundred would be his surplus applicable to the attainment of a balance of trade, and if so applied would draw from foreign nations money or property to that amount. But if he should be robbed of this surplus, he could not contribute any thing towards this object. Extend the supposition "to all the individuals who compose the nation" and, though each should, by his industry, procure a surplus beyond his expenses, yet if all are robbed of their several surpluses, none would have any thing applicable to the attainment of a balance of trade. The application is obvious. Whenever the profits of industry are transferred to monopolies, exclusive privileges, or public extravagance, the same amount is deducted from its means to procure for the nation a balance of trade. If the people of the United States are at this time paying thirty millions annually to banking pensions, the protecting-duty monopoly, and unnecessary public expenditures, it takes from individuals the same sum, which would otherwise have been applicable to the object of obtaining a favourable balance of trade, and applies it to the very different object of enriching a capitalist. Thus the theory is a *felo de se*, and inconsistent with the principle of tracing "political economy to the conduct and interest of individuals." It traces it on the contrary to the conduct and interest of a combination of factory capitalists. It proposes to acquire a balance of trade by transferring the means for doing so, to a totally different object. Would not individuals be more able to contend for this balance with thirty millions, or whatever the sum transferred may be, than without it? Besides, in this contest they would receive an equivalent for their surpluses, which would advance their own interest, and that interest is the end of true political economy.

But when their surpluses are transferred by laws to enrich any minor class in society, they get no equivalent for them, and their conduct has nothing to do in the affair. They are only passive instruments of fraudulent laws. It is unimportant to true political economy or national prosperity, whether the surpluses of individuals shall be applied to getting money or commodities from foreign nations, to building houses, or to other improvements; applied in either mode it is a substantial political economy, and a sound item in computing the balance of trade. But if these surpluses are transferred to exclusive privileges or lavished upon a sect of capitalists, they cannot be applied in either mode towards advancing this kind of political economy. During our colonial state, though the pecuniary balance of trade was against the provinces, the political economy of not transferring the surpluses of individuals to unproductive legal creatures, overbalanced the loss, and caused commerce to be so highly beneficial to the provinces, that they speedily grew up to be a match for the mother country, and surprised the world by the celerity of their improvement. Now, the fraudulent species of political economy transfers these surpluses to a large family of unproductive legal creatures, and our prosperity stops, because the profits of labour, heretofore applicable to the objects of drawing money or property from foreign nations, or improving our country, are diverted to, and exhausted by, this consuming family.

To obtain a distinct view of the oppressive system of commercial restrictions commenced about thirty years ago, and prosecuted to an issue widely different from what its authors contemplated, until it has made matter for another Paradise Lost, we have only to recollect that human happiness must consist of temporal gratifications. We can only extract from human nature itself a perfect test, by which to distinguish the honest and true, from the false and fraudulent species of political economy. If such a test is not to be found in the difference between privations and gratifications, I know not where it lies. A political economy for securing and increasing our gratifications, as we pass through this world, is exactly the adversary of a political economy for inflicting and increasing privations. One must therefore be a true, and the other a false, species of political economy. We have only to ask ourselves whether our gratifications or privations have been increased by commercial restrictions, to discover the species of political economy to which they belong. The embargo preceding the last war cost me, by a calculation which I believe to be correct, considerably more than my proportion of the expenses of the war itself. But it enriched capitalists. Commercial restrictions are all partial embargoes; but they will also enrich the capitalists. A complete embargo is a respectable witness to prove what are the effects of partial embargoes, because the latter only graduate the effects produced by a general policy of the same nature. These probably deprive individuals of as much annually as would pay their taxes, or purchase gratifications to the same amount. A species of political economy which inflicts privations on the present, under pretence of bestowing gratifications upon some future generation, is false, because it robs men of the only gratifications of which they are susceptible, and it ought to be distrusted, because it is not exposed to the least responsibility. If it fails to fulfil its promise, who are to be impeached? Its authors are in the grave. It may promise whatever its designs may require, without being deterred even by the fear of reproach, because the excuse "that the time is not yet come to exhibit the goodness of the system" is always ready. But when the temptation of acquiring wealth, is added to its incongruity with human nature, and to the absence of responsibility, it becomes highly suspicious. The political economy of the Committee inflicts innumerable privations on the existing generations, defended by a promise of making compensation after the Committee and the sufferers are dead; and also bestows eagerly-solicited gratifications on the existing sect of capitalists. As to the capitalists, it adheres to the principle of true political economy, in dealing out present gratifications to living people; but as to the rest of the nation, it rejects this principle, and adopts that of the false species of political economy, by dealing out present privations to living people. But justice requires that a system of political economy, like a system of government, should be founded in one principle, so as to operate upon all the living members of the society equally, and not dispense wealth and gratifications to a few, and poverty and privations to a multitude, under pretence that the account shall be settled with the unborn, and the balance paid by the bankruptcy of the grave. Gratifications should be bestowed upon all living people, or upon none, by a true political economy; and it should also inflict privations upon all, or none, because it is the very essence of tyranny to inflict privations, in order to reap or to bestow gratifications.

It is unnecessary to prove that political economy, in all countries, is capable of being founded in the same principles, and ought to result from the same theory; and it is sufficient to show a difference in the circumstances of different countries, in order to evince the species of political economy practicable in each. All the European writers upon political economy have extracted their systems from, and laboured to accommodate them to, local existing circumstances. Taking England for an example, and comparing it with the United States, these are so dissimilar, that a system of political economy, for that country cannot be suitable for this; and therefore an imitation by either of the other would be preposterous. England has two great interests, landlords and tenants, which are extensively computed in moulding her system of political economy; the yeomanry of the United States are land-owners, and must long continue so; wherefore rents are not an item of any importance, in moulding our system of political economy. Labour in England is environed by a multitude of laws, and must therefore be regulated by its system of political economy; being free here, it requires no such regulation. England abounds in political orders and exclusive privileges, of an influence to be considered and provided for: the United States have no such orders, and ought not to have any such exclusive privileges. These English orders and privileges are so interwoven with the form of government, that their preservation is a primary object with the English system of political economy, which must be calculated either to effect this end or to produce a revolution; nothing equivalent to these orders or privileges is interwoven with our form of government by our constitutions, and to create and provide for them by a legal system of political economy, would be a substantial revolution. We have no tribes of tenants, labourers, and mechanics, panting for a revolution, and breaking out into frequent seditions to be restrained by a system of political economy; England is under the necessity of maintaining a standing army both to repress their turbulence and for self-defence against powerful neighbours. These and other local circumstances are dictators to her writers upon political economy, but no dictators to us; and therefore neither reason nor power requires us to adopt the system of political economy, which they are compelled by both to defend and recommend.

Let us now proceed to a separate examination of the answers given by the Committee to certain objections urged against the restrictive system, which they have selected as most answerable. They amount to nine, namely: that the protecting-duty system is unconstitutional; injurious to morals, and productive of pauperism; improper to be extended; [a cause for smuggling;] a tax on the many, and a bounty to the few; a restrictive system; a destroyer of revenue; ruinous to commerce; and destructive to agriculture. Of all these crimes, the Committee contend that it is as innocent as the child unborn. If it can yet hide its future features in the womb, or excuse its present frolicks by its childhood, when it has grown up to maturity, it will hardly be acquitted, by an impartial judge, of any one. In considering the allegations of the Committee under these heads, an occasional recurrence to the principles we have passed over, will be unavoidable for the sake of their applications to new suggestions.

❧

Arguments Against the Protecting Duty Summarized Through an Analysis of Its Major Consequences

I. PROTECTING DUTIES ARE UNCONSTITUTIONAL

To make them constitutional, the Committee have adopted the present fashionable mode of construction, which considers the constitution as a lump of fine gold, a small portion of which is so malleable, as to cover the whole mass. By this golden rule for manufacturing the constitution, a particular power given to the Federal Government, may be made to cover all the rights reserved to the people and the States; a limited jurisdiction given to the Federal Courts, is made to cover all the State Courts; and a legislative power over ten miles square, is malleated over the whole of the United States, as a single guinea may be beaten out, so as to cover a whole house. Unfortunately, this political manufacture being encouraged by allowing bounties paid in power and money, these bounties have engaged successive factories in the occupation; and, from the sedition law, for controlling the use of our tongues, down to the protecting-duty law for controlling the use of our hands, it has been cultivated with successful pertinacity.

Why should some tongues and hands be oiled with power and money, and others rusted with penalties and taxes?

The protestation of the Committee against constructive limitations of power, applies with equal force against its constructive extension. No, says the new system of construction. Power has the double privilege of being exempted from any constructive limitation, and also of extending itself by construction. If an article in the constitution does not verbally reach the end in view, it may be wire drawn up to it by construction; but if it does verbally reach it, then it is to be construed as if the constitution had contained no other words, and is by no means to be explained or controlled by other articles, or by the primary principles of the instrument. Accordingly, the Committee pin the question on the power of Congress to regulate commerce as if it was isolated; and exclude the consideration of all the limitations in the same instrument, intended to prevent Congress from exercising an unlimited power of transferring property from State to State, from the nation to exclusive privileges, from class to class, and from individuals to individuals. And what has been done, without regarding what ought to have been done, is considered as affording precedents sufficient to confer these unconstitutional powers.

Thus they render several particular articles, and the true intention of the constitution inefficacious and nugatory. Of what value is the prohibition to impose a tax or duty on articles to be exported from any State, if Congress can impair or destroy this right of exportation, for the sake of enriching a local class of capitalists; of what value is the prohibition to bestow preferences and implicit partialities by a regulation of commerce or by modes of revenue, if Congress can establish preferences which shall make States tributary to States, the whole nation to capitalists, classes to classes, and individuals to individuals? Waving a verbalizing mode of discussion—the resource of imposition, and the detestation of common sense, we need only recollect that the intention and end of the constitution was to "secure the blessings of liberty to ourselves and our posterity." Can any construction, by which Congress may destroy the liberty of ourselves and our posterity, be true? Yes, say the Committee, it may be true, because "it is extremely difficult to point out the rate of duty when revenue ceases, and protection becomes to be the ruling object; to define the line which shall limit the constitutional powers of Congress." Does it follow that these powers have no limits? Yes, say the Committee: and to prove it, they echo the following terrifying words of the supreme court. "A power to tax, involves a power to destroy." And thus these echoes between Congress and the court are considered as the only constitutional limitations. This repercussion is the only security against Federal usurpations. "A power to tax, involves a power to destroy." This echo has destroyed the right of taxation reserved to the States, and extended ten miles square to the size of the United States. "Congress has a right to regulate the conduct and interest of individuals," because it is necessary for the sake of political economy. An echo from the court, can also establish this boundless power, and complete the catastrophe of the drama. Here, then, a combination of powers is asserted by these self-created guardians of the constitution, which expunges all the limitations thought by its framers necessary to preserve a free form of government. "The only security against this combination of limitation-destroying powers," say the Committee, still echoing the supreme court, "is the structure of the Federal Government." But neither the court nor the Committee have ventured openly to inform us, whether it lies in the whole structure, or only in some portion of it. Do they consider the State Governments as component parts of this structure, enabled to resist its threatened destruction; or do they believe the Federal Government to be compounded only of Congress and the supreme court. Whether they admit or reject the State Governments as balancing or checking portions of the structure, they allow that a security against destruction is deposited somewhere; and if the destroyer himself is tacitly meant, it may still be useful to entreat this angel of death not to destroy the securities for a free government, because it is extremely difficult to define his powers. The difficulty may place the honourable men and real patriots in Congress, in a nice and delicate situation; but, however hard it may be to split straws for the purpose of defining the exact line which limits their powers, it does not follow that they ought to demolish pillars. Some lines are so very visible, that they may be clearly seen. That of changing the principles of the constitutional structure, by a legislative reconstruction of a society by monopolies and exclusive privileges, is one of these. Will this reconstruction "secure the blessings of liberty to ourselves and our posterity?" Will it be the same structure created for this primary end? If not, how can it be constitutional to hammer it out of any particular article?

Another of these destroying powers, when construed without any regard to the real design of the constitution, may be found in the right of borrowing and appropriating money. If Congress should borrow and give to capitalists, its might be verbally constitutional, but substantially it would be taxing the nation for their benefit, and not for the general welfare. Commercial restrictions which beget the necessity of borrowing, for the purpose of giving them bounties, amount to the same thing. If Congress cannot find a line which prohibits it from borrowing and appropriating money to monopolies and exclusive privileges, I do not see why they may not create a king, since the maintenance of one man at the public expense will undoubtedly accord better with the principles of political economy, than the maintenance of such combinations.

The Committee have borrowed, from mere declaimers, an argument, which, if reiteration could make truth, would be forcible indeed. They say "that manufactures which, in all other countries are cherished as the most valuable offspring of human industry, have become with us a spurious progeny, born with a constitutional malediction, to struggle under legal disabilities. The constitution designates no national interest in preference to another, but throws all alike on the discretion of Congress." How are such assertions to be treated? Must I take off my hat, make a bow, and say "all this is very true?" Or ought I honestly to reply, "not a word of all this is true, except that the constitution designates no national interest in preference to another?" Had they substituted agriculture for manufactures, their assertions would have been diametrically different. Had they called that the most valuable offspring of human industry; had they asserted that it was treated as if it was under a constitutional malediction, and that it had to struggle with legal disabilities, they could not have been contradicted. To struggle with foreign industry is common to both occupations, and no legal disability to either. But the capitalists add insult to injury to roar out, whilst they are lashing agriculture and commerce with legal restrictions, like Sancho lashing the trees, that they are themselves receiving the blows they inflict. As the constitution designates no national interest in preference to another, it could not have designed that such preferences should be established by legislation, and a species of despotism created which it has carefully avoided and utterly neglected to provide for. But lest the forbearance of the constitution to recognise preferences of some national interests, should be considered as a constitutional rejection of that tyrannical policy, the Committee have supplied the omission, by gratuitously allowing it to have invested Congress with a power, which it forbears to exercise. "It throws," say the Committee, "all national interests, on the discretion of Congress." Thus undefined legal preferences of national interests rejected by the constitution, are entrusted to Congress; that body may legislate without limitation, their own discretion excepted, in creating them; and, by extending its power of legislation to objects excluded from the constitution as inconsistent with the principles of liberty and justice, the Committee have proved that the laws for bestowing lucrative preferences upon a capitalist interest to a great amount, are constitutional, however unjust or tyrannical. But under the sweeping doctrine "that the constitution throws all national interests on the discretion of Congress," what becomes of the interests reserved to the States or the people? Are not these national interests? What becomes of all the interests intended to be secured beyond the reach of Congress by limitations and restrictions? What becomes of the declared intention of securing liberty by these precautions? What becomes of the security of property? What a foolish and useless labour does this doctrine charge the convention with undergoing? According to it, all that was necessary was to form a Congress, and to add one line, saying "that all national interests should depend on the discretion of that body." As this assertion is thought necessary by the Committee to prove the constitutionality of the protecting-duty monopoly, its constitutionality and the assertion must stand or fall together. It places the question on its true ground. Will a power in Congress to manage all national interests and distribute preferences among them according to its discretion, preserve the Union, or secure liberty? Is it constitutional because the supreme court declares it to be so? Was Algernon Sydney constitutionally put to death, because it was done by a supreme court? Is the constitution subject to a similar jurisdiction, without the chance for reprieve, except from the prosecuting power? Whether it can be fairly so construed as to lay its limitations, its design and its life, at the feet of "a discretion in Congress," is the ground upon which this point is to be decided.

2. MANUFACTURES ARE INJURIOUS TO MORALS, AND PRODUCE PAUPERISM

This the Committee deny: and, to sustain their denial, reject the evidence of the great foreign factories, and rely on that of the Waltham factory, consisting of two hundred and sixty persons. I shall not attempt to prove that this little experiment is less to be relied on, than those made on a great scale, nor to overhaul the fact and opinions coinciding in the conclusion, that these factories degrade human nature. But leaving to the Committee all their arithmetick for estimating the thefts of the poor, it is yet necessary to remind them, that in wandering through its mazes, they have entirely overlooked political immorality, by which vices more pernicious to society are produced, and which also causes many of those peccadillos, admitted by them, and allowed by me to be bad enough. Laws for creating exclusive privileges and monopolies corrupt governments, interests, and individuals; and substitute patronage, adulation, and favour, for industry, as the road to wealth. If it be true, as the Committee believe, that the preferences and partialities of such laws, will not produce a correspondent impoverishment, which will reach the poor and deteriorate their morals; yet it cannot be denied that they will reach the rich, and corrupt the morals of the best informed, and of the officers of the government; in which three classes reside, the power and the influence, by which the morality and the liberty of nations are sustained or destroyed.

As to pauperism, the Committee quaintly contend, that it is not produced by hard labour. Daily wages earned by hard labour, do not prevent it. One of these general assertions balances the other, and they unite in showing how little is proved by either; and neither can diminish the force of the fact, that pauperism and crimes are more frequently produced by hard labour for daily wages, than from any other source; because it usually expends the wages of to-day in the subsistence of to-day, and is too improvident to lay up a defence against the occurrence of disability, or the temptations of necessity.

In a pamphlet lately published at Philadelphia, in defence of the system proposed by the Committee, we are informed that the poor list of the city of New-York has risen to fifteen thousand persons; being about an eighth of the whole population. We have also learned from State documents, that its prisons are crowded with felons and debtors. We have seen it too published in the newspapers, that one hundred and eleven persons were last year sentenced to death in four counties of England. In England the gallows groans, or ships are laden with convicts. In New-York the penitentiary overflows with them. In both, the prisons abound with debtors. And in both the proportion of paupers is about one person in eight. In England, fictitious capital, legal privileges, factories, and monopolies are abundant. At New-York they are probably more abundant, than in any other part of the United States. I have said that a partial accumulation of fictitious or legal capital in any one State, at the national expense, would not promote the general happiness or wealth of the people, even of that State. If the proofs of the assertion in England lie too far off to be seen, that at home is visible. If a local and individual accumulation of capital united with factories, will diffuse honesty and wealth within the sphere of its influence, why do we see most crimes, most debtors, and most pauperism, wherever this policy is most prevalent? May it not therefore be possible that this policy itself generates the crimes and pauperism by which it is attended? At least we must discern, that by whatever names exclusive privileges call themselves; however earnestly they assert that they are not monopolies, and only honest encouragers of industry; that they are not chafferers for selfish acquisitions, but pleaders for general good; that far from causing crimes, they are political moralists; and that far, also, from causing pauperism, they make people work harder than they could otherwise be made to do; that yet they are constantly attended by phenomena, which very plainly contradict all these professions. Bonaparte as devoutly declared, that he was not a military despot, but a patriotick consul.

Political economists in Europe, and especially in England, have forborne to consider the effect of political immorality upon national prosperity, or its influence in begetting both individual pauperism and crimes, because they could only build their systems upon the foundation of governments so thoroughly corrupted, that they despaired of producing a reformation by a true system of political economy; and could only seek for inadequate alleviations of evils, necessarily caused by the firm establishment of the system of patronage, monopoly, and exclusive privileges. Compelled into a reverence for these abuses, they have kept at an awful distance from adversaries so dangerous and unconquerable, and contented themselves with attempting only to soften their baleful influence upon human happiness by temporary expedients. In these endeavours, though they have exhibited great ingenuity, they have been unsuccessful; and, as the causes remain, the effects follow in spite of their wisdom and philanthropy. Here, we are yet able to apply the axe to the causes themselves, which in other countries have generated bad morals and grinding poverty, in spite of fine soils and good climates.

3. No Further Protection Necessary

If the proposition had been differently stated, it would have exhibited the question in plainer language. Suppose it had been objected, that further protection was not wanted. The Committee might have replied with truth, that the capitalists did want more money. The objection means that the capitalists do not need more money, and the Committee state that they already have more than they know what to do with, but that they want more still. From these facts, the plain question is, whether the nation, though reduced itself to pecuniary distress, ought to give more money to the capitalists because they want it, although they have already more than they can use.

The first reason for doing so urged by the Committee is,

> that if a factory occupied in a single manufacture, should ask Congress for further protection, or a further bounty, it would be a partial monopoly, and justify the objection, that protecting duties tend to create a privileged order of great capitalists, supported at the expense of the nation; but that if Congress grant to all factories the same

favour, that it will not be a monopoly, nor tend to create a privileged order of great capitalists, but only be a general and equal protection of national industry.

Thus they have reduced the point to a plain matter of fact. They say that a bounty to one factory would be a partial monopoly, and would create a privileged order of great capitalists, which would be unjustifiable; but that a bounty to all the factories is not a monopoly and will not create such an objectionable order. One bishop would be a hierarchy, but an hundred bishops would be religious freedom. I had thought that separate social interests, like separate nations, were individual with respect to each other. It would seem to common sense, if one privileged factory would suffice to create a dangerous exclusive interest, that a hundred factories combined by a common bounty, would create an exclusive interest an hundred-fold more dangerous. If each received its bounty by separate laws, each law would create an unjustifiable monopoly say the Committee, because they would be uncombined by law, however they might be united by interest; but if all these factories are combined both by one law, and a common interest, then the combination changes the whole mass from a monopoly into a protector of national industry, and will not produce a privileged order of great capitalists. Whether there are more or fewer factories than one hundred in the United States, it is excessively wide of truth, and excessively humiliating to all occupations, to apply to them exclusively the phrase "national industry." By doing so, the Committee have taken a substratum for their system, to be found in no other treatise which has ever appeared, and which is crushed by the weight of the plainest fact imaginable. In the old systems of political economy, land, labour and corn, have been considered as comprising the chief sources or items of national industry, and have been selected as the measures of national prosperity. But the Committee, in the face of every body's knowledge to the contrary, assert that the whole mass of national industry, is concentrated in a few factories, and that of course a bounty to them is a general and equal protection to national industry. If the fact was so, the bounty would be inert. Paid by national industry to national industry, it would only be the case of a man's giving money to himself.

Their idea, however, is, that these factories, though by no means constituting national industry, will afford general and equal protection to national industry. It is borrowed from the old idea of protection for allegiance, being only protection for bounties. One man pretended to protect a nation, if that nation would bountifully make over to him its liberty and property. One hundred factories offer to protect all the numerous branches of national industry, if the nation will be equally bountiful to them. I know not which is most to be coveted, the protection of a monarch, or of a pecuniary aristocracy. Writers upon political economy, as far as I recollect, have wholly neglected to recommend either. All of them consider branches of industry as separate and distinct; and allow, that some may be oppressed by exclusive privileges or bounties to others, because they must pay whatever these others receive from partial laws; and none assert that factories and agriculture are one and indivisible. The Committee subscribe to the same opinion in admitting that one factory endowed with a bounty would operate unjustly upon other national interests. In England, agriculture and factories are considered as interests so clearly distinct, that two violent and contending parties have been created and kept alive by bounties and monopolies occasionally given to each. Neither of these contending interests have ever asserted, that bounties to one, were bounties to the other; and the difficulty has been, to adjust the compensation for the injury sustained by one, from partialities to the other. At this very time the manufacturers are complaining of the corn monopoly, which, though created to encourage the most important branch of industry among men, and in England particularly, is fraudulent and oppressive upon all other branches of national industry, and protects them, just as they are protected here by our factory monopoly; by enriching itself at their expense. The English landlords have never had the assurance to assert, that their corn monopoly made bread cheaper to consumers. It has been tried much longer than our factory monopoly, and instead of making bread cheaper, has increased rents and enriched landlords at the expense of bread consumers. Our factories have asserted, that their monopoly would make manufactures cheaper. But after a considerable trial, its effects are found to correspond with those of other monopolies. It has only enriched capitalists and impoverished other occupations. The Committee admit that our moneyed capitals have increased even more rapidly than English rents; that they have grown up to an exuberance which cannot find employment. The English landlords do not complain of an exuberance of rents, nor crave an extension of their monopoly for its employment. The enormous growth of individual capitals, and the pecuniary depression of all other interests do not sustain the hope of the Committee, that a factory monopoly will be "a general and equal protection of national industry."

Whence came the redundant capitals allowed by the Committee to exist? If from commerce, it must have been highly lucrative; if from a system of internal legislation, that must have been excessively partial. Had commerce begotten this redundant capital, a correspondent prosperity of agriculture or other occupations must have been visible, unless it can be proved that a lucrative commerce will impoverish a nation. The Committee, by urging a balance of trade as the cause of national prosperity, have admitted that commerce is the instrument by which it is to be obtained; and by admitting the existence of redundant capitals in the hands of individuals with a concurrent national distress, it follows, either that these redundant capitals have been brought in by a favourable commerce, or bestowed by partial laws. Under the first supposition, there exists no reason for endeavouring to make so lucrative a commerce better by home monopoly; under the second, there is still less reason for increasing the national distress, to add to the accumulations of individual capitals.

But the Committee have endeavoured to blend the mercantile and capitalist occupations, so as to conceal the distinctions by which their very different effects are produced. They assert, that the protection afforded to commerce has enabled merchants to acquire princely fortunes, and leaving us to imagine that this protection is a bounty to merchants, infer that they are uncharitable in opposing bounties to factory owners, since they receive them. It is strange that the heat of controversy should have elicited an assertion, that protection to commerce was a bounty to merchants, when the benefits arising from it must so evidently be reaped chiefly by the owners and consumers of the commodities which it is the occupation of merchants to exchange. But the Committee had forgotten that the commercial and capitalist occupations are essentially different. The business of one is to exchange property, of the other to transfer it. One coincides with the good soul of money, in regulating these exchanges by free will; the other combines with its bad soul, by using it to promote transfers without equivalents. If the legislature should lay a duty upon imported commodities to be paid to merchants, then, and then only, would the two occupations produce the same effects, because it would be similar to the excise paid to capitalists, collected for them by restrictions and prohibitions. There are no such bounties given to merchants, and therefore the mercantile occupation, instead of inflicting general penury to promote partial wealth, has the effect of diffusing general prosperity by cheapening human comforts. It is in fact one of those occupations by which nations are enabled to exist under the property-transferring policy in its several forms. Had the capitalists requested Congress to increase the extravagance of government, in order to extend and protect the system of borrowing, for the purpose of giving employment to their exuberant wealth, they might as justly have charged the mercantile body with injustice for opposing the application, as in the present case. The same charge has been frequently urged against the farmers, and admits of the same answer. In both cases it results in the following doctrine, considered in its favourable aspect. Merchants and agriculturists are made rich by free industry and fair exchanges, but this operation is too slow for capitalists, and therefore it is ungenerous in the two first classes to oppose the enrichment of the third by monopolies, without exposing it to the toils which the two must undergo or remain poor.

All advertisements for recommending quack physick either to the body natural or body politick, are exposed to detection, because they are suggested by the same design. The Committee have represented the mercantile occupation as creating princely fortunes, but they have not said that these fortunes have been obtained by means of legal transfers of property, nor informed us by what operation so lucrative a commerce can impoverish the rest of the community. Other capitalist writers have filled pamphlets with computations to magnify agricultural wealth; but none have attributed this supposed wealth to a property-transferring monopoly. What an enigma is here exhibited. Merchants and agriculturists are wonderfully rich, yet a country in which these classes constitute a great majority is in terrible distress. At one time these doctors say that the superabundant blood of agriculture and commerce ought to be drawn off; at another, that they are expiring for want of blood, but that bleeding is still necessary. We are assured as usual by these doctors, that the same physick will cure both emptiness and repletion; that it is equally good for the most opposite complaints, and equally beneficial whether merchants and farmers are rich or poor. They were indeed pretty well and tolerably rich, whilst they forbore to swallow bolus after bolus compounded of commercial restrictions, prohibitions, embargoes, exclusive privileges, and monopolies; and have become sicker or poorer the more these drugs have been administered to them. But what of that? The Committee say, "we risk much by acting on the belief that the English nation does not understand its interest; and protection should end then, only after securing employment for all." These declarations are appalling. The drug recommended is that which the people of England are forced to swallow by a corrupt government, and we are desired to take it until employment is secured for all, which has never been effected by it. The reason given for it is curious. Commerce and agriculture are informed that they are sick, to induce them to take the physick; and that they are rich, to induce them to pay the doctors. If they should agree to pay a vast annual tax to the capitalists, until their prescriptions shall secure employment for all, especially for growing capitals, there are two tolerably strong reasons that the tax will last for ever. One, that the proposed object is an impossibility; the other, that the capitalists would never effect it by their prescriptions if they could, because they would thereby lose their fees. Employment must be nurtured by free exchanges, like commerce, or it flags. Commercial action and re-action constitute its food. Take away one and the other languishes. A nation deprived of the excitements arising from commercial reverberations, loses the creator of employment, as well as of civilization, knowledge, and comforts; and recedes towards savageness. Even with the aid of these excitements, employment for all can never be established. The fluctuations caused by war, seasons, fashions, and the wonderful catalogue of human passions, will reach employment and prevent that permanency no where to be found; but these fluctuations left to be met by free industry, are themselves excitements of genius and talents, and awaken exertions into life. Which generate most employment, all the inducements which propel the mind and body to make the utmost efforts they can, or the protecting-duty system which destroys most of them?

4. THE INCREASE OF DUTIES WILL LEAD TO SMUGGLING

And it might have been added, that it will inculcate an opinion, that smuggling is a virtue; and that the smuggler, if not an actual, is at least a comparative patriot. How an impartial casuist might determine the degrees of immorality between the two cases of pilfering industry, to enrich capitalists, or of supplying it by pilfering the pilferers, with necessaries and comforts at a cheaper rate than it could otherwise procure them, I shall not enquire; and only suggest that the parties interested will never believe themselves to be less moral than the capitalists, in uniting to defeat a monopoly operating upon themselves. The smuggler does not pilfer industry, but buys and sells under the check of free will, and the consumer only retains his own property by buying cheaper than the monopoly will sell to him; yet they both commit the crime of evading an oppressive and fraudulent law. If the enhancement of price is moderate, and is only produced by the fair object of revenue, both the parties will view it in a different light; nor will the temptation be of the same extent, as when it is magnified by the avarice of exclusive privileges. We need not go with the Committee in search of affidavits, to determine whether smuggling and high duties are allied; we need not call upon the casuist to decide whether the tempter or the tempted is most wicked; and we need not look for truth either in a cup of tea, or in the Isle of Man, though it is somewhat larger than the tea-cup; when it has been ascertained by unchangeable principles. Some people will for ever believe that there is no immorality in eluding oppression; others will for ever be tempted by pecuniary acquisition to pardon their consciences, especially if they can get a law to sear them; and commercial restrictions will for ever multiply smugglers and watchers of smugglers. I know not which of these occupations will do most harm. It often happens that not a single case of smuggling can be proved, whilst a country abounds with interpolated commodities, and the treasury announces its extent, by an enormous defalcation. What but intemperate zeal could deny the inseparable association of smuggling with the system advocated by the Committee; and who can consider it as at all important, whether the tax imposed upon his industry goes into the pockets of the smuggler, the capitalist, or the watchers of smugglers?

5. A TAX ON THE MANY, A BOUNTY TO THE FEW

This objection, the Committee admits "would be conclusive if true; that a permanent tax to encourage manufactures would be radically wrong; but that disclaiming the word bounties, as wholly inapplicable to any part of the bill, they are willing to test it by the principles of its active and intelligent opponents." On the next page, however, they observe "if there were no manufactories, and government could build them up by imposing duties on foreign fabricks, such duties would not be a tax on the farmer, but an efficient bounty, by giving a value to his otherwise useless products." The first suggestion they use in support of these assertions, is exactly of that character employed in pleading a cause. It is an extract from the report of a Boston Committee, admitting that in some cases, an argument may be found in favour of encouraging particular employments by bounties and taxes. Upon this admission the Committee have seized, as an acknowledgement that bounties to exclusive privileges, constitute a wise and just policy. But it may have happened that the admission itself came from an exclusive privilege. Some capitalists, contented with the existing protecting-duty monopoly, or fearful of pushing it further lest it should burst, are opposed to its augmentation. When the policy of bounties, monopolies, and exclusive privileges is introduced, those deriving emolument from any item of it, may find an interest in opposing another, but they will never contend that the policy itself is bad, and ought to be abandoned. Neither the landlord nor capitalist-interest in England, will admit that the system of bounties and exclusive privileges is radically vicious, though each will contend that its antagonist gets too much, and itself too little by it. Of what value can the authority of either, asserting that a system is good by which both get money, be to an enquirer who is considering whether it is also good for a nation? Such admissions are a vice in the system itself, because they are purchased concessions, not for disclosing truth to advance the public good, but for concealing it to enrich combinations. However the family of exclusive interests may quarrel among themselves, yet they will unite when the whole craft is in danger; and even when at variance, they will be careful to advance arguments in favour of the principle which sustains their common interest. Leaving, therefore, this extract from the report of the Boston Committee, as proving nothing, let us proceed to the words of the Congressional Committee, and consider what they prove.

The frequent occurrence of contradictions in their report, bewilders the understanding and perplexes the subject. They say "bounties are wholly foreign to their bill, and yet to build up manufactories by duties on foreign fabricks, would be an efficient bounty to the farmer." To build up these factories, by such duties, is the avowed object of the bill; and, when thus created, they will be bounties to farmers, the very fact upon which the Committee and its other advocates have rested its defence. And the same Committee deny "that the word bounty is applicable to any part of the bill; contend that the bill bestows an efficient bounty on farmers; and admit that a permanent tax to encourage manufactures, would be radically wrong." An advocate for the freedom and happiness of a nation, will not become the partisan of a particular interest. Why are the Committee, after having candidly admitted that a permanent tax for the protection of manufactures must be radically wrong, instantly converted into advocates for an efficient bounty to farmers? Having disclaimed the hateful term *bounty,* they instantly resume it in favour of farmers, whilst they renounce the propriety of thus endowing manufactures, although equally meritorious. If duties paid by the consumers of foreign fabricks to build factories would be no tax on the farmer, yet the efficient bounty thence accruing to him must be a tax on somebody; unless indeed the new discovery of the Committee, that such duties paid to support government are not taxes, which must be the case if they are not taxes when imposed to build factories; can obliterate all the received ideas of taxation.

Bounty certainly implies a payer as well as a receiver, and when it is bestowed by a government, it implies taxation on the people, considerably exceeding its amount, on account of the misfortunes to which public money is exposed, and the expenses of collection. As the proposed bounty to farmers could only be paid by some kind of tax, and the Committee assert that it would be wrong thus to encourage manufactures, it follows that it would be wrong also thus to encourage farmers. If a permanent bounty could not exist without its accomplice, a permanent tax, then the bounty promised to farmers, as resulting from building factories, distant as it is, must vanish the instant it arrives, or inflict on some interest the reprobated permanent tax. With the factories the case is very different. These are to be built by taxes on foreign fabricks, which must, inevitably, fall on consumers of the substituted domestick fabricks; but the farmers, far from paying any portion of them, are to be reimbursed by an efficient bounty. If so, the tax paid for building the factories, would be more glaringly unequal and oppressive, as other occupations and professions will pay all the tax, whilst the farmers will receive all the efficient bounty. But this whimsical mode of reasoning is gotten over, and the admission of the Committee, that the protection of manufactures by a tax on the community, is wrong, virtually retracted by the magical influence of the word "permanent." A tax on the many to raise a bounty for the few, is allowed by the Committee to be radically wrong, if the tax is permanent. It is impossible to find a better argument in favour of abuses, because it will fit all. The conciliating candour of acknowledging a policy to be bad if permanent, is a solicitation of confidence in the assurance that it is good, if temporary. Few things in this fluctuating world are less permanent than the promises of statesmen and the calculations of financiers; and the nation which submits to exclusive privileges, bounties, monopolies, and other abuses, because they are told they will not be permanent, instead of obtaining felicity like ancient wiseacres, by bestowing their temporary property on priests, will obtain the most permanent political machine we know of; a machine invariably constructed by temporary abuses, namely, a bad government.

"A permanent tax to encourage manufactures would be radically wrong, but the word bounties is inapplicable to any part of their bill, and to build up factories by duties on foreign fabricks, is good policy." There is some difficulty in simplifying this confusion of ideas. Would a permanent tax be radically wrong only because it was permanent, and a temporary tax be right only because it was temporary? A radical imposition must be made so by some principle, and not by the duration of the imposition. If a permanent tax to encourage manufactures would be radically wrong, it can only arise from the injustice inflicted on other occupations, by conferring an exclusive benefit on one at their expense. But whatever may be the principle which convinced the Committee that such a permanent tax would be radically wrong, the same principle must pronounce a temporary tax for the same partial purpose, to be also radically wrong. The temporary tax for the encouragement of manufactures is denied to be a bounty, by the assertion that the word bounties is inapplicable to any part of the bill. Why would the tax be radically wrong if permanent? Undoubtedly because it would be a permanent bounty. If the tax, being permanent, would be a permanent bounty and radically wrong, the same tax, though temporary, must be a temporary bounty, and equally wrong. A tax may be imposed for two objects; one to sustain a government, the other to enrich individuals. The idea of a bounty cannot be severed from the latter object, and the Committee labour against language and an indissoluble affinity, to prove that a tax not imposed for the use of government, but to encourage manufactures, does not imply a bounty. A feeble attempt, if such was the design, is made to find a subterfuge from conclusions so inevitable, by speaking of building factories with duties on foreign fabricks. Not a cent of such duties has gone or can go towards their fabrication. All the duties received on foreign importations go into the treasury, and are applicable to public uses, and the enhanced prices obtained on domestick fabricks from domestick consumers, by diminishing the amount of duties produced from foreign fabricks, are the architects of factories, and constitute the bounties to capitalists.

A great curiosity of the discrimination between good and evil, attempted by the words permanent and temporary, consists in its being addressed to temporary beings. Build factories for capitalists, because it is only a temporary radical wrong, and you will be reimbursed by what man can never get in this world; a permanent good. Why not build houses for farmers and professional men, because it may permanently foster agriculture and science? The consolation, that abuses may be only temporary, is ingeniously used to inflict them; and the sound principle, that temporary abuses are an introduction of durable evils, is to be abandoned. Factories are now to be built by bounties to capitalists, in order by and by to bestow efficient bounties on farmers. One abuse is proposed as a remedy for another, and these two occupations are to be provided for by successive bounties, radically wrong if permanent, but right if temporary. No compensation is even suggested for the others which share in the taxes to raise these bounties. Indeed this omission is of no consequence, for if these factories should deliver manufactures from the grasp of their own monopoly, the farmers could never obtain the alluring bait of an efficient bounty in their turn, unless corn and their other products had ceased to be exported; and could only hope to be reinstated upon the ground of free and fair exchanges.

The promise of future compensation for present wealth is the cunning offer made by the capitalists to the farmers. Build factories and give bounties to us now, and we will restore to you the blessing of free exchanges the moment we can no longer extort from you an enhanced price for our fabricks. Such is the basis of their arguments, and such the boon by which they are endeavouring to bribe the farmers, without paying any respect to other occupations. Is there any man in his senses who would make such a bargain with another man? No day of payment is prescribed. No security for performance is proposed. After all other interests have enriched the capitalist interest, it may break its promise, cease even to manufacture, and retain the wealth acquired by its bounties. Suppose lawyers and doctors could persuade the nation to build palaces for them, and buy their law and physick at double prices, under a promise that when these employments were overdone, it should get their physick and law cheap. What speculations can be equal to these? Vast estates are purchased by a promise, and no obligation to pay any thing for them is incurred. Indeed no payment can ever be made for them, except a restoration of free exchanges and fair competition, suspended to bestow them. The utmost compensation to be expected is that of taking off the suspension. Why then put it on? To take away a social right, in order to restore the same social right, is worse than nothing, by the amount of the intermediate loss incurred by the suspension. Whilst the business of building factories is made lucrative by bounties, the capitalists will pursue it; when it ceases to be so, they will give it up. If other occupations should escape from their toils and become profitable, by receiving either patronage or justice, the capitalists will transfer their wealth from the worn out, to the new patronage, or at worst, employ it in free and fair exchanges upon equal ground with other wealth. Money emigrates without difficulty from one exclusive privilege, or from one occupation to another; it is neither nailed to the soil, nor to a factory; it follows the scent of profit; and the cry of capitalists upon the track of exclusive privileges, like hounds in pursuit of game, grows louder as the scent grows stronger. A nation when caught does not indeed lose its life, but it loses the precious castor which is the object of the chase. The policy of transferring property by law, is only a series of speculations, like a series of monarchical successions, inflicting, it is true, temporary evils only, but which always last as long as we live. It is the system for keeping the birds in its hand, and sending the mass of a nation to look for them in the bush. The Committee, however, deny that it is a tax on the many or bounty to the few, and admit that if it was, it would be radically wrong. They only defend this denial, and elude the admission, by the use of the words permanent and temporary. The objection does not assert that which could not be foreseen, namely, that protecting duties were a permanent tax on the many and a permanent bounty to the few; and the Committee feebly deny, that which is quite visible, namely, that they are a temporary tax on the many and a temporary bounty to the few. They admit the truth of the objection by seeking for a refuge from it under the word permanent; and if all monopolies, exclusive privileges, bounties, and political abuses, are by nature temporary; if they beget successors, like other tyrants; if the bad principles, by which they are defended, are permanent; this vail is too thin to hide the fact stated in the objection, or to make that conceded to be radically wrong, according to permanent principles, radically right, because of a hopeless possibility that it may be only temporary.

The Committee have asserted "that there is no instance of an increase in the price of any articles, the high duties on which have secured our market to our own manufactures." Nothing is more easy than for the capitalists to make out accounts favourable to themselves. Who would lose a cause, if he could garble the evidence, much less if he could fabricate it? Nails and a few other articles are selected to prove the assertion. But how could its truth be established, except by the expelled test, competition? Prices may have fallen in other countries below those paid here, but it cannot be ascertained, except by the rejected test. It is therefore quite safe to make the assertion, when the means of detection are excluded. Yet for still greater safety it is equivocal. The price of articles secured against competition has not risen. This may be nominally true, and substantially false. The value of money has doubled, and if the prices of the selected articles remain undiminished, they are substantially doubled also, so as to acquire a great enhancement from being protected against foreign competition, if the same foreign articles have been reduced in price by the appreciation of money. If, however, protection against competition does not enhance domestick prices, then there is no reason for protecting duties. To establish the fact that it does not, the Committee have selected two or three articles, and left us to infer a general rule, generally false, from these meagre exceptions. Our situation would have been unexampled, if we had not possessed some internal manufactures, the prices of which would not be enhanced by protecting duties, or the exclusion of competition; but these furnish no evidence applicable to manufactures, the prices of which will be enhanced by this exclusion. To blend them, in order to misapply evidence furnished by the class of manufacturers, placed by domestick facilities beyond the influence of competition, to that class exposed to it for want of these facilities, is evidently incorrect. I could furnish the Committee with many articles, more conclusively establishing the fact they assert, than those they have selected. The price of flour has not been increased by a monopoly of that manufacture and the absence of competition. But would the low price of that article prove, that a monopoly would not enhance the prices of other articles? In like manner a selection of any other articles, the prices of which have not risen, from causes distinct from protecting duties, is insufficient to prove that such duties do not enhance prices, and a mode of reasoning entirely delusive. It is quite the case of one party making up the evidence for both.

The Committee observe that "it is not easily conceived, that duties, short of prohibitory, can easily operate as a bounty to manufactures." Having previously asserted that duties amounting to a prohibition do not enhance prices, and now that duties short of a prohibition do not operate as a bounty, they come to the conclusion, necessary, as they imagine, to sustain their policy, that no duties whatsoever will have any such effect. If their assertions are true, then these duties will be wholly inoperative, except for producing expense, and extending patronage; if false, it follows that they are taxes on the many for the benefit of a few; and whether true or false, the assertions suggest the conclusion, either that there is no reason for commercial restrictions or prohibitions, or that they are founded in a principle allowed to be radically wrong.

"Our best statesmen," say the Committee, "have laid it down as a maxim, that domestick competition will always tend to the reduction of price. It is not, therefore, without some surprise, that it should be so generally alleged by opponents of protecting duties, that they are a tax on the many, to enrich a few. If the price of the article advances with the duty, it still leaves the same profit to the importer." It is with no less surprise that I see a principle, directly adverse to monopoly, applied to its justification by the following mode of reasoning. All wise men agree, that competition will reduce prices, and therefore an exclusion of competition will reduce prices. As the Committee had previously endeavoured to make temporary evils good, by the instrumentality of the word permanent, they now endeavour to make competition a bad thing for the reduction of prices, by the instrumentality of the word domestick. But is not the competition between foreign and domestick commodities, wholly domestick? Will not the reduction of prices by competition be graduated by the extent of competition? How an enormous diminution of domestick competition can reduce prices, is inconceivable to me. The Committee, to prove that such will be the case, have imagined that the effect of protecting duties to capitalists, is the same as the effect of revenue duties to importers. Whatever are the revenue duties, the profit of the importers remains the same. I do not understand the observations they have deduced from this fact, but the difference between the cases is not so abstruse. In one case there is no monopoly; of the other, it is the basis. In one case the increased price occasioned by revenue duties goes to the support of government; in the other, the increased price produced by expelling competition, goes to enrich capitalists; one is a tax on the many for public benefit; the other a tax on the many for private emolument; one case is a transfer of property necessary for maintaining society; the other a transfer of property contrary to one of the ends of society. As to competition between importers, it is not affected by duties, because they all pay the same; but competition between commodities is destroyed, if so many of them are driven out of the market, as to enable the holders of the residue to enhance their prices by taking advantage of a scarcity. I cannot discern how two cases so clearly distinct, can be confounded, to make an exclusive privilege or a partial monopoly, bear the least resemblance to duties paid by importers. Confining the idea of competition to a rivalry between domestick factories, its great benefit, a reduction of prices is not to be expected. We cannot get manufactures cheaper by bribing capitalists, because these bribes are themselves an enhancement of price paid by the nation. If the factories should foolishly lose the bribes by a competition among themselves, yet a cheapness beyond that to be derived from keeping the whole field of competition open, could not be produced, because they would export their wares, if they should sell higher in foreign countries than at home. Thus the proposed policy consists of a tedious, heavy tax, to be paid to capitalists by excluding the domestick competition, begotten by the admission of foreign commodities, to enable them to carry on a war against natural laws, the utmost success of which cannot produce a degree of cheapness beyond that which would have existed, if competition had not been suspended, and no such tax had been paid.

Let us even imagine with the Committee, that these factories will be so many little nations, as incapable of being combined into one interest by an Amphictyonic council, as the little nations of Greece; and that they will be inspired with a spirit of rivalship, instead of combination, by the view of getting money; and also with a disinterested spirit of patriotism which scorns money, and intends only to make us independent of any nations but themselves. Yet even this wild supposition, could not enable these very small nations to create a competition among themselves, as operative in reducing prices, as a competition among all the trading nations of the world, added to their own, in supplying our wants. Independent of local and natural advantages possessed by the great nations, the vast difference in the number of competitors, would have an influence in the reduction of prices, exactly similar to the constant effect of plenty and scarcity; and carry the benefit of cheapness in articles of consumption, as far as possible, because the great disunited nations could not mould themselves into one combination, and carry on their operations against our pockets in concert, as may possibly be done by our little factory nations. If, then, it is the opinion of our best and greatest statesmen, that competition will reduce prices (to discern which common sense is as competent as these sages) the same sagacity will also discern, that the effect must depend on the plenty or scarcity of this competition. How, then, can an unprejudiced understanding, which admits that cheapness is a benefit only to be obtained by competition, contend also, that by contracting or destroying the remedy against the evil of dearness, and creating an artificial scarcity of competition, that it will not be melted down into a settled domestick monopoly, and produce effects exactly the reverse of those contemplated by able statesmen.

6. A RESTRICTIVE SYSTEM

The Committee, as usual, make new data for new doctrines. They say,

> the same measures may acquire a good or bad character, as they may be called a system of revenue or restriction. Impost, as a means of taxing the consumption of the country, for the support of government; prohibition, for the purpose of creating and maturing the subjects of an excise, are fiscal measures. Taking England as an example, and asking ourselves by what other means she could, from a small popula-

tion, extract as large a revenue as would keep in operation the immense machinery of her mighty empire, we must admire it as a masterly effort of human policy. With less than double our number, she meets an expenditure 50,000,000£ by the receipts of her treasury. Her corn-laws revenue, and commercial systems, tend to the same great object. The former is the basis of the land and income tax; the latter of excise and customs.

That is, the English policy throughout, is contrived for effecting only the end of taxation. I have met with many persons as wise, honourable, and worthy, as the gentlemen who composed the Committee probably are (for I have not the pleasure of an acquaintance with them) who have eulogized the English system almost as highly as the Committee have repeatedly done, but yet much as I admired the men, I could not concur with them. Our opinions are moulded by so many different circumstances, not to be traced even by the party himself, that it is impossible for one individual, to carry back those of another up to their sources. Favourite projects, local views, popular temptations, or a love of distinction, may sometimes mould even the opinions delivered in grave and patriotick legislative bodies; but the Committee have vindicated themselves against the suspicion of any such inferiour motives, by avowing their affection for those charming features of the English policy, which have enabled the government to expend fifty millions of sterling pounds annually. An enormous revenue extracted from a small population, by means of corn laws, commercial restrictions, land tax, income tax, excise and customs, is the mistress whom they adore, as a masterly effort of human policy. In my eyes, this beauty of theirs, appears to be a painted courtezan, who corrupts and plunders her admirers; and though we cannot account for different tastes, that especially called love, it seems impossible to discern even a probability that the United States will gain an addition of present or future happiness, by divorcing the healthy and chaste country girl whom they first espoused, and of whose integrity and frugal management they boasted for thirty years, to marry a second-hand town lady, so diseased and ulcerated, that the English people are heartily willing to part with her. The Committee, indeed, blinded by love, like a zealous and deluded cully, have selected a feature of their mistress, so beautiful as in their opinion to hide all her sores; and are transported by her enormous extravagance and taxation, as a masterly effort of human policy. One man often loathes what another loves. In my view, this is the most hateful feature of her whole countenance. Yet the taste of the Committee is not original. It is that of all the European and oppressive governments in the world. Taxation is, they believe, the end of government; and they concur with a distinguished American statesman in believing, that governments have occasion for all the people can pay. Hence, the system of the Committee is, to discipline the people of the United States into a patient sufferance of this doctrine.

The Committee have not only suppressed the disgust of the European people, for the mistress adored by their governments, but, in the phrenzy of their adoration, they have lavished upon her contradictory eulogies. To amaze us the more with the masterly policy of enormous expenditure and taxation, they tell us that the latter is extracted from a small population, not double of our own. Yet they tell us also, that the British empire is a mighty one. Is it true that this mighty empire contains only the population described? I had thought that the British Asiatic possessions alone, contained more than double our population, independent of other populous dependencies. Or is it true that these provinces contribute nothing towards British revenue? I had thought that Britain considered them as her best cows, and milked them with care and skill. If a man worshiped the devil, in commenting on his religion, I would give the devil his due, but not more than his due. I would not flatter him because he was powerful. Do not the Committee flatter the British government by attributing to it the masterly policy of drawing fifty millions sterling from a population not double of ours? Or was the compliment exaggerated to increase the censure upon our own, for being so unskilful in expenditure and taxation. I shall hereafter endeavour to show, that it does not deserve the reproach, and that it has been no mean adept in this masterly policy. However this may be, the parallel plainly proposes an object of emulation. If to draw two hundred millions of dollars annually from a population not twice as numerous as ours, is a masterly policy, the Committee insinuate that our governments are dishonoured, unless they draw above one hundred millions from a population more than half as numerous, by adopting the same policy. But in borrowing the English exclusive-privileges, bounties, monopolies and extravagance, to rival them in taxation, we must borrow also their provinces, or fail in the competition. These are made to feed their exclusive-privilege bounties and extravagance, but the same devourers here, must be fed by domestick labour only. Reforming the comparison by these considerations, our governments in a combined view, can hardly be convicted of less sagacity than the British, in the masterly policy of transferring property from productive to unproductive labour.

Is it benevolence or tyranny to fleece the people of all they can pay? If it may be called a masterly policy, who are entitled to the compliment, the payers or receivers; the ingenious inventors, or the foolish sufferers? Caesar, Cromwell, and Bonaparte may also be called masterly politicians, but the eulogy to them, is a censure upon the nations they enslaved. What can be more disgraceful to the understanding of a nation, than a recommendation to submit to an oppressive system, that it may compliment its oppressors with the epithet masterly? Let exclusive privileges and governmental extravagance take your property by a masterly policy, as conquerors do by a masterly army, and it will make you a great nation, and turn you into a mighty empire. The term is an unlucky one, and the Committee, conscious that the people were not quite ripe for creating these rich British masters, have formally renounced a predilection for foreign opinions. They only recommend the essential principles of foreign tyrannies in the strongest terms, and propose their adoption for domestick use because they constitute a masterly policy.

National defence is the usual pretext for the policy of fleecing the people. Even contiguous governments might maintain a comparative degree of strength as well by frugality, as by extravagance and oppressive taxation. These are so far from being suggested by national defence, that taxation, however enormous, is uniformly swallowed by individual avarice, and nothing is laid by, even in times of peace, to meet the dangers, as a precaution against which it is pretended to be inflicted. The treasure extorted beyond the line of honest frugality, is uniformly diverted from the end of defending, to that of transferring property. What is still worse, the pretext of defending nations by oppressive taxation, defeats its object by its means. It weakens nations by indisposing the inhabitants of a country to defend it. And why should they, if this masterly policy already takes from them as much as they can pay? No conqueror or tyrant can take more. Common sense sees no difference between tyrants; and patriotism is neutralized and torpid, when victory promises no good. In our case, nature having exploded the usual pretext for oppressive taxation, drawn from the contiguity of tyrannies, a new one is ingeniously invented. It is said that though we have no neighbours to conquer us, yet we ought to subject ourselves to this masterly policy of extravagance, exclusive privileges, and excessive taxation, to preserve our independence against the dismal aggression of selling us comforts cheap, and the pernicious abuse of buying or not, according to our own judgments.

I have overlooked the first answer given by the Committee to the objection. They have endeavoured to make it a mere question of terms. Protecting duties, they say, are not restrictive; they are only a system of revenue. "As an impost, they are a tax for the support of the government; as prohibitory, they are only a fiscal measure for the purpose of creating and maturing the subjects of an excise." The conclusion is, that no commercial restrictions at all can exist, provided they are called a system of revenue; and having obtained this conclusion by a change of words which cannot change the nature of things, they instantly contend that such restrictions are necessary for creating and maturing the subjects of an excise, preparatory to the introduction of the English masterly system of human policy. A very few definitions would settle the whole debate. If we could only ascertain what monopolies, exclusive privileges, commercial restrictions, and protecting duties were, it would be easy to understand the subject. If they are shadows, or if each is a Proteus, they cannot be seized by any argument. A scarcity, for instance, artificially produced, by which people are enabled to obtain higher prices than they could otherwise have done, has hitherto been considered as a monopoly. Those to whom this monopoly is given, have hitherto been considered as receiving an exclusive privilege. And protecting duties have hitherto been thought clearly distinct from an impost for the support of government; because, if the government receives an impost, domestick manufactures are not protected against the competition of foreign, however their price may be enhanced by it. For want of definitions the Committee seem to me to have made a hot-bed, by mingling up a confusion of terms, and sown in it the seeds of oppression and tyranny.

7. DESTROY REVENUE

This objection, like several others, is mis-stated. It means that protecting duties impair the productiveness of revenue duties, and not that they will destroy other sources of revenue; and that the very consequence will ensue which the Committee think so desirable, namely, a resort to unlimited excises and other internal taxes, in order to supply the deficiency. This consequence is the evil deprecated by the objection, and the Committee admit that it will ensue, and justify it as a blessing, because it will enable us to rival the masterly policy, by which Britain is enabled to extract an enormous revenue from a few people.

They rest their preference of excises over duties upon a single comparison, from which they deduce an equality between them in that one respect, and exclude from their consideration every sound argument disclosing the disparities between the two modes of taxation. They suppose that the preference of duties to excises, rests solely on the notion, that one mode is less compulsive and more avoidable than the other; and contend, because both are avoidable by submitting to privations, that the two modes are perfectly equal in this problematical or humble merit. It might be contended that even this imperfect test chosen by the Committee, is insufficient to establish an equality so destitute of importance, because it is evidently easier to forbear the use of foreign luxuries than domestick necessaries; but waving this undoubted fact, it is sufficient to recollect that the comparison is wholly delusive. Neither duties nor excises are avoidable; if they were, they could not be relied upon for revenue. Both will operate as a general tax, and if some evasions by particular subterfuges may be practised under both modes of taxation, these confer no benefit upon those who pay the tax. The Committee admit that excises, at least, are a compulsory mode of taxation, by contending that they may be relied upon for a revenue. But let us enquire if other comparisons, more substantial, between the two modes of taxation, do not exist. The collection of duties is less expensive than the collection of excises; therefore the people must pay a larger sum by one mode than the other, to place the same amount in the treasury. To provide objects for excises to operate upon, bounties to an enormous extent must be paid to capitalists; thus the amount paid by the people, compared with what the treasury will receive, may possibly be doubled. Excises are keys to every lock, and penetrate like foul air into every recess; duties leave our homes unviolated, and our quiet undisturbed by the eternal intrusions of vulgar officers hunting for penalties or bribes. Duties are liable to the limitations of the importation, which cannot long exceed the demand; of an ability to pay which is the only lasting source of demand; and of the check arising from a certain degree of moderation to make them productive; excises are liable to no such limitations, and may be pushed to any extent. Duties fall chiefly on the rich, and on those who are most able to pay, because these classes are the chief purchasers of imported commodities, and the poor chiefly subsist on home products; excises will reach the poor in a multitude of consumptions beyond the reach of duties, and increase pauperism. Duties preserve a rule of taxation, between the States, fair and just, corresponding with the inhibition to tax exports, and unlikely to generate local dissatisfactions; by excises, irregularities may be created by a majority in Congress sufficient to shake or dissolve the Union. Yet the Committee say, "had the word impost been applied to domestick articles, and excise to foreign, the popularity of the two modes of taxation would have been transposed, for their operation on the people is the same." Transpose the names horse and rat, and their qualities would also be transposed. The rat, when called a horse, would become a useful labourer to supply the family with necessaries; and the horse, when called a rat, would gnaw our clothes, steal our food, infest our houses, and produce a great expense in cats, not to prevent, but to assist his depredations. In this, and many other instances throughout the report, the Committee have reasoned upon the ground that words make or change the qualities of things; and, having previously gotten rid of monopolies, and exclusive privileges by calling them regulations of commerce, they now propose in the same way to convert excises into imposts. Is it possible that the universal opinion of mankind, that excises are the most troublesome and oppressive mode of taxation, has been imbibed, not from an experience of their qualities, but from the sound of their names? There was a dog once in this State, famous for following and taking thieves. Upon one occasion, a thief and an innocent person were made to change clothes, and mingle with the crowd, into which the dog was sent to search for the thief. When he came to the clothes on the innocent man, he growled, but discovering his mistake, left him, continued his search, found, and seized the thief, though concealed in the borrowed dress. Do the Committee think that men are less sagacious than this dog?

The impolicy of borrowing, and the inability of the land owners to pay taxes, are two other arguments urged by the Committee in favour of excises, if not more profound, at least more conciliating. The national aversion to borrowing is courted by one, and its aversion to a land tax, by the other. Our system of revenue, they truly say, is at present composed of duties and loans, and they propose to exchange it for a system of excises. They ought in justice to have said for one of excises and loans; for two bad modes of providing revenue, instead of the best which can probably be devised. I summon all experience to testify, whether the mode of obtaining revenue by excises, has diminished or extended the mode of obtaining it by loans. Has the masterly effort of human policy in England had this effect? The reason why it has not, is plain. That policy is a system for transferring property, in which borrowing is an efficacious item; and an increase of taxes by excises is a mode of making it more productive to the gainers, and oppressive to the losers of the property transferred. By adopting it, we shall also adopt its effects, among which the additional funds it furnishes for borrowing, is most prominent.

Land holders must not be taxed, say the Committee, because the depression of agricultural produce forbids it; and it would be equally repugnant to the wishes of the legislature and the interest of the nation. They are too poor to pay a land tax, and yet rich enough to pay excises, sufficient to maintain and increase our present system of extravagance. How are they to pay these excises? With money. How are they to get this money? By the same depressed prices. These are not only to pay more than they now do to government, in order to prevent a recurrence to loans, but also more than they now do to capitalists, in order to create objects for excises to operate upon. Excises, like all other taxes, must chiefly fall on land and labour in the United States for some centuries; I might say for ever; and a suggestion to land owners that this mode of taxation will be a favour to them, is therefore evidently only soothing or cajoling. Whiskey itself, the example exhibited by the Committee, does not prove that excises will relieve the poor land owners from taxation. A tax upon it, reaches the grain of which it is made, the land which produces the grain, and the labour which culti- vates the land. The example, however, affords other testimony. Let those who remember how many officers were necessary to enforce this small excise, compute the number which will be necessary to enforce a general excise; and let the land owners recollect that they must chiefly pay this expense, in addition to the excises upon their consumptions; and then determine, whether the sympathy for their inability to pay taxes, expressed by the Committee, is genuine or delusive.

"The important question," say the Committee, "presents itself. Will the proposed changes be beneficial to the revenue, or is it necessary for its preservation and increase? The revenue from the customs has rapidly decreased. Consumption diminishes with the increase of popu- lation. A reduction of duties will not increase the revenue. When the expenses of a government exceed its income, there must be a responsibility somewhere." Loss to the revenue is, throughout the report, the great evil to be deprecated, and gain to the revenue, the great good coveted. Far from apprehending that the treasury will be starved by an excise, I agree that it must be fattened because it can feed upon every thing; and that the patronage of the Federal government will be vastly increased also, by the multiplication of tax gatherers, and the bounties to capitalists. But ought the liberty and happiness of the people to be overlooked, in the ardent pursuit of these jewels, however brilliant they may appear to those eyes fixed upon the object of getting money for themselves; and ought we not to pause upon being told, that the agriculturists are too poor to bear a land tax, and yet that their taxes ought to be increased to enrich the treasury, extend patronage, and pay bounties? This is said to be necessary, because consumptions, and consequently the customs, have diminished as population has increased. Are there no artificial causes for this phenomenon? Must not our ill-judged tariff, and other commercial restrictions be among them? The responsibility must lie somewhere. Can it be found any where but in bad laws? New laws must be the true causes of new effects. But the Committee, overlooking this truth, have ascribed our past prosperity solely to wars between foreign nations. If we could compare the losses we sustained from armed robbers, with the profits we reaped from these wars, it might be problematical on which side the balance would lie; but these enormous losses are suppressed to deprive our former republican policy of all its laurels, and to hide the visage of that which scowls more and more upon our prosperity, as it gradually supplants its rival. During the long experience which the United States had of the policy decried by the Committee, they found it good in periods of peace, as well as in those of foreign wars, and that it should now fail, must be owing to causes which did not then exist. Foreign commercial restrictions and prohibitions existed during these periods to a greater extent than now, but they could not prevent our prosperity; and therefore no causes, but those of a domestick nature, can account for the gradual disappearance of the national prosperity; then our elevation, now our regret. Do not the facts stated by the Committee, point directly to these causes? Why have consumptions diminished? Because the protecting-duty tariff has increased. Why have duties diminished? Because this tariff and other property-transferring measures, have diverted the profits of labour from being expended in consumptions, by which the public treasury would have been supplied, to enrich the treasuries of capitalists. Why are agricultural products so excessively depressed? Because of the expulsion of foreign commodities by the existing tariff, which would have enhanced the value of domestick products by multiplying exchanges. To these internal regulations, add our imitations of English extravagance, in the expenses of government, and both the causes and the remedies we are in search of must be very easily discovered. Restore our renowned republican frugality, reform our tariff for the object of revenue only, and suppress exclusive privileges; and our treasuries will no longer be empty, government will not be obliged to plunge the nation deeper and deeper into debt, taxation will be light, and the national happiness, gradually lost, will be recovered by a re-occupation of the principles gradually deserted.

The Committee have disclosed one great cause of the decrease of consumptions in proportion to population, by reminding us of the fact, that capital has increased in a few hands up to a redundancy. The same policy which begets this enormous transfer of profits or property, must beget a correspondent diminution of consumptions, by depriving labour of that portion of its income applicable to consumptions, and transferring it to the employment of accumulating capitals in other hands. Reversing the principle of a fertilizing irrigation, it collects the streamlets into a few lakes, and drowns many a fertile vale. These reservoirs of capital, drawn from the small profits of labour, and unfruitful to the treasury, can only have been created by legal mechanism. If the system for transferring property by banking, protecting duties, bounties, and political extravagance, has not done the deed, what has? Have foreign commercial restrictions, always existing, suddenly bethought themselves of inflicting upon us the two evils of exuberant, and empty purses? Why should they have operated so partially as to have enriched a sect of capitalists, and impoverished the rest of the nation? Why should this sect be encumbered with wealth by peace, and the people be reduced to poverty? Can the cessation of foreign wars have been the cause of both these effects? But if the accumulation of wealth in a few hands was not caused by foreign wars, it clearly follows that it is caused by domestick regulations; that this accumulation, and not peace, is the cause of that distress in which the capitalists do not participate, though exposed equally with other people to the cessation of foreign wars; and that it is this artificial accumulation which has diminished consumptions, impoverished both the treasury and the people, and suspended the improvements of agriculture. Can it be denied, that the more of their profits are expended by the great body of the nation which subsists by agriculture, the more of them will be employed in obtaining the comforts of consumption, and in aiding the revenue; and that the more of these profits are taken from this great body of consumers, and tax payers, and applied to the interest, bounties, and dividends which have created our exuberant capitals, the less can be applied to the other objects.

But instead of removing the causes of the disease, the Committee propose to increase them. The impost being crippled, by diverting the profits of labour from procuring the comforts of consumptions, to the accumulation of artificial capitals, they propose to bestow more bounties upon this accumulation. The tariff having produced less and less in proportion to population, as it has been raised and raised, the Committee assert that it would not again become productive, by being lowered, and that it ought to be raised yet higher. If they had asserted that the same productiveness of the customs, experienced when the duties were low, could not be expected so long as an infinitely greater amount of the profits of labour, were diverted from consumptions to accumulations, they would have been right. It would then follow that a diminution of the duties and a restoration of profits to the object of consumptions, united, would certainly increase the revenue; and on the other hand, that both an increase of duties, and also an increase of the policy of transferring profits to pecuniary accumulations, will diminish it. The Committee, therefore, had no design to assist the revenue, by increasing the rates of the tariff; and indeed they fairly acknowledge, that their object is still further to diminish the profits of labour, applicable to consumptions, by transferring more of them to capitalists, that they may be able to prepare objects for an excise.

The Committee have justly observed, that taxation, either by excises or imposts, must fall on consumptions. To consider them with an eye to this equality only, is a concession which grants all that could be asked, and more than the excise system can reasonably expect. From this position it is obvious, that the system of augmenting capital, by diminishing the portion of income applicable to consumptions, will cripple an excise, just as it has crippled the impost mode of taxation. Now as the policy of transferring property, coupled with imposts, has almost famished both the treasury and the nation, whilst it has created an exuberant capital in a few hands; it is but a dreary kind of comfort to be told, that the same policy, coupled with excises, also a tax upon consumptions, will fatten both. But the Committee go further, and say, that the transition to excises must cost us a new augmentation of capital, by monopolies of indefinite duration, to enable these monopolies to fabricate commodities for excises to operate upon; and as the bounties paid under these monopolies will still further reduce the profits of labour applicable to consumption, these excises must be applied to articles of the first necessity, and must be made more oppressive, in order to extort from necessaries, what could not be gotten from superfluities by the impost mode of taxation, when coupled with a monopoly, diminishing consumptions.

Upon this ground, the project of the Committee promises less than nothing. A change in the mere name of a tax, which is still collected through the medium of consumption, would leave us substantially where we were; but the payment of a great and indefinite bounty to capitalists, for this difference between names, and the additional expenses of collection, would make the remedy worse than the disease. One plan to relieve both the nation and the treasury, consists of frugality, free exchanges, free trade, and an abandonment of the policy of creating capitalists by exclusive privileges, bounties, and monopolies; general excises, and an increase of public expenditure, united with these universal instruments of tyranny, constitute the other. We have only to ask ourselves two questions. Which of these plans would be preferred by a patriot, and which by a capitalist? Am I a patriot, or capitalist?

8. Ruin Commerce

The phraseology adopted by the Committee in stating objections to the protecting-duty policy, is that resorted to at the bar, in stating the objections of an adversary. They are put in a hyperbolical dress, to exaggerate them into an aspect of absurdity. Comparative injury, and not absolute ruin or destruction, constitutes the true question as to the impression likely to be made, on revenue, commerce, and agriculture, by the policy of the Committee or its adversary. To understand the objection, we must consider what commerce is. Avoiding as much as possible the previous remarks applicable to its definition, it is necessary to remind the reader, that whether foreign or domestick, it ought to be an instrument for facilitating exchanges, and not for accumulating redundant capitals in a few hands by arbitrary and partial laws. Commercial accumulations flowing from extraordinary skill or industry, are merely means used by commerce, for effecting its beneficial intention; but using it as an instrument for transferring property, without suffering free will to compute compensations, destroys this essential principle for exciting its efforts, and extending its benefits.

One item of the policy of the Committee, is to destroy the end of commerce, for facilitating foreign exchanges, by exporting without importing; another, to substitute for this destruction a domestick commerce, not for promoting fair exchanges, but for effecting a great and lasting transfer of property. They imagine that foreign commerce will not be injured, by restricting it in an extensive degree, to exportation; and that domestick commerce will be encouraged by disemboweling it of its essential principle, and converting it into an instrument for effecting unequal exchanges, to enrich monopolists. Whether this novel system of political economy, will impair or nourish commerce, either foreign or domestick, or whether it has been the true cause of the evil days upon which we are fallen, may be illustrated by a further consideration of the nature of money. Currency, however fabricated, regulates value; and value, if left free, regulates currency, when it is used to facilitate exchanges; but when it is used to transfer property without compensation, it becomes an instrument in the hands of legislation, for fostering local and personal avarice. Domestick commerce, carried on by the instrumentality of currency, presents itself in two characters; that consisting of exchanges of value for value, settled by the medium of money with the consent of the exchangers; and that consisting of exchanging a less value for a greater, enforced by legal compulsion. The intrinsick value of the same commodities, never alters, but their prices are liable to fluctuations from their scarcity or plenty, whether occasioned by casualties, by the laws of nature, by improvements in fabrication, or by laws for transferring property. The value is of course liable to the same fluctuations. But if demand and supply are left free, these fluctuations, except the last, are encouragers of commerce, and money is a medium by which they are moderated, and reduced to an equilibrium, if not with exactness, at least with the fidelity of competition. In cases, however, of a legal enhancement of price, money is deprived of its equalizing utility, and is prohibited from diffusing this equilibrium of values, so evidently just, and so highly beneficial to mankind, both by invigorating their exertions, and extending their comforts. When wheat sold at six pence a bushel, both the raiser and consumer were in the same relative situation as when it sold at two dollars, if the fair equalizer of values was unbiassed by legal privileges; but if these were used, either to raise or lower the price of wheat, one of the exchangers of property was defrauded. Hence it appears, that relative, and not actual prices, constitute justice between occupations, and that the honest office of money is to adjust these relative prices. Whether the actual prices are high or low, the equalizing power of money, if exercised upon free exchanges, prevents any general calamity, and moderates to a great extent individual inconveniences. But laws for depriving money of its equalizing power, establish permanent inequalities of value between occupations, and create those very calamities; to prevent or moderate which, is the most valuable quality of money. The capacity of money to produce an equilibrium of values, operates between nations as well as occupations. The existing peace has diminished prices throughout the commercial world; but as money and commerce will equalize values, neither nations nor individuals sustain any injury from that circumstance. But if a nation shall prohibit itself from sharing in this universal diminution of prices, by crippling its own commerce; and shall moreover enhance by law the commodities for one occupation, whilst the prices of others remain depressed, all the individuals deprived of the compensation to be derived only from the capacity of commerce and money to equalize values, must be considerably impoverished. The government then undertakes to settle prices between occupations and individuals, and it loses sight of relative values, to destroy which is the only design of its interposition. By expelling foreign commodities, the United States are prevented from reaping any benefit from the universal fall of prices; and also deprived of the advantages of exchanging their own by the scale of relative values, which money soon establishes between nations; and by enhancing the prices of domestick manufactures, the relative values of domestick products are also destroyed, and the equilibrium which prevents a general fall of prices from producing any general or partial distress, is overturned; so that they cannot derive any compensations from the principle of relative values, or from commerce, either foreign or domestick. On the contrary, if these relative values were suffered to have an unobstructed operation, individuals would have the means of compensation in their own hands, and self-interest invariably finds it in some part of the commercial world, when not prohibited by governments from exercising its acuteness and industry.

If pecuniary income remains as high as it was when prices were double to what they now are, its real value is doubled, and a double portion of the profits or property of productive labour, absorbed by unproductive. It is by the branch of domestick commerce (if it can be called commerce) for the purpose of transferring property from productive to unproductive employments, that nations are oppressed and enslaved; and I do not recollect a single instance in the whole history of mankind, of a nation oppressed or enslaved, by leaving relative values to be settled by money and commerce. It is said to be necessary to establish this enslaving branch of domestick commerce, to counteract the teasings of foreign restrictions, which cannot enslave us. So far as these foreign restrictions counteract the power of money and commerce to equalize values, they resemble our domestick restrictions for the same purpose; except that the latter are infinitely more effectual, because the former are dissimilar, and the number of disunited nations enables a free commerce to shun, and often to benefit by them. But the relative capacities of foreign and domestick commercial restrictions to enslave nations, by means of a power in the government to regulate values, usurped from commerce and money, is very different.

The nature of a domestick commerce for transferring property, may be demonstrated by a few facts. In the time of Washington, wheat was worth two dollars, and the prices of labour and other property were equivalent. Then the Federal Government received three millions annually. For the sake of round numbers, let us suppose the price of wheat to be now one dollar, and the receipt of the Federal Government twenty-five millions. It is obvious that one dollar represents as much property as two did then, and that though the same equilibrium of value may remain in free exchanges; yet that the equilibrium in the commerce between productive and unproductive employment, or between industry and income, is excessively altered. Tyranny or oppressive taxation, is graduated by this equilibrium. For the same services, or nearly so, rendered by an indispensable species of unproductive labour, which then cost us three millions worth of property, we are now paying fifty millions worth of property. If we come nearer the fact by supposing the average price of wheat to be now seventy-five cents, and other property to be reduced to a relative value, productive labour is paying seventy-two and a half millions annually, for the same government which then cost it only three, estimated in property. The increased expenses of the State governments, have also contributed considerably towards augmenting the oppression arising from the property-transferring branch of domestick commerce. The difference between the amount of contributions to unnecessary, unproductive employments, in the time of Washington, and the existing amount, is still greater. If labour then paid to the infant policy of exclusive privileges even as much as three millions annually, and is now paying more than ten to banking alone, these ten by the same scale are now transferring twenty or twenty-five millions worth of its property instead of three. In the time of Washington, duties were chiefly confined to the object of revenue; now, they are extended to that of enriching capitalists. If these capitalists gain ten millions by this branch of property-transferring domestick commerce, labour is losing twenty or twenty-five millions more beyond what it then lost. It results from the estimate, especially if we include the State governments, that above twenty times more property is transferred annually from industry to unproductive occupations, than was transferred thirty years ago, being the difference between its losing six, or an hundred and twenty-five millions annually. The Committee say that foreign commerce ought to be diminished, in order to encourage and extend this property-transferring domestick commerce. If a European government, between one and two centuries past, when wheat was at one third of its present price, had in thirty years increased the contributions of labour to unproductive employments, twenty-fold, the effect would have been such as is felt here, from our excessive cultivation of the same kind of domestick commerce, and the appreciation of money. If the contributions of industry to unproductive occupations happen to be doubled or trebled by the appreciation of money, I see no remedy for the unforeseen calamity, but a reduction of these contributions to what they substantially were when imposed. What legislature would propose a great and sudden augmentation of taxation, when the value of money was uncommonly high, and the price of products uncommonly low? There is some strange defect in the structure of society, if such an augmentation can be made without any legislative act at all. It is still stranger that the Committee should think of legislating exactly like this invisible tyrant; of whose pernicious laws they are complaining; by proposing to augment the contributions of industry to unproductive occupations, further than his unconscionable conscience has gone. Some irresistible power has substantially doubled or trebled our taxes and contributions to exclusive privileges, without the consent, and contrary to the wishes of our representatives; and instead of advising them to resist this evil spirit, the Committee propose that they should become his accomplice by increasing taxes and bounties, because the means of paying them have greatly diminished. It is this policy only which causes peace to aggravate the distresses of nations, by making the domestick commerce for transferring property, infinitely more lucrative to unproductive occupations, and more oppressive to industry. The extravagances of war and the appreciation of currency, created capitals, bearing with less weight upon industry, whilst the prices of property were high; and the appreciation of currency, by depressing the prices of commodities, has correspondently increased the value of income. The Committee propose to increase capital and income like war, and to enhance their value like peace, by restrictions on foreign commerce, and domestick exclusive privileges.

To justify this scheme for a domestick commerce, they have repeatedly urged the argument uniformly resorted to by every contrivance for transferring property. Whatever local or individual injuries it may produce, they contend that it will beget national prosperity. For this doctrine, they might have referred to English authorities and examples, more conclusively applicable than any they have quoted.

Many English writers, and among others the venerable Adam Smith[6] himself, justify the enrichment of Britain by the wealth drawn from her provinces, by the assertion, that the provinces are integral portions of the British empire; and that the trade between them and the mother country, is therefore to be considered as of a domestick character, and ought to be managed so as to promote the prosperity of the empire. Whether this doctrine is to be ascribed to the partiality of British writers for Britain, or to the design of deluding the provinces into an opinion, that the British monopoly of their commerce was no local injury; whether it was suggested by an ardour for local popularity, conviction, or avarice, it furnishes a parallel of the question we are considering. Admitting it to be true that the commerce between Britain and her provinces ought to be considered as domestick, because they constitute a portion of the British empire, it does not follow that these provinces sustain no injury from the domestick restrictions and monopolies to which their commerce is exposed. These regulations make use of the transferring capacity of money, by inflicting on the provinces a legal necessity of selling cheaper to Britain, and buying dearer of her, than they would do if she was checked by competitors. This double compulsion to buy of Britain and to sell to Britain, creates a domestick commerce, governed partly by the good, and partly by the bad soul of money. So far as the relative value of commodities prevails, its good soul predominates; but whatever is gained by Britain from the provinces beyond this relative value, by means of her monopoly, is bestowed by the bad soul of money, and is an acquisition of property without compensation. The United States, whilst portions of the British empire, constantly felt, and often urged, the great losses they sustained from the restrictions and monopolies of domestick commerce; and Britain as constantly felt the wealth she gained by them, and justified her acquisitions by the same argument now used by the Committee, namely, that these restrictions and monopolies contributed to the national prosperity. Neither side could convince the other, although

---

6. Adam Smith (1723–1790), Scottish political economist, was "venerable" for *An Inquiry into the Nature and Causes of the Wealth of Nations* (2 vols., 1776). He also wrote *Theory of Moral Sentiments* (1759). See Foreword, p. xx.

the colonies, awed by power, would have made considerable sacrifices of their opinion, to obtain only partial alleviations of an oppression, of which they were quite sensible. For the sake of peace, they only contended that Britain ought not to compel them by law to buy, nor to collect in the colonies a tax for nurturing the property-transferring policy, which she had established between them and herself. But Britain, enamoured with this property-transferring domestick commerce, as our capitalists now are; and protesting that she was wholly uninfluenced by avarice, and only influenced by the national prosperity, as the capitalists now protest; continued to increase her restrictions and monopolies, as the capitalists have done, and are still striving to do. The parties therefore went to war to settle a question, which we are trying to settle by reason, as the colonies attempted to do, before that war commenced.

Let the capitalists or factories stand for Britain, and all the other occupations for the colonies, and very little difference between the two cases will appear. If domestick commercial restrictions could transfer property from the colonies to Britain, they may transfer it from these occupations to capitalists. If they were fraudulent and oppressive, though inflicted by the British Parliament, either as a regulation of domestick commerce, or a system of revenue, they may be also fraudulent and oppressive, though inflicted by an American Congress, also as a regulation of domestick commerce, or as a system of revenue. If such regulations transferred great wealth from British colonies to British capitalists, they will also transfer great wealth from American States to American capitalists, wherever they may be located. If a compulsion upon the colonies to purchase necessaries of Britain, was impoverishing to the purchasers; a compulsion upon States and occupations to purchase necessaries of capitalists, must be equally impoverishing on the purchasers. Are not cargoes of internal manufactures, attended by a prohibition against competition, equivalent to cargoes of tea and British commodities, forced upon the colonies without being attended by competition? Will strong and free States be insensible to the oppression of this property-transferring policy, which was seen and resisted by weak and dependent provinces?

The similitude of these cases cannot be evaded by the subterfuge of a difference between foreign and domestick commerce. They are both domestick, subject to the same principles, and made to transfer property by the same regulations. Domestick restrictions and monopolies, more effectually transfer property than foreign, because they can be more effectually enforced; and therefore these instruments are more extensively fraudulent and oppressive in domestick than in foreign commerce, and are infinitely more able to establish domestick tyranny, whilst it is quite uncertain whether they can obtain any species of profitable trade. There is no difference between a contiguity by land or by water, sufficient to make the policy of transferring property foul and oppressive upon British colonies, but fair and beneficial when applied to free States. Britain may, indeed, plead as she feels, that the oceans which separate her from her provinces, render them only half social; and that therefore she is justifiable in using restrictions and monopolies to cheat them of half their property in exchanging hers for it; but the capitalists cannot contend for an addition of fifty per centum to the price of their wares, because the imposition operates upon a sort of half-breed or mongrel citizenship, having only a right to half justice. The moral difference of representation, far from justifying the fraud, is the strongest argument against it. These States, when colonies, possessed a representation for internal purposes, and strenuously contended, that this representation was a provision against colonial oppression by commercial regulations, made by the British Parliament. Can it be possible, that this moral plea, deduced from colonial representation, could have been sounder than the same plea deduced from State representation, even if the latter had no auxiliaries? But are not the original sovereignties of the States, the reservation of internal rights of sovereignty, and limitations of the federal constitution, to prevent Congress from making some States tributary to others, powerful auxiliaries to the argument deduced from representation? Was not representation both State and Federal, instituted to prevent fraudulent transfers of property from State to State, and from the people, to exclusive privileges and legal combinations? If representation does wrong, the possibility of which is contemplated by every free government, some mode of correction is necessary. We have provided two; election, and a division of representation between the Federal and State governments, assigned to each distinct and independent powers, and divided the moral rights of representation, that one species may check the wrongs of the other. Had an accommodation with Britain taken place upon the ground of a representation in her parliament, and conferring upon it the same rights conferred on Congress, reserving to the colonies their local representations for internal purposes, could it have been fairly so construed, as to have rendered these local representations perfectly inefficient, and to have empowered the parliament, in virtue of a right to regulate the commerce between the colonies, to make one tributary to another, or the colonists generally, tributary to a sect of capitalists?

An argument applicable to the point of constitutionality, has been postponed to this place, because it is also applicable to the point of representation. The constitution empowers Congress "to regulate commerce with foreign nations, and among the several States, and with the Indian tribes." Under this authority it has undertaken to regulate internal exchanges between individuals, and to destroy the freedom of exchanges, by conferring monopolies upon some individuals operating upon other individuals. Foreign nations, States, and Indian tribes, are united in one article, and intended to be affected in one mode. Did this article empower Congress to make one Indian tribe tributary to another; to build factories in one tribe, in order to provide objects for an excise, and to destroy the freedom of exchanges between the individuals composing the tribes? Did it give to Congress the same power as to foreign nations? If foreign and internal exchanges, were not intended by the article to be regulated by Congress, neither were State internal exchanges between individuals intended to be regulated by Congress, because the power being equivalent as to each, the construction must also be equivalent; and the absurdity of a construction as to two of the cases placed on the same ground, demonstrates the character of the same construction as to the third. National and not individual regulations of commerce, between States as expressed, and not between individuals, were therefore meant; and the representation in Congress, is only a national representation of this national object, and not a representation of the freedom of internal exchanges between State individuals, any more than the British Parliament was, or would have been, had the proposed accommodation taken place.

The monopoly of domestick commerce outstrips that established by the British Parliament. The colonies were left at liberty to trade with Britain and her dependencies. This created a competition infinitely more extensive and effectual than that confined to our few factories. If the inferiour British restrictions crippled our commerce, will not restrictions more general, cripple it also? The British restrictions left the British portion of the world open to colonial commerce; the protecting-duty policy prohibits or restricts our commerce with the whole world, and opens it with a few monopolies.

The Committee do not deny that foreign commerce will be wounded by this policy. On the contrary, they admit that such has been, and will be, the case, by urging its decay as an argument in favour of a monopolized domestick commerce. From the numberless intimate connexions between foreign and domestic commerce, one is selected as a proof, that the wounds inflicted on the former, will reach the latter. Our coasting trade is greatly fostered, if not sustained, by foreign commerce. Heavy products are carried to a few large cities, from whence they are exported, and the returns pursue the same route. If foreign importations are prohibited or diminished, and factories scattered sufficiently through the States to become markets for culinary goods, it must diminish or render unnecessary this coasting trade. But if this should not happen, and these factories should be so partially located, as to make some coasting trade necessary, yet the insufficiency of their manufactures to meet the demand, and the diminution of exchanges, must greatly impair it. Either the vaunted coasting trade, or the vaunted neighbourhood markets, or both, must therefore be a delusion.

The case of tonnage duties, selected by the Committee to prove the wholesomeness of protecting duties, illustrates the confidence to which such selections are entitled. These duties are rather fiscal than prohibitory; and if they were prohibitory, our abundance of tonnage would render the monopoly as nominal as the monopoly of manufacturing flour. The protecting duties are prohibitory and not fiscal, except to capitalists, and create an operating monopoly. Tonnage duties do not foster a dangerous and oppressive moneyed aristocracy; bounties to factories, levied upon consumptions, do. Tonnage duties fall on consumptions and go into the Treasury; factory duties fall on consumptions, go into the pockets of capitalists; and, by expelling foreign ships, destroy or diminish the revenue drawn from them by tonnage duties. The design that foreign shipping should come here empty and pay a heavy tonnage, and that our shipping should return empty from foreign countries, having paid them a retaliating tonnage, is no bad epitome of the whole project. Have the Committee considered whether other nations will permit our ships to go to them loaded, if we force theirs to come to us empty? If we expel foreign ships, would not foreign nations expel ours? If we expel foreign commodities, will they not retaliate? Will these mutual expulsions foster commerce? We have been long engaged in what is called a war of reciprocity, and by the Committee a free commerce. Blow begets blow, and wound follows wound, and commerce is gasping in the battle. Now, say the committee, let us try "whether the transportation from one part of the country to another, of materials to supply our manufactories, and of manufactures back to the raiser of materials, and the export of manufactures, might not employ as much shipping and as many seamen, as the importation of foreign supply." It is thus admitted, that the policy of the Committee is to give a settling blow to foreign commerce, from a hope that an equivalent domestick commerce will grow upon its grave. To effect this, our factories and raisers of materials must live a great way asunder, to give employment to shipping and seamen in plying between them; and this ferry is to raise sailors and keep up a navy, until we can export manufactures. Foreign nations are of course to admit our ships and these manufactures, when we have gotten them to export, because we have expelled theirs. The fewer have been our expedients of this character, the more has our commerce flourished; and hence it is highly probable, that the most efficacious mode of defeating foreign restrictions to which we can resort, would be to establish a really free commerce, which would enlist the merchants of all nations to evade and counteract them. We have not gained a single victory in a twenty years' war of restriction against restriction, and the harder we strike the enemy, the more severely the blow recoils upon ourselves. Unless we assail him with a new weapon, success seems hopeless. The Committee propose to surrender our foreign commerce, and thus put an end to the contest. Suppose, instead of retiring within our shell from the combat, we should oppose free trade to foreign restrictions. We once tried it, and found ourselves fighting with swords against daggers. I know of no nation which has entered into a commercial warfare in this armour, that has not been victorious.

The Committee observe, "that nature has not denied to the immense region watered by the Mississippi, the Ohio and the Lakes, the means of ship-building, or the supply of cargoes. Man refuses them a market, because he looks only abroad. Foreign commerce can present no preference over domestick." This immense region must, for ages, probably for ever, be agricultural. No equally interiour country has ever yet been a considerable exporter of manufactures. If this is susceptible of success in such an adventure, that success must be at the distance of some centuries. It cannot even enter into a competition with maritime countries, until its deficiency in populousness is removed. In the mean time, ship-building will make its interest more thoroughly agricultural, than that of the Atlantick region. Ships, the product of the forest, freighted with the products of the land, are themselves and their cargoes, only rendered valuable by foreign commerce. But the committee say what I cannot understand, "man refuses them a market, because he looks only abroad." Do they mean that our merchants look abroad for agricultural ships and cargoes, rather than purchase them at home? As such is not the case, and as I cannot discern any meaning in the expression, I am forced to consider it as an empty barrel, thrown out to draw off the attention of the western whale. Is it not obvious that this very branch of western commerce, destined soon to become highly valuable on account of the cheapness of timber, and its dearness in foreign countries, depends for prosperity on foreign commerce? Would these ships and their cargoes be purchased and eaten by domestick factories, Western or Atlantick? Why do the Committee endeavour to inspire a hope so absurd, by adding, "that foreign commerce can present no preference over domestick?" Will an undeniable truth establish an undeniable error? If horses are preferable to oxen, ought we therefore to destroy or hamstring our oxen? Far from inferring from the fact, that foreign commerce is not preferable to domestick; that therefore the destruction of the former will advance the western interest, there seems to be no stronger case than this ship-building and loading which they have selected, to prove the close connexion between foreign and domestick commerce; and to show how necessary the one is to the prosperity of the other. Without foreign commerce, it is perfectly plain that the domestick commerce in western ships and their cargoes will dwindle and perish, even sooner than any other item of agricultural interest.

The objection is, that the protecting-duty policy will injure or destroy commerce, meaning foreign commerce, and the Committee justify this consequence by asserting, that a domestick commerce between factories and raisers of raw materials will compensate us for the loss, because foreign commerce can present no preference over domestick. Foreign commerce is then condemned to death by this policy, leaving its partner, agriculture, as a legacy to capitalists.

9. DESTROY AGRICULTURE

Neither ambition nor avarice could ever succeed in depriving nations of their liberty and property, if they did not by some artifice enlist the services of a body of men, numerically powerful. The general promises the plunder of a town to his soldiers; they take it; and he keeps most of it for himself and his officers. These are enriched, and the soldiers remain poor. A demagogue promises liberty to a rabble, and by their help makes himself their tyrant. And capitalists, by promising wealth to mechanicks, accumulate it for themselves, and become their masters. The Committee disclaim a predilection for factory capitalists, and an enmity towards agriculture. I balance this argument by disclaiming also a predilection for agriculturists, and an enmity towards mechanicks; but I avow an enmity against all modes for transferring property by exclusive privileges. As no man, however, can find the seeds from which his opinions have germinated, such protestations are frivolous, and they are also unworthy of weight; because the consequences, and not the origin of opinions, constitute their materiality. If it was important to decide, whether the policy proposed by the Committee or its competitor, could be convicted of foreign origin, the difficulty of the subject would not be increased; but I wave the unedifying enquiry, and proceed to the substantial part of the question, whether it will be most injurious to agriculturists or mechanicks. At the threshold of this enquiry, I have changed a term, by substituting mechanicks for manufacturers, to display truth more clearly. The term agriculture needs no such correction, because we have not the two conflicting classes of landlords and tenants, as we have of capitalists and mechanicks. Where the land of a country is owned by landlords, and worked by tenants, the phrase "landed interest" refers to the landlords, who may enjoy exclusive privileges of which the tenants do not partake; and the impoverishment of one interest may contribute to the enrichment of the other. In like manner, where the factories belong to capitalists, and are worked by mechanicks, the phrase "manufacturing interest" refers to the capitalists, who may enjoy exclusive privileges of which the workmen do not partake; and their impoverishment may contribute to the enrichment of the capitalists, as the impoverishment of tenants may enrich landlords. In deciding the questions, therefore, by the test of friendship or enmity, we ought to exhibit persons, and not confound distinct interests, as the objects of these passions. A cold calculation of the profit to be made by factories, may be a vice of avarice, but a friendly sympathy for the calamities of workmen, arising from the policy of making laws to accumulate this profit, can only flow from good will towards them.

The interest of mechanicks against the factory policy, advocated by the Committee, is infinitely stronger than that of farmers, because, they may more easily be swept into factories, and the profits of their labour more completely carried into the pockets of the capitalists, than can be effected in the case of land owners. These are so powerful as to be able, when they feel a loss, to give themselves a compensation, as the English landlords have done by the corn laws; and between the capitalists and landlords in that country, the mechanicks find poverty. A keen sense of misery fraudulently inflicted, is the cause of their frequent insurrections, and fixed hatred of the government. Why are soldiers necessary to protect their masters, their work-houses and their looms, against the mechanicks themselves? The great lexicographer Johnson, in defining the condition and character of an English mechanick, has called him "mean and servile." The definition is justified by the fact, that his best resource against ending his days in a hospital or poor house, is the shortness of his life. A mechanick employed in a factory rarely acquires a competence; opulence is out of the question;

and he is completely excluded from public employments, by being doomed to a situation in which he can never acquire a capacity for them. He can hardly be considered as a citizen. A code of laws draws around him a magick circle, by making mechanical combinations punishable, lest they should check capitalist combinations; and he is reimbursed by penalties for the loss of hope.

The condition of the mechanick in the United States has hitherto been extremely different. It neither excites insurrections, nor inculcates a hatred of the government. It does not require a regular army to cure the agonies of misery. It neither shortens life, nor devotes old age to an hospital. It never fails to acquire a competency by industry and good conduct; sometimes rises to opulence; and receives its due share of public employments. Instead of being deemed mean and servile, it is capable of respectability, and the whole magistracy is open to it. I have heard that the son of a mechanick has been a President; and I know that a weaver, a carpenter, and a carriage-maker (the two first from Pennsylvania, and the last from Virginia) were at one time for a long period, worthy members of Congress. Probably there have been many other similar instances. In State legislatures mechanicks are often seen, and as magistrates and militia officers, they abound. They are real, and not nominal citizens. How often do the hirelings of a factory in England, become members of Parliament, magistrates, or militia officers?

For these enormous differences between the condition of the mechanicks in England and the United States, there must be some cause. What can it be, except that the factory and capitalist policy, deprives them of the erect attitude in society inspired by the freedom of industry, and bears hardest upon them, as the chief objects of its gripe? Has this policy bettered the condition of mechanicks, even whilst it was creating enormous fortunes for their masters? If not, the strongest motive for resisting it, is the happiness and prosperity of the mechanicks themselves; though the success of this resistance will also contribute towards the happiness and prosperity of all other useful occupations, because the freedom of talents and industry, and the absence of a system for making both subservient to the interest of avarice, is the principle which must operate beneficially to all, though most so to that occupation most immediately assailed.

To counteract facts established by a double example, the same bribe is offered to land-owners here, which has created in England, a conspiracy between landlords and capitalists against mechanicks, by which they have been reduced to perpetual labour and perpetual poverty. The land-owners are told, that by coercing mechanicks into factories, the prices of their manufactures will be reduced, and that the land-owners will then be reimbursed for the bounties now paid to capitalists, by a future cheapness to be effected at the expense of mechanicks, thus coerced into factories. I do not deny that such would be the case, if the factory scheme could be carried to the same extent here as in England. This could not be effected, even if our populousness could furnish the materials, except by the English system of legislation to prevent mechanicks from breaking their factory chains, and compelling them to labour hard for low wages to supply the conspirators cheaply. But is not this coerced cheapness evidently imposed upon the mechanical occupation? If it could be effected in the United States, the first class of valuable and respectable citizens which would be ruined by it, would be the great body of mechanicks scattered throughout the country, who would be undersold by the factory capitalists, and compelled to relinquish their free occupations, and become hirelings at the factories. The promised consummation of the factory project, therefore, however tempting to farmers, would be a complete degradation of mechanicks from the equal and comfortable station they hold in society, to one much less desirable. Every present fraud offers a future bribe. The future cheapness offered to land-holders is too distant and uncertain, to induce them to enter into this conspiracy with the capitalists against the mechanicks; and besides, why should they get less than the English landlords for doing so? These have had their rents, and of course the value of their lands doubled or trebled into the bargain, and if without this additional bribe, cheapness would have been insufficient to compensate them for the evils of the capitalist-policy, the land-owners here may safely conclude that they will not be compensated by this promise alone, for co-operating in the conspiracy; and that to make a good bargain, they ought to have the price of their lands doubled or trebled, like the English landlords.

The solitary promise of future cheapness to farmers, to arise from the factory policy, is met by many formidable considerations: If it could be fulfilled at some distant period, the great injury to society from reducing the respectable and numerous class of mechanicks down to Johnson's definition of them; from creating a moneyed aristocracy; and from establishing the policy of exclusive privileges, in which few or no farmers can ever share, would alone suffice to prove that the bribe, if received, would bring along with it a far greater cargo of evils than of benefits.

The prices paid by farmers to the great number of free mechanicks, scattered throughout the country, and by these mechanicks to farmers, promote neighbourhood consumptions; create much domestick commerce regulated by free exchanges, and not by a fraudulent monopoly; stimulate mutual industry, and increase the value of property; but the prices paid to factory capitalists, so long as their monopoly operates, will to a great extent be employed in transferring and accumulating capital. A transfer of profit from industry to the accumulation of capital, whether the profit is agricultural or mechanical, is a mutual diminution of the fund, acting and re-acting between industrious occupations, and begetting mutual prosperity. The more of his profits the agriculturist can save from the capitalist, the more employment he will give to his friend and neighbour, the mechanick; and the more of his are retained by the mechanick, the more he will consume of agricultural products, or enhance by his savings, the value of land. In either case would domestick commerce be rendered more beneficial to the society, by diverting these funds from this intercourse, to the accumulation of pecuniary capitals?

Monopoly is a word sufficiently indefinite, to enable ingenuity to obscure its malignity, by extending it to property acquired by industry and free exchanges; and though private property begets civilization, society, and happiness, it is made, by calling it monopoly, to supply arguments for its own invasion. If monopoly, like money, does really reach every species of acquisition, yet it may also possess good and evil qualities; and a discrimination between them is necessary, to reap the good and avoid the evil. The monopolies obtained by industry, admitting the phrase to be correct, are, like earning money, beneficial to society; those obtained by exclusive privileges, like stealing money, are pernicious. These qualities of monopoly are hostile to each other. The latter species of monopoly takes away the acquisitions of the former. The most enormous monopoly is that of monarchs of all the land within their territories, once established in Europe by the feudal system, and still subsisting in Turkey and some Asiatic countries. This deprives industry of its power to acquire, to a great extent. Of the same nature is the protecting-duty monopoly. A monopoly of land, enables the monopolist to extract wealth from the produce of land; and a monopoly of mechanicks, enables the monopolist to extract wealth from the produce of mechanicks. The monopolist in both cases is able to enhance the price of land or its produce, or the produce of his mechanicks, at the expense of buyers. Land was monopolized by the feudal system, incidentally to monopolize labour; by the factory system, the labour itself is directly monopolized. Next to that of land, a monopoly of manufacturing is the most extensive and oppressive of which we can have a conception. It even appears to operate more widely than a monopoly of land, because all are consumers of manufactures. It does not indeed take away the land itself of agriculturists, but it effects the same end which the feudal monopoly effected; it obtains a portion of its profits. If a law was made to bestow all the lands of the United States upon a few persons, it would be equivalent to a policy for enabling capitalists to build factories, and monopolize mechanicks. We should then have the English policy complete; landlords and tenants, capitalists and mechanicks. I know but of two modes of ascertaining whether a monopoly exists. One consists of appropriation without compensation, the other of an appropriation obtained by compensation. The latter is only called a monopoly, in attempting to confound it with the former. Loss and gain without an equivalent determined by free commerce, is established between farmers and capitalists by legal coercion, and if this does not constitute the former species of monopoly, the Committee may be right in denying its existence.

But it is urged that manufactures are in their infancy, and require monopolies or bounties to make them grow. When is this allegation of the imperfection of arts and sciences to cease, as a justification of bounties and monopolies? How long will the world be persuaded that it is an infant, and ought to be scourged into knowledge? Europe is told that she is not fit for liberty, because political science is yet so imperfect, that she cannot bear it. Asia has been lashed from a considerable proficiency in arts and sciences, to a renovation of extreme ignorance. And the United States, as if they had blundered immaturely upon a free form of government, are retracing their foot-steps towards the alleged European unfitness for it. When will a maturity of arts and sciences arrive, to enable mankind to reject bad, and adhere to good principles, if they should have adopted them by chance? We are told, that many centuries past, when the mechanical arts were extremely simple and rude, bounties and privileges were expended for the sake of their introduction and improvement. We might also be told, that once upon a time mankind were so savage, that the feudal system was necessary for their civilization. Neither fact proves the propriety of bounties and exclusive privileges, or of the feudal system at present. The advancement of mankind in political science, and mechanical arts, has entirely changed their character in several countries, and a great proficiency as to both has certainly appeared in the United States. Our mechanical knowledge is so considerable in the opinion of the Committee, that they propose to create capitalists to monopolize it. Our political knowledge has even soared too high, and ought therefore to be reduced to the European standard. Will the time never arrive, at which arts and sciences can be entrusted with freedom, and left to their own unrestricted exertions? We have probably fewer eminent scientifick people than skilful mechanicks, compared with some European nations; would it therefore be wise to prohibit ourselves from a participation of foreign knowledge, and bestow a monopoly of the sciences upon a combination of learned men, as we propose to bestow a monopoly of the mechanical arts, upon a combination of capitalists? Are not such monopolies of an equivalent character? No, say the Committee, we will import from Europe its system of exclusive privileges, monopoly, and extravagance: this is a blessing; but we will exclude her manufactures; these are a curse.

Circumstances must be the same, to make examples worthy of imitation. When the Committee go back to distant times in search of examples, and overlook existing circumstances, they suppress the facts which ought to govern the conclusion. When England was ignorant of the art of manufacturing, it was wise to purchase information of foreign mechanicks, and obtain their instruction; but after she acquired the art, the end was obtained, and the only good reason for the purchase, ceased. The distinction between bounties for introducing the arts of manufacturing, and bounties for enriching a class of capitalists, after they are introduced, is manifest. The bounties in one case go to the mechanicks themselves; in the other, to masters set over them by laws. In one case the mechanicks are enriched; in the other, they are impoverished. One offers them a reward for their skill; the other, its degradation. The policy of rewarding mechanicks for introducing and perfecting manufactures, bears no resemblance to the policy of enabling a combination of capitalists to monopolize mechanicks. The suggestion of the latter policy, admits that our circumstances do not require the former. It is founded on the fact, that we have a sufficient number of mechanicks for the capitalist-monopoly to act upon, so as to make it highly lucrative. Our abundance of mechanicks, and not their scarcity, has suggested the speculation; and the same abundance refutes the application to us, of the ancient policy of purchasing mechanicks from other countries, and also the modern policy of purchasing a moneyed aristocracy at the public expense, composed, not of foreign artisans, but of native capitalists. It has been asserted, and perhaps truly, that the number of the mechanicks, and their families, amount to half a million. Whatever may be their number, it is sufficient to detect the misapplication of precedents for alluring mechanicks from foreign countries, to us; and also the pretence, that this important class of our citizens receive the bounties, bestowed on factories. Rewards to a few artisan emigrants are practicable; but bounties to one in about eight of our white population, of a sufficient amount to wed it to a particular occupation, are impracticable. A tithe is a heavy tax, but it is nothing compared with a bounty to half a million of people. The clerical class in England does not amount to one hundred thousand persons, and about one hundred and twenty people, support one person of that class. The project of the Committee is, to make about eight people here pay a bounty sufficient to weld one person to the manufacturing employment. This estimate cannot be so inaccurate, as to weaken the argument deducible from it. A bounty to a class so numerous, must either be an intolerable tax upon the rest of the nation, if it is large enough to effect its object; or if the bounty is so small, as to be a light tax to the rest of the nation, it must be insufficient to have any influence upon a class so numerous. Our protecting-duty bounty must be of one or the other character. Its insufficiency hitherto for the purpose of influencing our great artisan class, is admitted by the Committee. At each increase it has promised to do so, and all its promises have failed, as to its effects upon this numerous class, although a few factories have been created by it. Whence arises these disappointments? Either from the great number of the artisan class, which causes the bounties to be insufficient to influence it, or because mechanicks do not receive them. The fact is, that although our class of mechanicks is too numerous to be purchased like a few foreign emigrants, yet that the bounties insufficient to enrich half a million, are an enormous acquisition to two or three hundred capitalists, and awakens their activity, whilst it has no perceivable effect upon the mechanical class.

In order to keep up a resemblance between the old authorities quoted, and the policy of protecting duties, the encouragement of artisan emigrants, is, however, frequently urged. And yet we are told, that the few who have accepted the invitation, proclaimed by this policy, reject its blessings upon their arrival, and pass on into the western country, to exercise or renounce their trades. And how can it be otherwise? Will mechanicks flee from factories and capitalists in England to be monopolized by factories and capitalists here? Mark this argument of the Committee and their admirers. It is necessary, by a bounty, to induce mechanicks to exchange the English regimen for the American. The news of a bounty brings them here, and they find the same English regimen. It is that which the Committee profess to imitate, and propose to introduce. The disposition of the English mechanicks to fly from it; to abandon country and connexions to get rid of it; and to shrink into the western country from its resurrection in this country, where there are no parish nor penal laws to nail them to the loom, explodes the expectation, that the policy abhorred by mechanicks there, will be adored by them here. On the contrary, a horrour of factories and capitalists, carries emigrants as far from them as they can get, and also keeps native mechanicks at a distance from them. If our factories were as well filled as the English, cross desertions might take place, as men are prone to fly from one evil to another; but the deserters must still remain in the ranks, and be subject to the same oppressive discipline, whatever might be the bounties or pay of their officers, the capitalists, unless they could flee further, as they do here. Can such emigrations ever bear the minutest resemblance to the rewards and honours bestowed by wise kings, upon ingenious mechanical emigrants, when they were scarce; and their trades mysteries? Must not the emigrant mechanick fall into the ranks of the five hundred thousand, and can his pittance of the bounty, even if he could wrest it from the capitalist, have any influence over him? The factory servility will be as much hated here as in England; and the facility with which it may be avoided, unites with this hatred, to disclose the reasons why neither emigrants nor natives perceive the advantage of earning bounties for capitalists, and degradation for themselves. The difference between exporting slaves to Africa to make them free, and importing mechanicks to make them slaves to capitalists, is nearly the same, as that between purchasing ingenious artisans by great rewards to teach unknown trades, and tempting emigrants by promising to them the English inflictions. Would slaves wish to go to Africa to be again enslaved? Why not tempt emigrants by bounties, to work on our farms, as well as in our factories? New-York has swallowed more of the emigration quackery than any other portion of the Union. I know not whether it has filled her factories, her poor houses, or her jails; or whether the recruits raised by bounties to capitalists, prefer running away, to running after these intercepted bounties.

Having examined the effects of the protecting-duty monopoly to the mechanical class, to test its professions of friendship for that class, let us proceed to enquire how it will promote the interest of the agricultural class, for which its friendship is equally sincere—indeed it professes to be a general friend. We have seen that its effect in establishing a perfect monopoly of mechanicks by capitalists, does not promote the wealth or respectability of these mechanicks; and it is now to be considered, whether an imperfect monopoly of agricultural profits, though it does not enslave the persons of the farmers, differs from a complete monopoly of mechanicks, and the profits of their labour, except as partial pilferings differ from a total robbery. By supposing that the farmers were reduced to the situation designed for mechanicks, that is, to work for daily wages, we shall get a clear view of the nature of the protecting-duty policy. When a combination of capitalists can both coerce persons and reap the profit of their labour, we have seen that this perfect operation of their monopoly, does not promote either the wealth or respectability of these persons. Such a system, rendered perfect as to farmers, must of course operate upon them as it does upon the mechanicks. But it only operates upon farmers imperfectly, by transferring a portion of their profits to capitalists, by the simple but effectual mode of creating an artificial scarcity of necessaries and comforts, to be supplied by capitalists at enhanced prices. If, however, we include every description of income-men without labour, we may very safely conclude, that all the profits of farmers, like those of factory mechanicks, are now reaped by capitalists of some kind or other. The farmers then are already invested with half the situation of factory mechanicks; their persons are freer, but the profits of their labour go to capitalists. In fact the whole United States are, by the protecting-duty laws, turned into one great factory, and all the people are placed upon the factory regimen as to profits. These are transferred by laws to a vast pecuniary aristocracy, just as the profits earned by factory labourers go to an owner. If we admit that it is as hard to get out of our country as out of a factory, our persons also are under restraint like mechanicks in a factory; and the similitude between the mechanicks in a factory, and the farmers in their own country, under the protecting-duty policy, becomes complete. Both are sufficiently incarcerated to be under a necessity of yielding up the profits of their labours to a combination of legal capitalists.

Intricate as the science of political economy has been rendered, by the artificers of exclusive privileges, it yet contains some principles so undeniable, as to explode the whole mass of partial and perplexing calculations, used to conceal or evade them. Among these principles the most important is, that land is the only, or at least the most permanent source of profit; and its successful cultivation the best encourager of all other occupations, and the best security for national prosperity. If this principle can maintain itself against the sophistry of exclusive privileges in any country, it must be in the United States. If the cultivation of land flourishes, all other occupations prosper; if it languishes, they decay. Malthus in his late able treatise upon political economy[7] observes, "that the causes which lead to a fall of rents are, as may be expected, exactly opposite to those which lead to their rise; namely, a diminished capital, diminished population, a bad system of cultivation, and the low market-price of raw produce. They are all indications of poverty and decline, and are necessarily connected with throwing inferiour land out of cultivation, and the continual deterioration of land of a superiour quality." To prevent this general national decline, agricultural capital (the capital he means) is indispensable. If that is deficient, the most efficacious security against national poverty, and the most efficacious excitement of talents and industry, are lost. Profits are the rents of land-owners in the United States. The policy of diminishing these profits to increase the wealth of exclusive privileges, has already produced those indications which Malthus foretels. The cultivation of inferiour lands has been thus rendered wholly unprofitable. The lands of the United States are chiefly of this quality. Good land is continually impoverished. Both effects proceed from the property or profit-transferring machines, called exclusive privileges, and government extravagance. It is admitted by the Committee, that exuberant capitals have been accumulated in a few hands, but that agriculture wants them. What can have produced the want, but the accumulation? Then this very accumulation has produced our national decline, by robbing agriculture of the capital by which only this decline can be prevented. Why has the accumulated capital been unable to find employment in our spacious country, where capital has been so successfully employed for two centuries, under provincial disadvantages, and all the sufferings from foreign restrictions? It is because exclusive privileges, which bestow the capital, are too wise to invest it in an occupation, the profits of which are tapped perpetually by their various gimlets. Capital, like rats, deserts a falling house; and who can so well discover

7. Thomas Robert Malthus (1766–1834), British political economist, wrote *Principles of Political Economy* (1820). He also wrote *Observations on the Effects of the Corn Laws* (1814) and *Inquiry into the Nature and Progress of Rent* (1815), and is best known for his *Essay on the Principle of Population* (1798).

that the dwelling is ruinous, as those who are gnawing it down. Capitalists will no longer invest their money in agriculture, because that very money demonstrates to them, that agriculture can no longer be profitable. Is it not highly unreasonable that the capitalists should be continually pressing for augmentations of income, when the agricultural occupation is already reduced by the transfers of its profits, to such a state, that they will not in this wide country, abounding in a choice of climates, soils, and products, venture their money in so hopeless a business? And are they not perfectly right? Who in his senses would place his money where it would certainly be taken away by a combination of which he is himself a party?

Not pretending to any authority myself, it may be excusable to insert several other quotations from Malthus, the latest, and perhaps the ablest of the English economists. He vindicates to a great extent the doctrines of Adam Smith. But what is authority? Fashion only. A great man, discerning that the doctrines of Adam Smith or Malthus are hostile to his views, has only to say that they are calculated to do much mischief, and the watch-word is caught and disseminated by his admirers, his flatterers and accomplices. Avaricious or ambitious authority, purchased by bribes or patronage, is opposed to honest authority, only sustained by truth. The inquisition itself was defended by this species of authority, because it was a mode of getting power and money. Thus, the authority of all writers on the side of justice, liberty, and good government, is invariably undermined. It is perpetually assailed by exclusive privileges, monopolies, frauds, ambition, and avarice, to deprive mankind of the only beacons which can warn them of the approach of those enemies, by which their prosperity and happiness are destroyed. The following quotations from Malthus are therefore offered, not as authority, but as appeals to the understanding of the reader.

He observes,

> that the fertility of land, either natural or acquired, may be said to be the only source of permanently high returns of capital. In the earlier periods of history, monopolies of commerce and manufactures produced brilliant effects, but in modern Europe there is no possibility

of large permanent returns being received from any other capitals, than those employed on land. But that capitals employed on land, may sometimes yield twenty, thirty, forty, fifty, or even sixty per cent. A striking illustration of the effects of capitals employed on land, compared with others, appeared in the returns of the property tax in England, which yielded six and a half millions from their income, whereas those employed in commerce and manufactures, only yielded two millions.

Another most desirable benefit belonging to a fertile soil is, that states so endowed, are not obliged to pay much attention to that most distressing and disheartening of all cries to every man of humanity; the cry of the master-manufacturers and merchants for low wages, to enable them to find a market for their exports. If a country can only be rich by running a successful race for low wages, I should be disposed to say at once—perish such riches. The peculiar products of a country, will generally be sufficient to give full spirit and energy to all its commercial dealings, both at home and abroad; while a small sacrifice of produce, that is, the not pushing cultivation too far, would, with prudential habits among the poor, enable it to maintain the whole of a large population in wealth and plenty.

It will readily be allowed that an increase in the quantity of commodities, is one of the most desirable effects of foreign commerce; but I wish particularly to press on the attention of the reader, that, in almost all cases, another most important effect accompanies it, namely, an increase in the amount of exchangeable value. And that this latter effect is so necessary, in order to create a continued stimulus to productive industry, and keep up an abundant supply of commodities, that in the cases in which it does not take place, a stagnation in the demand for labour is immediately perceptible, and the progress of wealth is checked.

It cannot for a moment be doubted, that the annual increase of the produce of the United States of America, estimated either in bullion or in domestick and foreign labour, has been greater than that of any country we are acquainted with, and that this has been greatly owing to their foreign commerce, which, notwithstanding their facility of production, has given a value to their corn and raw produce, equal to what they bear in many countries of Europe, and has consequently given to them a power in commanding the produce and labour of other countries quite extraordinary, when compared with the quantity of labour which they have employed.

What I wish specifically to state is, that the natural tendency of foreign trade, as of all sorts of exchanges by which a distribution is effected, better suited to the wants of society, is immediately to increase the value of that part of the national revenue which consists of profits, without any proportionate diminution elsewhere, and that it is precisely this immediate increase of national income, arising from the exchange of what is of less value in the country, for what is of more value, that furnishes both the power and will to employ more labour, and occasions the animated demand for labour, produce and capital, which is a striking and almost universal accompaniment of successful foreign commerce.

It is unquestionably true that wealth produces wants; but it is a still more important truth, that wants produce wealth. One of the greatest benefits which foreign commerce confers, and the reason why it has always appeared an almost necessary ingredient in the progress of wealth, is, its tendency to inspire new wants, to form new tastes, and to furnish fresh motives for industry. Even civilized and improved countries cannot afford to lose any of these motives.

To interfere generally with persons who are arrived at years of discretion, in the command of the main property which they possess, namely, their labour, would be an act of gross injustice; and the attempt to legislate directly in the teeth of one of the most general principles by which the business of society is carried on, namely, the principle of competition, must inevitably and necessarily fail.

The natural and permanent tendency of all extension of trade, both domestic and foreign, is to increase the exchangeable value of the whole produce.

In leaving the whole question of saving to the uninfluenced operation of individual interest and individual feelings, we shall best conform to that principle of political economy laid down by Adam Smith, which teaches us a general maxim, liable to very few exceptions, that the wealth of nations is best secured by allowing every person, as long as he adheres to the rules of justice, to pursue his own interest in his own way.

These quotations have not been applied severally in the course of this treatise, because I had proceeded to the page where they commence, before I saw Malthus; and therefore the memory of the reader must be chiefly taxed with their applications. The unforeseen coincidences are remarkable, and they might have been greatly extended by other quotations, had not a fear of prolixity forbidden it. The leading principles; that land only can yield permanent and sometimes great profits, in the United States especially; that manufacturing in the present state of the world must yield lower profits; that arbitrary depressions of wages are necessary to obtain these low profits; that the products of good land, well cultivated, will bestow spirit and energy both on domestick and foreign commerce; that an increase of foreign commodities will both augment and enhance the price of domestick productions; that the freer are exchanges the more industry is encouraged; that restrictions upon this freedom produce stagnations of labour and check the progress of wealth; that the wonderful prosperity of the United States for two centuries has been owing to foreign trade; that this consists in exchanges of what they did not want for what they did want; that wants produce wealth; that laws against competition must fail, or cannot produce good effects, as we have experienced; that an extension of trade increases the exchangeable value of produce; and that the great principle of political economy is to leave to individuals the right of pursuing their interest in their own way; are all clearly asserted.

The fact, that the general diffusion of manufactures throughout the commercial world, both by home fabricks, and the competition of many nations, ought to be maturely considered, before we cripple agricultural profit, from a hope of reaping more profit by becoming adventurers in this overstocked market. A forbidding and permanent competition every where stares us in the face. If the competition in agricultural products was equally universal and permanent, yet the agricultural occupation would stand on the same ground with the manufacturing; but with us it possesses the exclusive advantages arising from the cheapness, freshness, and goodness of our land; from always having a surplus to be enhanced by occasional fluctuations of seasons; and from often having the value of its products increased by foreign wars, against being engaged in which our situation shields us.

But a comparison between fostering agriculture or manufactures, does not exhibit the true question in debate. The policy we have been pursuing for some years, is that of surrendering our agricultural advantages, and driving our best customers into other markets, for the sake of fostering the unproductive capitalist employment; and it must be confessed that we have succeeded in both objects to a great extent. I am not satisfied with the usual division of productive and unproductive

labour. It comprises in one class all bodily, and in the other, all mental
labours; and seems eminently defective as to the latter class, for want
of a discrimination between such mental labours as are good, and such
as are bad. By confounding both under the general term, unproductive,
they are artfully rested upon the same principles, however different in
their effects. There may be more perspicuity by dividing labour, first,
into physical and mental, and then dividing mental, into moral and
immoral labour. Mental labours cannot be correctly called unproductive, because they are certainly productive of good and evil to a
great extent. Government has been assigned to the class of unproductive
labour, but it produces much good by frugality and justice, or much
harm by extravagance and exclusive privileges. Philosophers, authors,
lawyers, physicians, and tutors, are assigned to the same class; but
they produce knowledge, justice, health, and instruction, and like
governments, render compensations for the money they receive. Merchants excite and satisfy wants, encourage industry, and enrich nations.
Exclusive privileges, monopolies, oppressions, and even thefts are also
worked by mental labours; but instead of compensations, they render
injuries for the money they obtain. The powers of physical labour
suffice to produce a surplus of subsistence beyond its own necessities,
and this surplus is apparently the provision made by the laws of nature,
for the maintenance of the mental labourers, necessary to the existence
of society. But a correspondence between natural and social laws, does
not justify the establishment of that class of mental labourers, which
produces social mischiefs. To distinguish true from false political economy, we ought to distinguish beneficial from pernicious mental labours;
and not comprise both under the common appellation, unproductive,
both because their effects are different, and also because neither, strictly,
deserve that character. But foreign economists have very ingeniously
used the fact "that consumption bestows value on production," not
only to justify the policy of sustaining by social institutions a class of
useful mental labourers, but also to justify all the modes for transferring
property or profit from useful labour, whether physical or moral, to
useless and pernicious immoral labour, upon the ground, that it is
beneficial in society that it should contain a class of consumers to
bestow value on consumptions. The force of the argument applied to

the bad class of mental labourers, is condensed in the assertion, that it would be thrifty for a man to give two dollars of his money to another, that this other might give him two dollars for a bushel of his wheat. The doctrine of purchasing consumers is adopted by the Committee; the object of which is to prove, that oppressive taxation and exclusive privileges will add to this class, and that it is of no consequence whether it is created *per fas aut nefas,* because it is a market for productions. It is a doctrine as applicable to highwaymen as to any other immoral capitalists; they are also consumers. But is it not better to get consumers by natural and voluntary modes, than by artificial and coercive modes; such as render compensations for their maintenance, than such as do not? If the individuals who compose a society, are left to arrange themselves into the two classes of physical and moral labourers, the supply of both will adjust itself to the demand; but if the supply of consumers is furnished by the Government, an overstock has never failed to appear highly oppressive to producers, who are forced by laws to maintain them. A sufficient stock of consumers will never be wanting, if men are left free, because the motive for acquiring wealth being to get into the class of consumers, or to get there by moral accomplishments, it is a class into which all are pressing as fast as they can, and more likely to be sufficiently filled without the help of laws, than any other in society. The pasture for consumers will be filled naturally up to the food; but when people are turned into it by laws, without the passport of talents, industry is used like a common, and grazed as close as possible. Out of these observations arises a very important distinction as to capitalists. Those who acquire capitals by material productions or moral services, are the really useful capitalist class, as consumers, as giving value to productions, as encouraging industry, and as extending comforts. If they use their capitals in improving the face of the earth, for which there is always ample room, they are most eminently beneficial to mankind. And if they give them to their children, they rarely fail, in a generation or two, to breed consumers sufficient to keep a supply of consumption equal to production, without manufacturing them by arbitrary laws, and without subjecting the public to any expense; on the contrary, capitalists or consumers created by exclusive privileges or fraudulent laws of any kind, are, unexceptionably, drones with stings.

Highly valuable as manufactures undoubtedly are, yet all writers upon political economy agree that they are secondary, and unite in allowing the first place to agriculture. Capital is essential to both occupations. If they were of equal value, nothing would be gained by transferring the capital of either to the other, and much would be lost by transferring the capital of either to the class of capitalists I have just attempted to describe. But if mechanicks are reduced to a state of vassalage, and both their profits and the profits of farmers are transferred to such a class of capitalists, according to our existing protecting-duty and factory policy, we have already obtained an enormous overstock of consumers of the profits of labour, as always happens when this family is created by laws, and not by free industry and fair social intercourse; and we are feeling that it grazes too close. Taxes are not burdens but blessings to this whole family, because they contribute less than they receive, and an increase of taxation is a new acquisition to them. Is it this fact which has influenced the United States to submit to the policy of a capitalist aristocracy? Neither bankers, nor pensioners, nor lenders to the public, nor receivers of factory bounties, pay any thing to the treasury as such, for their personal consumptions would exist if they were neither bankers, nor pensioners, nor lenders, nor receivers, of factory bounties. As capital is created by profit, and as the useful occupations cannot flourish without capital, each transfer of their profits, whether to the government by unnecessary taxation, or to exclusive privileges, diminishes their ability to promote consumptions, and the national prosperity; and establishes a domestick commerce by which the majority pays all, and receives nothing, and the minority receives all, and pays nothing. The rapidity with which such a domestick commerce impoverishes one party and enriches the other, is demonstrated by the present situation of the capitalists and the rest of the community. This, and not foreign commercial restrictions, is the cause of the public distress. Though prices have fallen, commerce, if undisturbed by domestick restrictions, would soon establish an equilibrium in the commercial world, leaving a profit less as efficacious in fostering individual internal improvements, as one nominally greater; if this inferiour profit is not taken away by the really unproductive families; but if these families continue to extract from the productive classes of both material and moral comforts, the same sum of money as when profits were higher, they are deprived of the only means by which they can advance the national prosperity; and as the classes producing neither material nor moral benefits, do not advance it at all, indications, of national poverty and decline, are the unavoidable consequence. This observation is sustained by the distinction between the capitalists and mechanicks, and between the capitalists and agriculturists, and is equally applicable to both the productive classes. Agriculture cannot be destroyed (the question as skilfully stated by the Committee) but it cannot flourish, by being deprived of its profits or capital. If profit is necessary (as the Committee insist) to make capitalists flourish, it must also be necessary to make farmers and mechanicks flourish.

But we are again met by the English example. Both agriculture and manufactures flourish in that country, and therefore it is inferred, that, by adopting the English policy, they may both be made to do so here. If the physical and moral circumstances of the two countries were the same, the argument would prove the practicability of the imitation proposed, and the inquiry would then turn upon its justice, and whether it was calculated to increase or diminish the happiness of mankind. But because a system is practicable in England, it does not follow that it is practicable here. That which is allowable for the ends of sustaining a monarchy or an aristocracy, may be tyrannical in a republic. Her populousness, the scarcity of land, and the difficulty of subsistence, are remorseless goads for driving industry to its utmost stretch, safely applied by landlords and capitalists to tenants and mechanicks, because they have been inured to them by the help of a standing army, and cannot flee from their inflictions. But here neither of these goads exist; and, instead of these resources for stimulating industry, we can only excite her by leaving her profits in her own hands, and suffering her spontaneously to create capitals for improvement, consumption, and reproduction. Whether this end is obtained by free-will or legal coercion, the effect in advancing national prosperity, might in some degree be the same; but the attempt here to obtain it by the impracticable legal coercive mode, has paralysed the practicable free will mode, without deriving any advantage from its substitute, consisting of a monopoly by landlords, capitalists, officers of government, and pensioners, of nearly all the profits made by tenants and mechanicks; and of a considerable portion of those derived from extraordinary mental talents. Our land-owners being the tenants of their own lands, far from having an interest to join in this conspiracy against productive labour, are its chief victims. An imitation of the English policy for transferring property from productive to unproductive classes, has taken away the profits and capital able to excite free industry, without being able to make any amends for its discouragement, because it has not the English scourges for lashing enslaved industry up to its utmost exertion.

The English coercive system being impracticable in this country, a substitute for it became necessary, which is attempted to be found by cutting commerce in two, for the end of establishing a compulsory mode of transferring property—oiling the wound with two promises; one, that the way to keep it alive is to kill one half; the other, that the reserved half will bring us more money than the whole. Suppose that these promises should bring us in ship loads of money instead of ballast. Whilst the depreciation produced by this expected influx of money, should travel faster than taxation and exclusive privileges, less property would be transferred; but the managers of the transferring policy, would very soon take care to make themselves amends for it, and when the ebb happened (for money cannot be converted into an inland sea without tides) they would find their incomes so much improved by its appreciation, that they would not love them less, nor be more willing to diminish them. We have had some experience of the effects of this money-importing project, supposing it should succeed, in a money-making project, which did succeed. A plenty of currency induced legislative bodies to increase their wages; governments to increase their expenses, extend their patronage, and bestow pensions; and capitalists to increase protecting duties; and has taught us, by woful experience, the effects of a redundancy of money. It is used by the property-transferring policy to augment its incomes, and ultimately to punish the credulity which believes that a plethora of money will advance the wealth or happiness of majorities. Our protecting-duty capitalists have had their appetites so whetted by the augmentation of their bounties arising from the appreciation of money, that they are craving still more.

The English system for transferring property, works by compulsion; ours by promises; but their effects are the same; they both transfer property from useful and productive, to immoral and unproductive occupations. Banking promised to foster commerce, and make us rich by a plenty of money—the money came, and made us poor. Protecting duties promised to bring us plenty of money by half-killing commerce, and patching a domestick monopoly to the other half—they have brought distress. What good could the promise of a second plethora do us, without an importing commerce? Both these promises have been substitutes for the English coercive mode of transferring property; and they operate upon farmers in this country, exactly as rents do in England upon tenants, except that they transfer the profits of the cultivators of land to pecuniary capitalists, instead of landlords. But the difference between the land-owners in the two countries is greatly in favour of the English. There they take care to benefit themselves by the property-transferring policy, make corn laws to increase their rents by enhancing the price of bread, and chiefly confine the factory capitalists to what they can make by their monopoly of mechanicks, and exporting their commodities. But here the factory capitalists have managed far more skilfully, by transferring to themselves the profits of agriculture in addition to those they may obtain from a monopoly of mechanicks; and the land-owners have discovered nothing of the dexterity, or self-defence, exhibited by the English land-owners. Hence the agricultural employment has become so unprofitable, that Hope, though an enthusiast, shrinks from it as forlorn, and the capitalists, as their object is profit, flee from it as desperate.

To this cause, in a great degree, must be ascribed the chief indication, according to Malthus, of the national decline which we regret. The translation of the profits of agriculture, which it ought to retain to prevent this decline, to the hands of unproductive capitalists, is effected by one of the plainest principles of political economy. Scarcity enhances, and plenty diminishes, prices. The scarcity of manufactures, produced by the protecting-duty policy, must of course enhance their prices; and the plenty of agricultural products, produced by shutting them out from foreign markets and prohibiting to them sundry foreign exchanges, must also diminish the prices of these products; and thus two screws are at work to diminish agricultural profit and capital. A legal, has the same effect as a natural, scarcity; and there is no difference to the sufferer, whether the loss inflicted on him proceeds from one or the other mode of effecting it. If a famine or a monopoly of grain, produces the same degree of scarcity, and the same enhancement of price, the purchaser would sustain the same deduction by either from his capital or the profits of his labour. What would the purchaser of grain think of a proposal to keep up an artificial famine of it for an indefinite period to enrich its monopolies, because they promised to make it cheap at some future day? That which a purchaser of manufactures ought to think of our policy for creating an artificial famine of these articles, almost as necessary as grain, because they also promise a future cheapness. Is it difficult to discern that artificial and natural famines operate in the same way, and that neither can be blessings to those who pay the enhanced prices, which both produce?

That may be true, the Committee might reply, but we propose to bring about a famine of agricultural products to increase their prices, and an abundance of manufactures to diminish theirs. These two cards are all they propose to deal out, and they suppose that those who hold them, will play very lovingly into each other's hands. The Committee do not observe that they calculate in the two cases upon contradictory principles. If the consequence of making manufactures scarce and dear, should terminate in their plenty and cheapness, an encouragement to agriculture which would increase its products, would not have the effect of increasing their prices or value. It is therefore a fallacy to suppose that agriculture can ever be compensated by future high prices, for those now extorted from it by capitalists, because if it derives encouragement from the protecting-duty project, that encouragement would have the same effect in diminishing its prices, as it is supposed it will have in the encouragement of manufactures. The modes resorted to for the encouragement of the two occupations are exactly opposed. One is to be encouraged by increasing prices, the other by diminishing them. If both should have the effect of producing plenty, cheapness ensues in both cases, and a compensation to agriculture for its temporary disbursements can never happen. In fact, however, the plenty and cheapness of land must, for many centuries, cause a plenty of agricultural products; and, as the principles of commerce will for ever annex cheapness to plenty, agriculture can derive no augmentation of its prices from the bounties it is now paying to capitalists. The project is therefore only a temporary transfer of property, which proposes, by giving high prices to manufactures and low prices to agricultural products, to produce a plenty of both, and then to leave this plenty to regulate future prices by the commercial principles of free exchanges, without even disclosing a possibility of reimbursement.

The spice-burning policy of the Dutch, if it ever existed, has been quoted to prove the wisdom of the destroying portion of the protecting-duty policy; and the manufacturing policy of England is relied upon, to prove the wisdom of its creating portion. Protecting duties will diminish the products of agriculture, and enhance their price by their scarcity; and they will increase manufactures, so as to make them cheap by plenty, to bear exportation. Now, it seems to me that by increasing the exportable surplus of agricultural products, we shall with more certainty increase their prices, than by diminishing them, provided we invite commodities from all parts of the world to exchange for them. The greater this surplus, the more it will be depended upon by foreigners, and this dependence will extend competition. If the surplus is small, its influence is trifling, and it may be abandoned by foreigners without difficulty. We have suffered by no error more severely, than by that of assigning too great an importance to our surplus of bread stuff, which has induced us to imagine that we could starve nations, and tempted us to contract markets which ought to have been extended, for the purpose of coercing them by a necessity which we supposed would be imperative, but which was hardly felt even as an inconvenience. Our soils and climates have not invested us with any article resembling spices, and as all our commodities meet with competition, plenty and cheapness, and not scarcity and dearness, must be our reliance for a profitable commerce. The Chinese tea-policy would be better for us, than the Dutch spice-burning policy. Instead of diminishing the quantity of this agricultural product, they increase it; and retain the trade by its plenty. If they should produce a scarcity by burning or by any other artifice, and enhance the price, they would induce other nations to cultivate it, and drive their customers to other markets, as we have done in the case of bread stuffs. All our agricultural productions are rivalled, and the competition can only be met by industry, plenty, cheapness, and a frugal government. Thus only can we avail ourselves of the plainest principles of political economy. Plenty begets cheapness, cheapness invites customers, customers produce competition, and competition enhances prices. Plenty is also ready for emergencies or casualties, caused by fluctuations of seasons or foreign wars, so frequently occurring in some country or other; and would undoubtedly, in union with a commerce freed from our own restrictions, constitute the best basis for political economy, of which the United States are susceptible. By diminishing agricultural products, to increase manufactures, we only surrender our best commodities for the sake of trying others, which others must be subject to the same commercial principles; and it is easier for us to rival other nations in agricultural than in mechanical commodities. The latter could only force their way by superior plenty and cheapness, and could never derive any assistance from an abundance of fresh land, foreign wars, or bad seasons, in other countries. As success in both cases depends on the same principles, economical, political, or commercial, we have only to compare the probabilities with each other, to determine our choice.

The English precedent, relied upon by the Committee to justify their project, defeats it. Manufactures constitute the occupation most able to produce exportable commodities, in their circumstances; agriculture is that most able to produce exportable commodities in ours. The English, far from endeavouring to diminish the mechanical productions, to enhance their price by a scarcity, endeavour to increase them, for the purposes of extending their commerce by plenty, and meeting competition with cheapness. This plenty and cheapness, by multiplying customers, procures for their manufactures more markets and better prices than could otherwise be obtained. Such is the English political economy as to their kind of exportable commodities. That of our restrictive policy, advocated by the Committee, is to burden agricultural products, constituting our species of exportable commodities, with bounties to factory capitalists; to diminish their quantity; to cut off their markets; and to disable them from meeting competition by plenty and cheapness; so as to extend our commerce and create new customers, as the best mode of keeping up their value. And it is very remarkable that the object of this project deduced from transitory circumstances, is to terminate in the very same political economy subservient to the laws of commerce, applicable to agricultural exportable commodities, namely, that of entering into a manufacturing competition with all the world, founded upon plenty and cheapness. The principles which must govern our competition, either in agricultural or manufactured exportable commodities, with commercial nations, being the same, the question is reduced to the plain computation, as to which class our means for success are most extensive. Had the English destroyed their manufacturing competition with the rest of the world, in order to create an agricultural competition, the precedent would have been exactly in favour of the political and commercial economy, advocated by the Committee; as they pursued a different policy, it is exactly against them.

But whether the prices of agricultural products are high or low, it equally furnishes arguments for exclusive privileges and unproductive classes. If they are high, farmers are able to pay high taxes and bounties to self-enriching projects; if they are low, it is for want of more of these projects to raise them. But political economists have never been able to discover any mode for securing high prices, or even a measure by which they can be regulated. Both money and corn are imperfect measures. It has been impossible to count the circumstances, or unravel the complexity, affecting the commercial intercourse among mankind. Climates, soils, population, wars, industry, fashions, discoveries, stratagems, and the whole mass of human passions, enter into the computation. Yet the Committee propose to govern this ungovernable complexity by local laws, and promise to farmers a compensation dependent upon a hopeless success. They have discovered that the existing low prices of agricultural products proceeds from the want of a sufficient number of endowed factory capitalists. But a fall in these prices is common to all commercial nations. England has experienced it. Was her decline of agricultural prices also occasioned by a want of such factories? If not, they are no remedy against it. Land has also fallen in price. Has this also been occasioned by the want of factories drawing bounties from land? Had prices been left to the umpirage of commerce and self interest (arbitrators so powerful as to prevent the fraudulent attempts to regulate prices by local laws, from being quite ruinous to nations and individuals, though they have uniformly suffered severely from them) we should have avoided the evils which these attempts never fail to produce. To conciliate the farmers towards their attempt to regulate prices, the Committee tell them that it will violate justice in their favour, by having the effect both of raising the prices of their products, and diminishing those of manufactures; but ought not a good government to protect the factory owners against their fatuitous ardour to obtain this double misfortune? The Committee have celebrated the acuteness of the Americans in discerning their interest, but instead of leaving this acuteness to take care of itself, they propose to render it inoperative, for the sake of showing their own acuteness in surmounting the impossibility of regulating prices. They will not suffer our "eagle-eyed" acuteness to discern which employment is the best, agriculture or manufacturing, whilst they leave it a competence to discover what species of manufacturing will be most profitable, trusting that the capitalists will pounce upon the richest prey, and not forget their interest in their eagerness. But the agricultural eagles are supposed to be too dim-sighted to see their interest. Local laws have never been able to regulate domestick prices, even by the aid of local currencies; how then can they regulate both domestick and foreign prices, by the universal medium of exchanges?

To subvert the unalterable laws of commerce, upon which political economy is founded, the Committee have selected several particular articles, the prices of which they say are reduced by the protecting-duty policy; such as manufactured cottons. The prices of these they assert are below what they could be imported at. If so, it is obvious that the reduction is owing, not to this policy, but to the primary and invariable cause of cheapness, namely, our plenty of the raw material. Cheapness being the natural consequence of plenty, could not have been caused by laws, which neither increased nor diminished the plenty of the material which caused the cheapness. Thus, our plenty of wood enables us to build ships cheaper than some nations can, and our plenty of wheat and tobacco, enables us to sell those articles in a manufactured form, cheaper also than they can be imported. The cheapness in all these cases results from the local plenty of the raw materials, and can by no means be ascribed to cunning laws. To impair the value of the surpluses remaining after supplying our own factories, by restricting the freedom of exchanges, and by prohibiting the acquisition on the best attainable terms of things which we want, in exchange for those surpluses which we do not want, causes a useless loss to the agriculturist, and a general loss to the nation. This exhibition of particular articles therefore, to prove the goodness of the whole cargo of the protecting policy, is that of a shop-keeper who puffs off two or three articles in his store; but credulity only believes that these two or three articles suffice to establish the goodness and cheapness of his whole stock. With people of understanding the artifice rather excites a suspicion that the rest are bad and dear. Of the same complexion is the artifice of selecting and retailing in debate a few articles, as a proof that an immense system, compounded of innumerable items, pecuniary and political, is good throughout. No project was ever so poor and dark, as to afford no glittering specks—no glimmering delusions. As the isinglass sometimes found in gypsum does not constitute its character, so a few glossy particles sprinkled in a widely-operating system, are no proofs that it will advance the national prosperity; but when these particles are stolen from the principle of plenty and cheapness, as in the cases of cotton, wheat, and tobacco, it is on the contrary a proof that the system does not even contain any glittering specks at all, but is opaque throughout.

Several of these retail cases are urged as if each was a new argument, though they all admit of the same answer. They seem however to be comprised in the assertions, "that it now takes as much wheat to buy one yard of linen, as would formerly buy four, and that foreign manufacturers and domestick importers will take nothing but our money for their goods." The Committee might have added, that in the spring of 1821, it took as much wheat to buy a yard of domestick cotton shirting, as would at one time have bought three or even four also. Such fortuitous occurrences are frequently arrayed against unchangeable principles, and if they could be thus destroyed, mankind would soon have none left to steer by. If these assertions are true, what further coercion can be necessary to drive people from the plough into the loom? Is not the price of shirting sufficiently high without enhancing it to enrich capitalists? If money only will be received for foreign goods, must not the trade end soon enough of itself, without hastening its death by restrictions, and infallibly effect one object of the protecting-duty policy—that of compelling us to manufacture. We have not exportable money enough to pay for one year's importation, and when our money is out importations must cease, if our agricultural products will not be received in payment; and when importations cease, manufactures will be in sufficient demand. But the fact is, that as commerce cannot exist without exchanges, so no nations which trade with us, will conceive the contrary; and though they will get our commodities as cheap as they can, yet this very cheapness will bring to us frequent opportunities of retaliation.

To get over so plain an argument, and to provide against inferences from their own assertion, the Committee suggest that we are indebted to some other markets, to enable us to buy English manufactures with money; and then they endeavour to prove that a circuitous commerce, by which we make one nation pay for what we buy from another, is of no importance, by presenting us with an Utopian picture as the model of their commercial and political economy. A nation, they say, "differs only from a village in extent," and that "the model of a society composed of an hundred men, following an hundred different occupations, dealing with each other," is a good commercial example for a great nation. This village policy overlooks all differences of climates and soils, and seems only designed for one of those fortunate islands when found, which contains every thing which man can want; but being apparently antedeluvian, or at least aboriginal, the Committee have thought proper to defend it by an encomium on household manufactures; observing also, that the greatest means of exchange, is said to be the most prosperous situation. This confusion of ideas is not to be reconciled. Why should factory owners receive bounties from farmers, if household manufactures are the best security for the prosperity of farmers? Why should the means of exchange be diminished, if the greatest means of exchange constitute the most prosperous situation? How can a mighty nation be compressed, morally speaking, into an insignificant village, if an insignificant village cannot be dilated into a great nation? But the merchant's ledger is the Pythian oracle ready to supply the Committee with the responses they suggest, in order to demonstrate that the policy of promoting exchanges, so good between one hundred villagers, will be bad between one hundred nations, or at least much worse than household manufactures. That manufactures promote exchanges; that the greatest means of exchanges constitutes the most prosperous situation; that household manufactures to diminish exchanges are still better, and that the means of exchange should be narrowed and compressed in a great nation until it resembles a village of an hundred men, are positions making, when combined, a very good oracle. It is true, that farmers, aided by commerce and exchanges, have frequently thrived by the additional assistance of household manufactures, but in no instance that I know of have they been able to thrive by household manufactures, without the aid of these two auxiliaries. These are the means by which industrious farmers certainly gain a considerable balance of trade from other countries for their own, by supplying many of their wants within themselves; and by prohibiting foreign commerce and free exchanges, these household manufactures have no longer the important effect of causing a multitude of surpluses beyond expense, silently to unite in procuring the envied balance of trade, and promoting to a great extent, the national prosperity. The experience of five or six revolutions between the liberty of free exchanges, and the coercions, accidental or legal, creating a necessity for household manufactures, have convinced me of their inefficacy for producing wealth, when uncombined with foreign commerce. We are not obliged to elect between foreign manufactures and household manufactures. Let all be free to individual preference; let our eagle-eyed people choose and abstain for themselves. They generally strive to make some surplus annually, and know how to effect it better than the government can inform them. Their surpluses constitute the only solid national profit, and therefore whatever defeats their efforts causes a national misfortune. With this freedom of commerce the ledgers of the farmers will be hard enough for the ledgers of the merchants. So far as my experience has extended in Virginia, I believe that a balance is always due by the mercantile to the agricultural class; and that the latter class suffer more from the bankruptcies of the former, than the former class does from those of the latter.

But however this may be, even our household manufactures, eulogized to curry favour with the agriculturists, will be cut up by the policy of excises; proposed as a substitute for the loss of duties. They must operate entirely in favour of the factory monopoly, and deprive the agriculturalists and many other people, of the comforting household manufacturing resource, against fortuitous misfortunes, and premeditated legal contrivances to foster an oppressive aristocracy. Excises are quite convenient to factory, and excessively teazing to household, manufactures. An excise is reimbursed to the factory owners by the consumers, whereas it falls upon household manufactures as a direct tax, without any reimbursement. In England, an excise is a *bonum* to capitalists, and a *malum* to farmers. In the United States, it will be particularly oppressive upon the whole inland district; the few villages excepted where factories are established; and equivalent to a tax upon the land itself, imposed by the acre, and not according to its value. Under the excise system of raising a revenue, a man who cultivates poor land, pays as much for the same article taxed, as he who cultivates rich: it is therefore a tax by the acre, if the article taxed is produced by land. If an excise is laid upon corn, wheat, rye, hops, and many other articles, it must be by a measure common to every quarter of the Union, because the constitution requires uniformity; and this uniformity would compel the raiser of corn, and most other agricultural articles, to pay twice as much tax, in those districts where a barrel of corn is worth only one dollar, as in those where it is worth two. Such would be also the case in an excise upon many other domestick manufactures or products. The tax upon them when they are consumed in the family, is completely a direct one, except that it cannot be regulated by the rules applicable to a land tax, and must therefore be excessively unequal, locally and individually. If factories are dispersed throughout the inland district, it will not alter these effects, because excises must either extend to a great number of household manufactures, or these factories could not furnish objects for an excise to act upon. If farmers consume the factory manufactures, they must pay the excises laid upon them, which would be equivalent to the payment of the same taxes upon household manufactures. If they do not consume them, but fly from these excises to household manufactures, the excises must follow them, or more unavoidable modes of taxation must be resorted to. Either way the inland districts will be the chief sufferers. Direct taxes upon land are paid by the census of a State, and not by the profitableness of geographical situation; whereas the mode of raising revenue by duties, is apportioned by the relative ability to pay between maritime and inland districts. Nor is there any injustice in this, because, if household and factory manufactures were both free, the maritime districts can avail themselves of either, or do better. Taxes on foreign commodities, such especially as are most costly, when their consumption is not prohibited, fall on opulent cities or wealthy individuals; but excises on home manufactures, fall chiefly on the labouring classes. Duties for revenue only, are subject to a wholesome limitation, because, if they are pushed too far, their end is defeated. But excises on domestick necessaries, seconded by commercial restrictions, may be made exorbitant; whilst duties to a great extent are the voluntary contributions of wealth and luxury, if they are not excluded from gratifications by unjust and impolitic restrictions. But these arguments, it must be confessed, admit of an answer; the protecting-duty policy will make the whole of the United States an inland country, and then excises and other direct taxes will fall with equal severity upon every portion of it, as geographical advantages will no longer exist.

Household manufactures are complimented by the Committee, to insinuate that their encouragement was one design of the protecting-duty policy; but the very reverse is intended and must happen, or their eulogy upon factory manufactures and excises cannot be realized. Manufactures made for sale only, receive the bounties bestowed by protecting duties, and those made and consumed in the family do not receive a cent of it. Could the amounts of household and factory manufactures be ascertained, it would probably appear, that the former exceed the latter an hundred fold; at least the difference would be very considerable. And yet it is proposed to inflict an excise upon household manufactures, to foster the factory manufacturers, though of so much less value. Does not this demonstrate, that the prosperity of capitalists, and not of manufactures, is the object in contemplation? The more valuable household manufactures are, as an appendage to agriculture, the deeper will agriculture be wounded by transferring taxation from duties to excises.

The Committee have repeatedly urged the effects of the late war, and the war duties, as proofs that it will be wise to nurture factories by prohibitions upon commerce, because, during that period they flourished exceedingly, by deriving excessive prices from a casual prohibition, producing a temporary famine or scarcity of manufactures; by which a few capitalists who made them for sale, and not those who made them for family consumption, were enriched. This accidental discovery has suggested the idea of a permanent famine or scarcity, as a substitute for the war which has ceased; and equally beneficial to capitalists. The new war ought to be estimated by others as well as by the capitalists, according to their experience. Those who gained wealth by the old war, undoubtedly loved it, but those who only got poverty from it, must as certainly be glad that it is over. It is easy for those who felt the calamities of the old war, to determine whether their revival by a new war against their property, ought to be coveted. War is the casualty which most extensively transfers property, and by that effect most sorely oppresses nations. It invariably generates a class of men, who wish for its continuance, however injurious it is to the people generally. The very plain language put into the mouths of the capitalists by the Committee, was never surpassed, nor perhaps equalled in point of candour. "We were wonderfully enriched by a temporary manufacturing war monopoly, therefore secure to us the same income by a permanent legal monopoly." Commissaries and contractors might petition Congress for bounties on the same ground. The claim of the gallant officers, soldiers, and seamen who fought our battles, is tenfold stronger. They lost more blood, and got less money than the capitalists. Which of these two classes, if we were obliged to keep one, ought to have been disbanded? The Committee state so very fairly, the nature of the war which has been substituted for that we were glad to get rid of, that it cannot even be called a war in disguise. This new war is to be carried on by foreign and native capitalists. The foreign combatants for capital or wealth, receive great bounties or high pay from their governments; therefore, say the Committee, we ought to give great bounties, or high pay to our domestick combatants, for capital or wealth, "or they will not have fair play." As the victory consists in getting most money from the people, whether the play is fair or foul, it will undoubtedly be a very pleasant war to the two armies of capitalists. Instead of losing blood, they are to get money. These foreign and domestick armies are perpetually exclaiming to their governments, "more pay, more pay!" As pay only can win the victory, we must lose it, say our capitalists, unless our government augments our pay as fast, or faster, than the British do that of their army of capitalists. Can there be a finer war for the two armies? The effort is, which government can give its army most wages, or open most purses to their chaste and patriotic fingers. And this kind of war is called by the Committee, "protection to agriculture, which the people have a right to ask of the government." Let us exhibit the nature of this protection in figures. The English give a bounty or wages to their capitalist army of more than one hundred millions of dollars annually, therefore this species of protection requires our government to give as much to our capitalist army. If they increase their bounty, we must increase ours. The number of people in England and the United States is nearly equal, therefore their bounties to the respective capitalist armies, must be nearly equal also. But who pays these merry pipers—the people or their governments? Let us shrink from the idea, that our government can protect or enrich us, by transferring our property to capitalists, with a siren song. When nations depend on themselves for protection and wealth, it is a proof that they are free; and when governments claim a power to give them either, it is a proof that they are not free. They become the slaves of an army of soldiers, or an army of capitalists, commanded by the government. But what is the protection afforded by the protecting-duty policy? Simply to transfer some millions from the people to capitalists, for which, if not transferred, they would have received an equivalent from foreign nations. The reason alleged for this protection of our property by transferring it to capitalists, is, that the bounties paid by foreign governments to their capitalists, enable them to sell manufactures cheap to us; if so, we get the bounty. In this view, it would be beneficial to us that England should increase her bounties, until their capitalists could sell us manufactures at half their value, or even give them to us. But the Committee, with great magnanimity (and this seems to me the best argument in favour of their policy) propose fairly to reciprocate the kindness by giving bounties to our capitalists, that they may also sell cheap manufactures to foreign nations. No, says this policy, the domestick bounties are given to enable our domestick capitalists to sell cheap to ourselves, and also to prevent foreign cheapness from acquiring a monopoly among us.

This argument deserves some attention, in order to detect some share of plausibility. We must recollect the existing circumstances of the manufacturing world to estimate its force, because, though it might have been sound under some circumstances, it may be weak under others. It might have been wise to purchase arts, sciences, philosophers, and artisans, by temporary rewards, when a nation was without them; and unwise to convert them into permanent exclusive privileges or a pecuniary aristocracy, after they were acquired. By suppressing this distinction, a superficial force is bestowed on the argument which it does not deserve. A knowledge of commerce, arts, and sciences, is now so generally diffused among a certain number of nations, that ignorance does not subject any one of them to the necessity of obtaining information at the expense of great sacrifices, either political or pecuniary; nor is any member of this informed catalogue of nations so exclusively wise or skilful, as to be able to establish a monopoly upon another. The United States undoubtedly belong to the commercial, manufacturing, and enlightened catalogue of nations; and therefore they are neither under the necessity of purchasing any branch of knowledge, nor exposed to the danger of being monopolized on account of their ignorance. With respect to the mechanical arts, they are admitted by the protecting-duty project to be so well informed, as to be even able to expel foreign competition; and the art of agriculture is supposed to be so far advanced, as to enable us to exercise a coercion on our part over foreign nations, by withholding from them its products.

Under these circumstances, it is said, that sound policy dictates to us the establishment of a manufacturing monopoly at home, lest we should be exposed to a manufacturing monopoly from abroad, to be obtained in future by bounties giving us cheap manufactures at present. Much has been said by the Committee to strip the subject of the two ugly words "bounty and monopoly," respecting our native capitalists or factories, whilst they apply them to foreign capitalists or factories. They contend that foreign monopolies are created by bounties, enabling factory owners to undersell competitors at present, and to obtain an exclusive market in future. They also contend that domestick bounties ought to be given to domestick capitalists or factories by protecting-duties, that they may also undersell competitors at present. But they deny that the domestick pensioned factories will obtain an exclusive market or monopoly, by the very same means which they suppose will bestow it on foreign pensioned factories. Yet it is evident that they will be more able to do so, assisted by law, and unexposed to any competition except among themselves, than any foreign nation without legal assistance, and kept in check by all other foreign nations. However this may be, it is evident that success in either the foreign or domestick project must produce the same consequences to consumers. If one case constitutes both a bounty and a monopoly, the other must also constitute them. The cases being the same, the terms applicable to one are applicable to the other; and a disavowal of this mutual application, is merely an endeavour to alter the nature of things, by altering the words used for defining them. The true question is, whether the fear of an English monopoly should drive us into a domestick monopoly. The Indians, towards the north-west, have, it is said, an ingenious mode of taking deer: by frightful but harmless appearances they drive them into real toils and certain destruction. Our mechanical skill, and the competition between foreign nations, will secure us against the ugly English monopoly, and also save us from the destructive toils of a domestick monopoly and permanent excises, if laws did not force us into them.

Let us compare the evils resulting from foreign and domestick restrictions, bounties, and monopolies, to discern which are the worst; for both are undoubtedly bad. By foreign bounties, consumers are enabled, for a period, often a long one, to buy cheaper; by domestick they are compelled to buy dearer. Foreign monopoly, the design of foreign bounties, is certainly diminished or defeated by the competition of independent nations; by our power of transferring our commerce from a nation attempting it, to those nations which do not; and by the progress of our internal mechanical skill. Domestick monopoly, the design also of domestick bounties, cannot be defeated by the competition of all manufacturing foreign nations, because this competition is expelled by protecting-duties; nor by a power of transferring our dealings from the monopoly to free exchanges, wherever to be found, because this power is taken from us by law; nor by our internal mechanical skill, because that skill is to be monopolized by the capitalists, who will very easily effect it, by the help of a general excise. Our mechanical skill, if not monopolized, would itself be a full match for foreign competitions, when aided by freights, revenue duties, and the cheapness of materials; and to force it into undertakings where these advantages will not suffice, can only produce a loss or a fraud. Foreign bounties and monopolies cannot create a moneyed aristocracy here, able and willing to corrupt the principles of our government—domestick can. Foreign regulations of commerce cannot be uniform among all nations, and however restrictive, their dissimilarity will always afford us a better market, than can possibly be afforded by a single capitalist combination at home. But the Committee contend that all these foreign nations will receive money only, and that the domestick monopoly will receive our agricultural products. This is the great argument by which the protecting-duty policy is defended, and if it is unfounded in fact, the error of that policy becomes apparent.

Where are our capitalists to get money to purchase the flour, grain, cotton, tobacco, fish, and all our exportable articles, exclusive of those they manufacture? The idea of their being a competent, or even a tolerable market for all these articles, is either a very high computation of their present wealth, or an appalling intimation of that which they expect to get by their monopoly. If they have not the money with which to buy all these exportable articles, it is obvious that their monopoly will not yield us money; if they have, it is as obvious that they have no occasion for the monopoly. It is possible for us to get money of those that have it, for our commodities, but not from those who have it not. The fact is, that these capitalists will themselves be extractors of money from the people, and mere compilers of unproductive capital, because they will require but a very inconsiderable portion of agricultural products, for manufacturing or consumption, and beyond that portion must be paid in money only for their wares. Thus, the trade to be introduced for the sake of enriching the capitalists, is coerced by the protecting-duty policy, into the following course: The surplus of all our commodities, beyond the inconsiderable portion of them which the factories can consume, is to be exported to bring back money only, and this money is to be paid to the capitalists for the surplus of their wares, exceeding the value of their inconsiderable consumptions. Its effects are, first, to diminish excessively the value of agricultural products, by depriving them of the enhancement produced by a freedom of exchanging them for foreign commodities; by doubling the price of factory commodities, or increasing it far beyond what the foreign would cost under a freedom of exchange; and by doubling the expense of freight upon our exported commodities, for want of the return cargoes which would have divided it. Secondly, to increase enormously capitals in a few hands, by a constant current of the money thus to be procured, into the pockets of capitalists, and cause pecuniary accumulations which will not be employed in reproduction, because they will not be invested in agricultural improvements, since profit from them will, by the system, be made more and more hopeless. Thirdly, to continue the destruction of the impost mode of obtaining revenue, so as to enforce a resort to more oppressive modes of taxation, and to loans, which will be successfully advocated by the great moneyed influence thus to be created, for the two purposes of increasing the profit of its monopoly, and finding employment for the capital it brings, by lending it to the government. Fourthly, of increasing the expenses of government by new and internal taxes, and by the facility with which loans will be obtained from the capitalists. And lastly, by throwing this whole accumulation of expenses on all other occupations which have least money, and absolving the capitalist occupation which has most money, from bearing any share of them.

Such is the course of the proposed trade, supposing that foreign nations both can and will give us their money for our commodities, though they are said to be giving bounties to their capitalists, in order to come at our money, by enabling them to sell cheaply to us. If the money they thus get of us, does not exceed in amount the bounties they pay to get it, the speculation is so absurd as not even to deserve the lowest of all compliments; that of being fallacious. The same compliment is due to our speculation for getting their money, if we fail to get enough to reimburse us for the money we pay to our capitalists to come at it. But as it is impossible that the greediness of all commercial nations should be levelled at our little stock of specie, and not at our great stock of commodities, our commercial policy would stand upon safer ground, if it was modeled upon a supposition of the latter greediness, than modeled as it is upon a supposition of the former. In that case, there would be no occasion for a domestick sect of capitalists, to save our specie, and subject our commodities to depreciation. Let us, say the Committee, turn the tables upon these foreign speculators, and aim only at their specie, as they aim at ours. If their speculation will diminish the value of their exportable commodities, by depriving them of their exchangeable value in our markets, the same speculation will, in the same way, diminish the value of our exportable commodities. In this project for overturning the only principle by which commerce can subsist or be useful, the Committee propose, first, to be as cunning as foreign nations, by refusing to admit their commodities, lest they should take away our money; and then to outwit them, by sending our commodities to take away theirs; never recollecting, that as we have discovered this profound stratagem of theirs, they may possibly discover it when turned upon themselves. Should they do so, and imitate the Committee, as the Committee propose to imitate them, our commercial surgery will be like that of a British soldier captured by the Indians, who induced them to cut off his head, as the means of procuring his liberty. The project is internally inconsistent, by supposing that commercial nations will combine to get our money, and reject our products which they want, and can use; but that our domestick factory owners will not combine to get our money, but will buy our products which they neither want nor can use, except to an inconsiderable extent; so that the mass of these products must remain on the same ground, as if the domestick monopoly had never existed. We cannot turn the tables on these factories, by forcing them to give us money; on the contrary, their owners are empowered by law to force us to give them money. Our exportable commodities, which serve without pay, will be better soldiers abroad, in carrying on a commercial war with dissimilar foreign restrictions, if they retain a freedom of exchange, than an army of capitalists at home, created and paid for carrying on the same war. The surplus of these is the whole fund for acquiring of foreign nations what we want, but the surplus of capitalists which we have created, acquires nothing. Commerce subsists by exchanges of indigenous for foreign surpluses, and though our surpluses of commodities may sell low, our surplus of capitalists will sell for nothing. By whatever regulation the exchange of our surplus for a foreign surplus is obstructed, national wealth is diminished, because it consists of things which we want, and not of things which we do not want.

The fallacy of the notion, that foreign nations will regulate their commerce for the purpose only of getting the specie in the United States, is demonstrated by the maxim advanced by the Committee. "That foreign nations will buy what they want, and will not buy what they do not want." Is not this concession sufficient to show, that our commodities stand on the only firm commercial ground; that foreign wants are the true pledges for our commerce, and that to surrender those pledges for an exclusive privilege at home, is a wild and unnecessary speculation. Do we mean by it to force them to buy what they do not want? That they will buy what they do want, is acknowledged. Money, intrinsically, is not a want, considered as currency; but the representative of wants. If a foreign nation does not want any of our commodities, and we cannot supply it with money to satisfy their wants by resorting to other countries, no commerce can exist between that nation and ourselves. If it does want any portion of the surplus useless to us, we must elect between the policy of encouraging its wants by exchanges which will supply our own, or discouraging a direct commerce by demanding money, which is of no use except to send to other countries to procure, indirectly, things to satisfy our wants. If we will not exchange the surplus of our industry for the surplus of their industry, we render it as impossible for foreign nations to take our surplus, as it would be for us to take theirs, without such an exchange. Money alone cannot sustain a commerce between two nations, even if both had gold and silver mines. To give money for money would be no commerce at all. Mechanical and agricultural commodities constitute the basis of exchanges, and these exchanges constitute the essence of commerce. As they are the means by which alone commerce can exercise its comfort-distributing office, to deprive it of these means, is evidently to stab commerce precisely in its vital part. Both are produced by people, both are manufactures, and exchanges of one for a surplus of the other, will equally reflect an additional value on both, as on any other exchanges of useless surpluses. Indeed, between them they comprise all things which can be exchanged, and therefore, a policy which asserts that it is wise to destroy exchanges of agricultural products for manufactures, asserts also that it is wise to have no exchanges at all. If it is the interest of any foreign nation to take an agricultural surplus of us, because they want it, we must also pursue our interest in taking of any foreign nation its manufactured surplus, should we want it. Neither surplus would be of any value except for such exchanges. The enquiry, which species of surplus may be most valuable to a nation, is worse than hypothetical, where one does not exist. It tempts a nation to lose an existing, in pursuit of an imaginary, surplus. Further, if we consider the skilfulness of all occupations in computing profit and loss, we may safely conclude that it has been applied to these two, so as to have produced an equilibrium of value between them. Suppose, however, we should obtain a mechanical in lieu of our agricultural surplus; would it promote or wound the interest of the mechanicks, still to adhere to the policy of discouraging exchanges? If this policy would discourage the production of a mechanical surplus, and render it less valuable, it must have the same effect upon the existing agricultural surplus. Even this hypothetical enquiry, would not result in the conclusion, that a mechanical surplus would have more effect in advancing the prosperity of a nation, than an agricultural surplus. Adam Smith observes, "that the interest of the land-holder is closely connected with that of the state, and that the prosperity or adversity of the one, involves the prosperity or adversity of the other." Malthus agrees with him, adding "that as the increase of the land-holder's capital increases population, improvements in agriculture, and the demand for raw materials by commerce, it seems scarcely possible to consider his interests as separated from those of the state and the people." It is therefore impossible that a mechanical surplus, should contribute more to the prosperity of a nation, than an agricultural surplus, even where they are equally attainable; but where they are not equally attainable, no policy can be worse than to break the right, and drive the wrong nail. If the English should by compulsory laws diminish their mechanical surplus, they would imitate our policy in diminishing our agricultural surplus; nor would their mechanical surplus be of any value, should they refuse to exchange it for such foreign surpluses as they want.

A single consideration will suffice to assuage our apprehension of a conspiracy among foreign nations, not to take our agricultural surplus in exchanges. Foreign commercial regulations are all made by governments for the purpose of getting money, and this end is a full security that none will be made, which by destroying commerce, would defeat it. They will never destroy their best instrument for fleecing industry, by an entire prohibition of exchanges; for though they will use it as far as possible for effecting transfers of property, yet they will never forget that actual commodities only, and not prohibitions, will bear shearing. Even those governments which manage commerce for the end of transferring property, will not kill it to effect that object, like our protecting-duty policy. If left free, it brings most comforts, but creates fewer exuberant capitals. Under the guardianship of domestick exclusive privileges, it transfers more property from the people, than it could do to foreign nations, if it was made free at home, to take every advantage of their conflicting and countervailing stratagems. Why should we buy the cunning of exclusive privileges to defend us against the cunning of foreign restrictions, when the domestick cunning will cost us more than the foreign cunning; like a man who spends his estate in learning of lawyers how to keep it? To make productive labour pay as much as possible to unproductive, is the European policy; that one should pay to the other only so much as is necessary to sustain a free government must be ours, or we must exchange those political principles which we have hitherto called free, for those which we have hitherto called tyrannical. If the two combatants were left to grapple upon these terms, victory would not be doubtful; but productive labour having surrendered the armour of free exchanges, and her unproductive adversary having acquired that of exclusive privileges, she is easily chained to the property-transferring policy, like Hercules to the distaff of Omphale. His submission to the degradation cost him his life.

Exchanges of necessaries, conveniences, and especially luxuries, and not mere acquisitions of money, constitute the great impulse, which has caused human nature to make those exertions by which civilization has been extended, knowledge produced, refinements discovered, wealth obtained, and a love of liberty inspired. Leave this impulse undiminished; this moral steam-engine to operate; and its force will be sufficient to drive our commerce, our wealth, and prosperity along, in spite of all the little foreign currents setting in many different directions, which may endeavour to impede them. But take away from us this moral discovery, destined to be our glory or our shame, and we sink back into the mob of tyrannies, and lose at once these features of distinction, to which we have been hitherto indebted for our progress in arts and sciences, and for the share of reputation we enjoy amongst men.

The Committee conclude with a mental reservation, "out of deference to the opinions of those who differ from them," by observing that their bill is only "a foundation to be built on hereafter." If it would have been disrespectful to shock their opponents by a full display of their project, yet the concealment is not calculated to suppress apprehension or obtain confidence. How can the nation judge of an entire system, by inspecting an acknowledged fragment, better than they could of the size of a pyramid, by seeing one of its stones? How can taciturnity be examined? If the partial disclosure is awful and alarming, what must be the reservation? It would certainly have been divulged, had the Committee thought that it was calculated to win the favour of the public. Ought a nation to risk its own fate, by deciding without having the whole truth before it, and under the acknowledgement of a suppression, likely to be offensive? Our progress in imitating European governments, is sufficient to exhibit this something behind to our imaginations, as a dismal gulf, in which we can see no bottom; especially as the Committee allege that they are only driving on a wedge already entered. Is it not time that the United States should be informed how far the wedge is intended to be driven? Does not common prudence dictate the precaution of knowing how far it is intended to plunge us into the European policy, or ought we to plunge into it blindfold?

I have not left the report where the Committee have left their project, in the middle; but persevered to its end, endeavouring to select and examine its essential principles; and to anticipate some consequences, which the Committee have prudently concealed.

One paragraph, in reference to the cloud of pamphlets and essays, which have from the motives of love, pity, and friendship, been launched at the mechanics and agriculturists. They so nearly resemble the eloquence in the Vicar of Wakefield, of Lady Blarney and Miss Carolina Wilhelmina Skeggs, from London city, that the intelligent and uncorrupted readers of these classes must very often have borrowed the exclamation of honest Burchell upon that occasion. Are these classes such children as to be seduced by promises and flatteries, like poor Olivia? A sample of this city reasoning, will suffice to show at what rate our rural understandings are estimated. Capital invested in factories, is liable to more risks, than that invested in agriculture, and therefore agricultural capital ought to pay bounties to factory capital. Old nations require a different regimen from young nations, and therefore, as we grow older, we ought to revive old abuses. The lands of Europe are exhausted by age, and therefore the inhabitants of our new and fresh country are able to bear heavier burdens than the Europeans. Agriculture is rich, because she is skimming the cream of a rich country, and she is poor for want of factories. As she is rich, she ought to pay bounties to the owners of factories; and as she is poor, the factories are necessary to make her rich. I will only confront these assertions by a few facts. Capital invested in agriculture, is exposed to equal risks, from fire and fluctuations in price, as that invested in factories. It is moreover exposed to numberless exclusive risks from bad seasons. Invested in either, it is equally exposed to want of industry or extravagance. It is better that each occupation should be its own insurer, than that either should be bribed by the other to become idle or wasteful. All occupations, calculate their risks, in fixing their prices, and this calculation is the only fair, honest, useful, and impartial underwriter of the risk attending each. All nations, at all times are composed of people of correspondent ages, equally young and equally old; and as one generation passes away, another succeeds, having the same wants, and the same capabilities. There are some principles always good, and others always bad. Time improves arts and sciences; it cannot therefore be made a good reason for reviving frauds and abuses. Time improves agriculture; therefore what are called old countries are more able to bear burdens, than those called new. The whole earth is of the same age. The soil of the United States being poorer and worse cultivated than that of many other countries, and of England in particular, the people are less able to bear taxes, and farmers have the more need for their small profit to improve it. Is it not therefore better for them to consider themselves as the Switzerland of the world, and to flourish by the principles objected to, because adopted in their supposed minority, than to ape the expensive policy of old England? If principles and the earth are deteriorated; if an existing generation must be pilfered and enslaved, because other generations have preceded it on the same surface; if improvements are to be abandoned because they are new, and errors revived because they are old; and if the people of a newly settled country ought to be grievously taxed, and subjected to exclusive privileges, because they are skimming its surface, because they are rich, and because they are poor; there remains no situation fit for liberty, and no age fit for political morality. When God gave a land to the Israelites flowing with milk and honey, he did not defeat his beneficence, by a revelation, that this milk and honey ought to be transferred from the nation to a few individuals, by heavy taxes and exclusive privileges.

☙

A General Discussion of Tyranny and the Choice that Americans Face

The preceding answer to the report of the Committee is offered as one proof that tyranny is at hand. If its arguments are sound, the conclusion would certainly follow, except for the uncertainty as to the meaning of the word "tyranny." Had we possessed a precise definition of this single word, or known exactly how the people of the United States understand it, we should have a test for the arguments already advanced, and for those which are to follow. But as we are without these guides for our enquiries, each of us must form his own idea of tyranny, and apply it to the reasoning advanced or to be advanced. It is therefore necessary for me to express my ideas as to what constitutes tyranny, because their correctness or incorrectness, will either sustain or defeat the arguments by which they are enforced.

Theoretical and actual tyranny generally subsist together, but they are not inseparable. Actual liberty may subsist with theoretical tyranny, and actual tyranny with theoretical liberty. These States when British Provinces, were a proof of the first position, and revolutionary France of the second. Liberty and tyranny are neither of them inevitable consequences of any form of government, as both depend, to a great extent, upon its operations, whatever may be its form. All that man can accomplish, is to adopt a form, most likely to produce liberty, and containing the best precautions against the introduction of tyranny. An absolute monarch may occasionally dispense liberty and prosperity to a nation, and a representative government may occasionally dispense fraud and oppression. Such events under both forms of government, may be rare, but history proves that they are possible. If liberty consists in cutting off heads, the United States are as free as any other countries, but not more free than some; if in not transferring property by unnecessary taxation and exclusive privileges, they are less free than when they were provinces, and have nothing to boast of when compared with some other countries. As provinces, both their heads and their property were safe for nearly two centuries; in revolutionary France, with a popular representation, neither heads nor property were safe for two years.

A passion for carnage, is the tyranny of savages. Ambition and avarice are the passions which produce civilized tyranny. A policy for encouraging the latter passions, is like one for training savage nations to become bloodhounds. If ambition is cultivated by feeding it with excessive power, it extorts from industry the fruits of its labour; if avarice is cultivated by feeding it with excessive wealth, it acquires political power to pillage industry also. Enormous political power invariably accumulates enormous wealth, and enormous wealth invariably accumulates enormous political power. Either constitutes a tyranny, because the acquisitions of both are losses of liberty and property to nations.

Tithes to established churches have had these effects, although they are far less powerful engines for transferring property and power to a separate combined interest, than exclusive privileges, because they are limited in amount. They are also less pernicious in suggesting new abuses, because the establishment of one church, does not beget an endless establishment of churches, each endowed with tithes; and less injurious to national manners, because opinion, as in the case of female chastity, imposes a demeanour on the ministers of religion favourable to virtue. All other modes of transferring and accumulating wealth by law, are perpetually growing, and inculcate frauds. If they do not usually cut off heads, they invariably combine in themselves two of the three worst characters of tyranny. They transfer property and nurture vice.

By our political theory, the people are supposed to be the patrons of the government, and not the government the patron of the people. A theoretical reversal of this principle, is a theoretical advance towards tyranny; and a practical reversal of it, either by an assumption of power by a government, to prescribe constitutional regulations to the people, or to use their property in donations to individuals or combinations, is in my view, both theoretical and actual tyranny.

Having thus endeavoured to establish an idea of tyranny, theoretical or actual, let us proceed to enquire whether we are verging towards it in one or both forms. In its latter aspect the inquiry is most important, but this importance reflects great weight upon the enquiry as to its theoretical aspect, because tyranny in form is the first step towards tyranny in substance; and because great reliance is reposed on the argument "that our good theoretical system of government is a sufficient security against actual tyranny." Admitting that the argument has great weight, it becomes more material to preserve a theory which is good, and to prevent it from sliding into a theory which is bad. The moment this takes place, the argument fails, because its basis is gone. It even recoils upon those who urge it; since, if a good theory is a probable security for a free government, its gradual change into a bad one, will probably introduce tyranny.

The theoretical maxims best established by our political principles, is, that the people by special conventions have a right to make or alter their constitutions or forms of government, and that the government itself can do neither. If the entire government, or any department of it, shall exercise either of these powers, the essential principle of theoretical liberty, and all the securities against tyranny deduced from it, is destroyed. This primary maxim ought therefore to be vindicated, if violated in the slightest degree, because its preservation is indispensable for the preservation of liberty. Nobody asserts that either Congress or the Supreme Court, or both united, can make a constitution for the United States or for any one State. It is also conceded, that they cannot separately or in union, alter constitutions already made. Both prohibitions result from our primary maxim; but both are cyphers, if either can be evaded.

An alteration of the Constitution of the United States by Congress and the Supreme Court, would undoubtedly be an evasion of one prohibition. It is founded (to borrow from a former work) in the distinction between political and civil law. The people enact the former, legislatures the latter, and the judges act upon what legislatures enact. Political law is intended to restrain governments; civil, to restrain individuals. By adhering to this distinction, we are enabled to detect the attempts of governments to destroy the first principle of theoretical liberty, not less subversive of it, than if the people should undertake to make civil laws.

But the difficulty is to distinguish between civil laws and judgments, and political laws and judgments. This difficulty was foreseen and provided for by our system of government, by establishing divisions and limitations of power, as the only means of establishing theoretical liberty. For that purpose the divisions and limitations of power between the Federal and State governments were established. That such a constitutional division has been made, is not denied; but if no means for its preservation have been provided; if one of the departments or copartners has a power to usurp rights allotted to another; it is obvious, that this next most important principle of our theoretical liberty, is wholly nugatory and ineffectual. It would be perfectly evident that no security was obtained for it by divisions and limitations of power, if Congress or the Supreme Court, or both, could exclusively determine, whether their laws or judgments did or did not destroy the two principles of division and limitation. To say that these principles are left to be enforced by the people only, that they alone can keep political departments within their spheres, and that these departments cannot check each other, amounts to an assertion, that our theory for the preservation of liberty is grossly defective; far more so than the English; as not containing any internal means for self preservation. The argument, if sound, defeats all the checks, limitations, and divisions of power, to be found in our theoretical structures for the preservation of liberty. If the State governments should violate the limited theoretical powers, given to the Federal government, or if the Federal government should violate those reserved to the States, the argument asserts that our theory contains no internal provision against either violation, and that there is no remedy save that of going back to the people for a new theory. The consequence of this doctrine is, that no theory could be devised, capable of self-execution; and that every check which could be contrived for the preservation of liberty in current affairs of government, would be useless and inoperative; or only operative in requiring perpetual appeals to the people upon every collision of opinions between political departments. If either the legislative, executive, or judicial departments should usurp powers, one from another, the injured party would possess neither a right, nor the means of self-defence; and in all such cases, this theoretical imperfection would make it necessary to consider society as dissolved, and to go back to the people for a new one. To me however it seems that such collisions have been foreseen and provided for by our constitution, as perfectly as the case would admit of, by its checks and divisions of power. Far from designing to establish an imperfection so glaring, as that of perpetual appeals to the people upon every collision of opinions between departments, it has invested each department or division of power with the means of self-defence. If such was the design of the constitution, in order to secure theoretical liberty—by destroying these means, the theory itself is destroyed; and if the theory established by the people for the preservation of their liberties is destroyed, it can be no longer capable of effecting the intended end.

If the State and Federal governments are political departments, considered theoretically, as important for the preservation of liberty, as the legislative, executive, and judicial departments of these same governments, it cannot be even imagined, that a limb of either was intended to be invested with a power of overturning the entire structure of the other. It would be like telling a stranger, that the chamber of the Supreme Court was the whole Capitol, because the architect had covertly invested that chamber, with a power of swallowing up all the rest. Nor would this new notion in the art of building be much mended, by supposing that architect had, by some magical contrivance, invested the great Capitol at Washington, with a power of swallowing all the little Capitols of the States.

It is said, however, that the political architecture of the Federal constitution, must be considered as having copied such imaginary models, because it is extremely difficult to distinguish between laws and judgments which will change our political theory, and those made in subservience to it; and that it would be also highly inconvenient to be without a tribunal invested with a power of deciding whether laws or judgments were constitutional or not. Both the difficulty and the inconvenience is admitted. This very difficulty of distinguishing between laws and judgments for dispensing justice, or for destroying constitutions and liberty, demonstrated the magnitude of the danger, and the necessity for a remedy able to withstand it; and the inconvenience of having no such remedy was too obvious to be overlooked. It was this very danger and inconvenience which suggested divisions of power and distinct political departments, as independent tribunals for arresting that species of laws and judgments intended to work out a political revolution. As the Senate and House of Representatives are each an independent tribunal to judge of its own constitutional powers, so the State and Federal governments are independent tribunals to judge of their respective constitutional powers. The same principle is applicable to the legislative, executive, and judicial departments, both State and Federal. It never could have been forgotten or disapproved of in the formation of the State and Federal departments. Being an essential principle for preserving theoretical liberty, used by the Federal constitution, it never could have designed to destroy it, by investing five or six men, installed for life, with a power of regulating the constitutional rights of all political departments, or at least of the most important. Suppose the Supreme Court should attempt to settle collisions of opinion between the Senate and the House of Representatives: are not the political rights of all the States as important for the preservation of theoretical liberty, as those of one of these houses? It was foreseen by the framers of the constitution, that the difficulty of distinguishing between political laws and judgments, and those intended for the distribution of civil justice, would not be diminished by the supremacy of a concentrated power, and that it required the acuteness of collateral powers to detect and control it. The remedy provided for this difficulty, is the only remedy hitherto discovered; and has been interwoven in some shape with the texture or forms of all governments, pretending to a construction at all calculated for the preservation of liberty. It consists of a mutual veto. All our checks, balances, and divisions of power, are founded in the difference between a negative and affirmative; and the only practicable mode by which one department of any form of government, can be prevented from usurping the rights of another, is that of investing each with a negative able to stop such usurpations. The great difference between a negative and an affirmative power is, that one can only prohibit, whilst the other can create; and this difference has settled the judgment of the soundest political writers in estimating the inconveniences resulting from a negative power, able only to prevent laws from being enacted or having effect; or from an affirmative power able to enact and enforce laws, contrary to the theory established for the preservation of liberty, without being subjected to any negative check. All such writers have united in the opinion, although these negative checks may produce occasional inconveniences, that an affirmative creating power without them, will produce inconveniences much greater and more lasting. No form of government has ever pretended to any merit, or been allowed to possess any recommendation, except what has been derived from negative checks. The Roman tribunitial veto, however imperfect as a novel experiment, was considered by the people as the best safeguard of their rights; but by a senate installed for life, as highly inconvenient. The veto of the English king is the security for his prerogatives. The mutual negative powers of the two legislative chambers, is the security for their respective rights. An executive negative preserves executive power. And the negative pronounced by the judges on unconstitutional laws, preserves the judicial department as established by the constitution. In all these cases it is well established, and universally admitted, that the rights of a political department cannot be preserved, unless it is invested with a defensive negative power; and theoretical rights, unattended with the only means by which they can be preserved, are considered as equivalent to no rights at all.

Can it then be imagined that the States, when forming a constitution, and reserving a considerable share of political power to themselves, could have intended that this reservation should be merely didactick, and utterly devoid of the only means by which it could be preserved? Such a doctrine amounts to the insertion of the following article in the constitution: "Congress shall have power, with the assent of the Supreme Court, to exercise or usurp, and to prohibit the States from exercising, any or all of the powers reserved to the States, whenever they shall deem it convenient, or for the general welfare." I cannot perceive that a negative, able to prevent such aggressions, which may alter the theory of our government, is less necessary for the preservation of liberty, if the integrity of the State rights is necessary for that purpose, than the tribunitial, regal, executive, senatorial, representative, and judicial negatives. All these negatives are considered as necessary to preserve rights and powers, constituting portions of sundry theories contrived for the purpose of securing civil liberty, and unite to prove, that without this practical mode of defence, theoretical reserved rights and a division of powers, are insufficient for that end. It is equally inconceivable to me, that our State governments will be more corrupt than tribunes, kings, presidents, senates, representatives, and judges, and are therefore less worthy of being entrusted with a negative power for self-preservation. If such was the opinion of the framers of the constitution, why were they entrusted with so much power; but if they were thought trust-worthy, as to the powers given and reserved to them, could they have been considered as unworthy of being trusted also with the same means of preserving these powers, conferred on all other political departments? It might even be contended that they are less likely to corrupt the principles of the constitution than the Federal government itself, and that therefore a negative power in their hands for self-preservation, would cause fewer inconveniences, than an affirmative power in the Federal power to change the constitution, unsubjected to any State check. But whether the State political departments are necessary or unnecessary, convenient or inconvenient, good or bad, they have been established, however erroneously, upon a supposition that they were really very important members of our political theory for the preservation of liberty; and, therefore, whilst they last, we ought to reason upon the supposition that they are so. We must then conclude, that if a power to preserve the rights conferred on them for this end, must attend the rights, or they cannot effect the end, the want of such a power, or whatever may render them dependent on another constituent of the same theory, must be a movement towards theoretical tyranny.

The answers to this reasoning which I recollect, are, first, that an express power is given to the legislative and executive departments to control each other, but not to the Federal and State governments. The reply seems easy and conclusive. The mutual negatives between our two legislative chambers, and that given to the President, are expressed, because they do not result, exclusively, from the inherent right of self-preservation common to all collateral political departments, but from an intention to organize the legislative formulary, to prevent the passage of inexpedient laws. But no form in passing them was intended to make unconstitutional laws obligatory, and no reason existed, for declaring that these negatives were given to arrest such laws, because they would be as void after they were passed as before. Such a declaration would have admitted, that if neither house of Congress, nor the President, stopped a law or bill by a veto, it was to be considered as constitutional. No express negative upon unconstitutional laws is given to judges; yet they claim and exercise a negative over them. Of the same nature is the negative power of the States. Being at least as much political departments as the courts of justice, they derive from that character the same power to reject unconstitutional laws, as the judges do from theirs. So far this right of rejection is equal, but in other views, that of the States is infinitely the strongest. As contracting parties to the Union, this right is an appendage of that character. If they are not to be so considered, it goes to them as representatives of the people, because it is an appendage of the political powers with which they are invested by the people. It is absurd to allow that they were entrusted by the constitution with these powers, and yet prohibited from looking themselves into the constitution, that they might exercise them faithfully. The States possessed political powers antecedent to the constitution, as is acknowledged by their reservation. These State political powers previously possessed, never surrendered and expressly retained, inherently comprised a moral right of self-defence against every species of aggression; and the constitution, instead of saying that they may be taken away by the Federal government, expressly declares that they shall not; that they are without the compass of that instrument, and not embraced by it at all. Here then is a positive constitutional veto, clearly precluding both Congress and the federal court from touching the reserved State rights. Is this veto to be considered as a mere didactick lecture, or was the moral right of defending the powers, reserved with the powers themselves, so as to convey positively to the States the right of resisting unconstitutional laws for their own preservation? Thus the State political departments appear to have a much sounder right to disobey and resist unconstitutional laws, than even the judicial department. That State reserved political powers exist, is not denied, but it is contended that their moral right of self-defence is constructively taken away because it is inconvenient to the Federal government that it should exist, against which the reservation was directed. If that government may suppress one part of the constitution, because it is inconvenient, it may apply the same reason to any part it pleases. The Roman consuls and senators, when committed to prison by the tribunes, for resisting their right of veto, doubtless thought it very inconvenient that these tribunes should use the means necessary to sustain the right. When the inherent moral right of self-defence as to the reserved powers, is invaded, and the States are told that it will be inconvenient if they resist the invasion, they have undoubtedly to elect between the alleged inconvenience and the loss of the right. The State governments are in fact tribunes of the people, entrusted with rights bestowed for the preservation of their liberty, and if they surrender these rights, by surrendering the power of defending them, they will be as faithful to the people, as the Roman tribunes would have been had they surrendered their veto to the consuls and senate, or to the praetors. But what will be said to the silence of the constitution, as to any right in the Federal government to resist unconstitutional State laws? Certainly, that the donation of federal powers by the people, carried with it the indissoluble moral appendage of a right to resist aggressions upon those powers. Another donation of powers was made to the State governments by the same donors. How came these to be deprived of the same appendage? The people gave to each of these governments a fine horse to parade on: but it is said that the tail of the horse given to the State governments did not pass, and that the Federal government, as representing the people, have therefore a right to cut it off. If so, the State governments will soon be ashamed of their horse.

But it is answered, secondly, that an inherent right of self-defence, is an appendage neither of the Federal, nor of State governments, and that the Federal court is the guardian of the rights of both governments, with a power to cut off the tails of both their horses; that is, that the people divided certain powers between these governments, but withheld from both a right to defend its own allotment, and invested the Federal court with a power of making new divisions from time to time. This tremendous power is not expressly given to the court by the constitution, and is claimed by a string of inferences. If they can be made to reach such a power as this, it is surely time to enquire where they will stop. I have never heard before so novel a political doctrine, as that courts of justice are instituted to dispense political law to political departments. It is to be found in no writer; it has never been a component part of any government; and it is highly probable when the constitution was made, that not a single person in the United States contemplated the idea, of its having empowered the Federal Supreme Court to divide political powers between the Federal and State governments, just as it does money between plaintiff and defendant. Why should truth be suppressed? There is probably not a man in Congress who would subscribe to this doctrine, and who would not indignantly resist the least effort of the court to transfer Federal powers to State governments. Is it the power of impeachment which causes Congress so patiently to receive State powers through the same channel? The question is, whether the general idea attached to judicial power is, that its office is to distribute justice between individuals; or, whether it has been considered as extending to a right of distributing powers between political departments. It is contended that the great latter power, never before thought of by any political theory, has been tacitly conveyed by the constitution to the Supreme Court without any provision against its abuse. The novelty of the doctrine, the silence of the constitution, and the absence of any effectual check upon a power so enormous, are strong proofs, that the rights of both Federal and State governments, were not intended to be surrendered to six men, so as to make them administrators of powers to political departments, and guardians of the guardians of liberty; as well as of justice to individuals. Had the constitution considered the Supreme Court, as a political supervisor of departments entrusted with the preservation of liberty, it would have devised some security for enabling them to discharge a trust so important, in case the court should have interrupted their efforts for effecting the great end of society. None was devised, because the universal idea of judicial power confined its operation to individuals, and had never extended it to political departments. The inherent right of self-preservation was considered as attached to the State and Federal departments, and of course there was no reason for prescribing the mode by which it should be defended against judicial aggression, especially as no power was given to the court to aggress at all. There is no difficulty in distinguishing the power of the court to disobey unconstitutional laws, from a power to govern political departments. It is comprised in the difference between civil and political law; and the difficulty is gotten over, if it is the office of the court to dispense justice to individuals, and not to dispense powers to political departments. Whenever the constitution operates upon collisions between individuals, it is to be construed by the court, but when it operates upon collisions between political departments, it is not to be construed by the court, because the court has a power to settle the collisions of individuals, but no power to settle those of political departments. Suppose a collision of opinion to happen between the Senate and House of Representatives, or between Congress and the treaty-making power; could the court settle these collisions, or must they be settled by these departments themselves? Suppose Congress by a law should dissolve the State governments, or consolidate two States into one, and enforce the law by an army: could the court settle these collisions? An utter incompetency in the court to settle a multitude of collisions between political departments, is a proof that they were not empowered to settle any. The argument of inconvenience is as strong in those cases of collision which they cannot reach, as in those which they can; and had their supervisorship been contemplated as a remedy for such collisions, a mode of applying it to all would have been devised. Can the State governments defend themselves against a usurpation of those rights by the federal court, which the federal court is unable to preserve, but not against a gradual absorption of them, which the court is able to accelerate? If they may constitutionally defend themselves in the first catalogue of cases, it must be in virtue of an inherent right of self preservation. Where is the distinction to be found by which they are entitled to apply this right to cases of the first character, but not to those of the second? Good theories for the preservation of liberty are most liable to be destroyed by piecemeal; bad ones, by a single blow;

and therefore as ours is exposed to most danger from the detail mode of destruction, it is more important to the States to possess the right of self-preservation against the insidious enemy, than against one which dares not even show his face.

Let us apply the right of mutual veto to some of the constitutional questions which have occurred, in order to estimate the inconveniences attending its existence or abolition. In the bank case, which is most detrimental to our theory for the preservation of liberty—that a State should negative the establishment of an exclusive privilege within its territory, or that Congress should acquire an affirmative power of abolishing the State right of taxation? The State veto only prevents the introduction of a new political machine; the affirmative power impairs, and is a precedent for destroying a right given to the States, without which they cannot exist. In the lottery case, the State veto only prohibits an immoral practice; but the extension of an absolute power over ten miles square, to the whole United States, abolishes the distinction between limitation and reservation. On which side do the inconveniences in these cases preponderate? In both, affirmative federal powers are conferred by the court, containing political innovations radically assailing the powers reserved to the States, considered as essential for the preservation of liberty; whereas their prohibition by the State veto, leaves our political theory unaltered. These two cases themselves prove, that there is no danger in a mutual State and Federal veto. Would our liberty be lost by suppressing banks and lotteries, and are the States to be considered as dangerous usurpers for resisting either? The cases, indeed, discover a difference of opinion between departments as to the regimen necessary for its preservation, but surely the States are not so egregiously in the wrong, that they ought to be deprived of their constitutional right of self-defence.

A State attempt to destroy a Federal tax, is equivalent to a Federal attempt to destroy a State tax. A mutual veto can defeat both attempts. The Federal tax law may be executed by the Federal courts, and the State tax law by the State courts. As the Federal courts would disregard the interposition of the State courts, to prevent the exercise of a right conferred upon the Federal political department to tax, so the State courts ought to disregard the interposition of the Federal court to prevent the exercise of the right to tax reserved to the State departments; both courts acting upon the same principle of self-preservation, because the constitution has not extended it to one department and withheld it from the other. There is no uninferred Federal power that I recollect, except one, capable of being interrupted by the State resistance to Federal laws, upon the ground of unconstitutionality; because the Federal government possesses internally a power to execute all laws founded upon powers expressed. If a State can prevent by exerting any of its reserved powers, the execution of a Federal law, it is a presumptive proof that it is unconstitutional. The power of exercising expressed Federal rights, is a security for the Federal government; but a veto against unconstitutional Federal laws impeding the exercise of State rights, must belong to the State governments, or the exercise of State rights must depend on the will of the Federal government. A correspondent power of exercising their respective rights must be mutual to the two governments, because if either should exclusively possess such a power, it will swallow up the other.

But may not the States pass unconstitutional laws? In answer to this question, I shall select the chief case of their having done so. The stay-laws as they are called, are admitted to be of this character, and they serve to illustrate the provision made by the constitution, against State unconstitutional laws. The first and chief provision, is the internal capacity of the Federal government to carry into execution all the Federal powers expressed. The second consists in its jurisdiction between citizens of different States, given for the purpose of preserving union between the States. But the expression of this jurisdiction excludes a jurisdiction over the internal operation of local laws between citizens of the same State, and therefore these stay-laws do not in that case fall under the jurisdiction of the Federal courts. How much stronger is the case of a State tax law? The third provision against unconstitutional State laws is the oath taken by State judges to observe the Federal constitution, by which they are entitled to determine upon the constitutionality of State laws. A fourth provision is, that a State government cannot pass unconstitutional laws, which will operate externally, but the Federal government can pass unconstitutional laws operating upon all the States, or upon a single State; and if there exists no remedy against them but an appeal to the joint supremacy by which they are made and executed, a consolidated government is their inevitable effect. The excepted case is that of the Massachusetts militia during the late war. This case I suppose to have been an executive act. As checks upon this violation of the constitution, if the Federal power over the militia is insufficient to meet it, which I do not admit, the Federal government can both refuse to pay misemployed militia, and also raise armies. But this is a case which demonstrates the incapacity of the Supreme Court to supervise the unconstitutional acts of either the Federal or State governments. They could not make the militia march. And an incapacity to restrain the unconstitutional acts of these departments, which might be carried to a great extent, was, therefore never thought of as the guardian of the constitution.

The mutual veto of the Federal and State governments, or the mutual inherent rights of self-preservation, is rendered infinitely more safe, and less inconvenient or dangerous, than the exclusive veto claimed by the court, by the check of election. This is a powerful control upon unconstitutional laws passed by either, and may be applied against an improper resistance by the people of a State, without dissolving society and appealing to a convention; whereas no such control exists to prevent the Supreme Court from altering the constitutional division of political power. Can there be the least difficulty in deciding between the safety, inconvenience, and danger, attached to the mutual vetos of the State and Federal governments, when both are frequently exposed to the restraint of public opinion; or to the judicial veto, exposed to no such restraint? The Roman tribunitial veto was exposed to the same popular control, and thus only rendered useful towards preserving the liberty of the people. The veto of the English king is liable to no such control, and therefore it is used, not to advance liberty, but to gain and preserve power. The veto upon State laws assumed by the Court, is of the latter character. It is under no responsibility to foster and defend liberty, and may, without control, disorder and subvert the primary division of power, established to preserve it. Departments for its preservation, over which they retained a control, were confided in by the people; but the Court step into the place of the people, substitute themselves as controllers of these departments, and make them responsible to a tribunal by which they are not elected. It was somewhat erroneous to say, that the assumed judicial veto was of the same character with the regal. It is in fact infinitely more dangerous, because judgments are affirmative as well as negative. They can make as well as abrogate laws. Their capacity to do both displays forcibly the difference between civil and political laws, and discriminates very clearly one from the other in the hands of a few men not responsible to the people. If the Supreme Court should misconstrue a civil law, or make a new one, the legislative power is able to correct the error; but if they make or misconstrue a political or constitutional law, the injured legislature has no power of correction. Hence arises the necessity of a mutual veto in the State and Federal governments, since otherwise the Supreme Court would be able to alter both State and Federal constitutions, transfer the allegiance of representatives from their constituents to themselves, and deprive the people of the most valuable jewel attached to election, namely, its power to preserve their constitutions.

The only argument urged to prove that a veto in the Supreme Court, is better than a mutual right of self-preservation in the Federal and State governments, responsible to the people for its proper exercise, is the liability of the judges to be impeached by the House of Representatives, and removed by the Senate of the United States. The State departments can neither impeach the judges, nor bring them even to trial, for any violations of State rights, however flagrant; whilst the Federal department can do both, and also dismiss them for any violations of Federal rights, however trifling. These two are the chief classes of powers which can come into collision, and these judges are said to be safer guardians of them, or more impartial arbitrators, than a mutual right of self-preservation under the control of the people. I deny that there is a single man in the world, who can possibly believe this to be true, or who would risk his tooth-picker upon such jurisprudence. Let us make a case of it. A and B are at law with each other. A has six men employed by great salaries to do his business, whom he can accuse himself, try himself, condemn himself, and dismiss himself. He proposes to B these very men as arbitrators between them. There is not a B in the whole world who would not laugh at the proposal. Gentlemen lawyers, is there one of you who would advise a client to listen for a moment to it? The check of impeachment, as it is called, is a threat to impartiality, and an admonition against justice, in deciding Federal and States collisions. It is oftener used as a party instrument, than to secure judicial independence, even in cases where neither the accusers nor triers are parties in the controversy; and is oftener an engine of persecution, than an encouragement of integrity. What then is its security to one rival for power, when wielded by his adversary? If not a single man in his senses, not a single B can be found, who would submit his property to such arbitrators, can we make out even a possible case to sustain this doctrine, by supposing whole States to be Bs, so utterly ignorant of man and his passions, and so infatuated by the word "impeachment," as to have created A's officers for arbitrators of collisions foreseen and feared with this same A? Would they not have retained some choice in the appointment, the accusation, or the trial of arbitrators, able to deprive them of their whole estate? Would they not have secured for themselves at least a trial *per medietatem lingua?* Could Massachusetts have forgotten that she had rejected as an insult upon her understanding, the idea of confiding in judges paid by the king; and all the other States, their concurrence in the same opinion? Considering the extreme jealousy of the States lest the Federal Government should encroach upon the reserved rights, they certainly never meant to say, by not saying "let Congress and the Federal Court cut and carve among these rights at their pleasure." We must either charge them with an absurdity so egregious, or believe that they meant to retain an inherent power of self-preservation. If this was their opinion when they established the constitution, no verbal inferences, however plausible, can accord with its intention; and any construction at enmity with the intention of the contract, is unexceptionably erroneous. If it was not the intention of the States, or of the people, to invest the Supreme Court with a power to deprive the former of their powers, and the latter of their elective influence; in fact, to model society according to its own pleasure, without being under responsibility to the people or to the States, the question is decided; and, unless this was not their intention, we must conclude, that language is unable to express the design of contracts.

The impeachment of Judge Chase demonstrated the inefficacy of that mode for preventing unconstitutional Federal laws, by which State rights are invaded. The opinion, that the sedition law was unconstitutional was so general, as to effect a revolution of political parties. Having changed the majority in the House of Representatives, it is highly probable that the new majority concurred in opinion with the people, when it impeached Judge Chase; but a love of power was too strong even for party spirit; and therefore his having executed an unconstitutional law and fined and imprisoned men without law (for it is admitted that unconstitutional laws are not laws) was not even made an article of his impeachment. This omission was a tacit acknowledgement that the sedition law was constitutional, and will be quoted to prove it, whenever a party may have occasion for another. Thus the event has already confirmed what the States must have foreseen, namely, that no Federal judge would ever be impeached, much less removed, for executing an unconstitutional Federal law; and experience justifies what the theory plainly predicts, that impeachments of Federal judges, far from being a check upon such laws, are the most effectual means for sustaining them. It is therefore impossible to imagine that the States ever intended to surrender their inherent right of self-defence, for the sake of holding their powers by tenure of the impeaching power, exclusively given to Congress. The fact has already fully disclosed the nature of such a tenure. The court has nearly established the doctrine, that it is almost impossible for Congress to pass an unconstitutional law; and positively asserted, that no law of a State, which contravenes a law of Congress, can be constitutional.

We may obtain a correct idea of the piecemeal mode of destroying theoretical liberty, by supposing that the first Congress under the present constitution, had published a declaration in the following words:

> Congress has power to assume the State debts; to confer on bankers a vast annual income by a monopoly of currency; to endow capitalists with an equal bounty by a monopoly of manufacturers; to pass alien and sedition laws; to prohibit negro slavery; to make roads and canals; to prohibit the importation of all foreign commodities; to provide for the poor by pensions; to try all individual claims for public money; to give public money gratuitously, and as a sinecure, to whomsoever it pleases, without limitation; to model State constitutions; to give away the public lands; and to legislate internally without restriction,

in virtue of its power to legislate for ten miles square. No State can pass any law which shall contravene a law of Congress. No State possesses a right of self-defence against encroachments of the Federal government. The supreme Federal court can abrogate any State law, and reverse any State judgments. It can regulate and alter the division of powers between the State and Federal governments: and it can constitutionally execute unconstitutional Federal laws by which State rights are infringed.

How would such a declaration of powers have been received, when the principles which had dictated our theoretical system for the preservation of liberty, were fresh? Should we not have heard the universal cry of "consolidation and tyranny." Because it is safer to pull down a fortress by piecemeal than to blow it up once, lest the fragments of the explosion should knock in the head some of the engineers, it does not follow that the fortress will not be destroyed by the first mode. Had all these successive blows been thus condensed into one, would it not have been considered as an attempt to blow up at once, our theoretical fortress for the preservation of liberty, and have produced a general and animated resistance; or should we have submissively petitioned the Supreme Court to protect us against the threatened calamity? Yet all these blows have been successively given to our theory; proving that the gradual and piecemeal mode of destroying it, and for substituting a tyranny in its place, is the most dangerous because it is the least alarming.

It is not expressly asserted, that the Federal court may constitutionally execute unconstitutional Federal laws, by which State rights are infringed, and only that should it do so, the States have no remedy, and must surrender their rights. But is not the latter power perfectly equivalent to the other? Would not the court act unconstitutionally, by executing an unconstitutional law of Congress? Have the States no remedy in such a case, whatever of their rights such a law might take away; and must these political departments, or sovereign States, or whatever may be their title, tamely surrender the powers confided to them by the people for the benefit of the people, and submissively betray the sacred trust? Even the individual right of suffrage, being a political right, is not left to be extended or contracted by the civil law courts; but as a subject too high for their jurisdiction, is exclusively entrusted to popular representatives. How then can it be possible to suppose, that the same system, so wary in withholding this political right of an individual from the jurisdiction of the Supreme Court, could have intended to have invested it with a jurisdiction over all the political rights of the States, and incidentally to weaken extremely the right of election itself?

The insufficiency of the constructive judicial power to regulate political departments, may be further demonstrated, by considering to what extent it can operate upon the Federal department. Were the powers of this department made subservient to the jurisdiction of these six men? If not, the check would be insufficient. Are some of the Federal powers subservient to this jurisdiction and others not? Then the unsubservient may be used by the Federal department to invade the powers of the State department. Suppose the Federal department should use its military power against the State department; it is obvious that the Supreme Court could not prevent the aggression. Such would be the case also, if the State department should assail the rights of the Federal department by its military power. In both cases, the judicial power would be unable to preserve the rights of the department attacked. Whence does this imbecility arise? From its civil nature; from its action having been limited to private cases; from its incapacity to govern these political departments. Could the constitution have relied upon this imbecility for their preservation? Why has it divided military power between them, except to confer on both the means for exercising the mutual right of self-preservation? In establishing this mutual check, it recognises the existence of the right. Powers must be equivalent, to be able to check each other. If the judicial power is unable to govern these two political departments; or if it can govern one and not the other; it could not have been contemplated as the means for preserving the powers of both. The constitution, when it bestowed these powers, must have contemplated some better means for their preservation. What these can be, except the mutual rights of self-preservation and self-defence, is not discernible. If one of them does not possess these rights, neither can the other; and by establishing their political subordination to the court, we should exhibit to the world the political phenomenon of two governments, neither possessing a right of self-preservation, and both subjected to six men, not elected by the people, but nominated by one man. Had the Supreme Court consisted of one man, he would have been a very powerful monarch, invested with the right of making, or which nearly amounts to the same thing, of modeling constitutions, claimed and exercised by a few of the monarchs of Europe. The court therefore resembles a holy alliance of six monarchs.

The Amphictyonick council of Greece, created by a union of seven states, was instituted for the purpose of preserving peace, and providing for the general defence; and not to model the internal governments of the States forming the Union, or to meddle with their local laws. It never claimed a right to do either, because it was composed of representatives from these United States. If it had been made subordinate to the Areopagus of Athens, one of the united and rival states, we should have had a precedent for that species of security for state rights, now contended for. This supervising tribunal constituted by one rival state, would have been equivalent to our six judges, appointed and removable by a rival department; except that an Amphictyonick council would have been selected from all the confederated states, whereas our supreme judges may be selected from one, and must be selected from a minority of the United States. Their removal by the Athenian department, would have rendered them subservient to the ambition of that department, when directed against its rivals. Such a Grecian-federal theory, for the preservation of the liberty of the confederates, would have been sufficiently unpromising, but we are endeavouring to make ours more so. It is said that our federal theory bestows supreme power on six men, not one of whom are appointed by, or representatives of any of the confederates. Congress are our Amphictyonick council; but this doctrine places over it a superiour council, constituted as the Grecian council would have been, had it been appointed and removable by the Athenians alone, able, it is said, to govern both the confederates themselves, and their representatives. The Grecian Amphictyonick council however, strongly resembled our judicial political council, in being unable to prevent, though it could easily excite wars between the confederated States.

The tribunitial veto at Rome was sometimes entrusted to six men; but this precedent does not sustain our novel doctrine, because the tribunes were annually elected by the people. Had the senate indeed appointed and removed these tribunes to prevent senatorial aggressions upon the rights and liberties of the people, and had such a theory prevented the senate from committing them, it would have forcibly supported the project of preventing the Federal political department from trespassing on the State political department, by the newly invented veto of judicial tribunes, appointed by, and responsible to, the Federal department.

We may, however, very nearly find a precedent for our judicial negative, in the imperial theoretical system discovered by Bonaparte for the preservation of liberty.

By reserving to himself the exclusive right of proposing laws, he obtained a previous veto upon every effort by the representatives of the people, for the good of the people. But his veto was not quite as objectionable as the judicial. He could prevent, but not create unconstitutional laws; the court can establish or even create them by construction. His was only a negative, theirs is a power affirmative as well as negative. Bonaparte's legislative power had a negative upon the laws proposed by him: Neither the State legislatures nor State courts are supposed to have any negative upon unconstitutional laws established or created by the court. Bonaparte prohibited debates; the Supreme Court only render the deliberations of the State legislatures and courts, idle and useless. The veto of the English king can strangle usurpations in their birth: the veto of the court cannot prevent their conception and delivery, but it can give them life and power. The vetoes of Bonaparte, the English king, and the Supreme Court, are alike in being exercised by characters, neither representing, nor responsible to the people. But they are unlike in a very material feature. Bonaparte was not the creature of the French senate and tribunate. Instead of his being their instrument, they were his instruments. They could neither appoint, impeach, nor remove an emperor, who should oppose their love of power. The English king, in like manner, is independent of the lords and commons, and these imperial or monarchical vetoes being both free, might dare to do right. The Supreme Court under the influence of the Federal government, is neither independent nor free; and it cannot dare to do right for any length of time, or it will display a degree of boldness and disinterestedness, never yet practised by any body of men exposed to an equal influence. It will therefore be easier for the Federal government to use it as a sham court for advancing its power, than it was for Bonaparte to use his senate and tribunes as a sham legislature for feeding his ambition.

The enormities of the French revolution planted a diffidence in republican theories, which has spread its branches to the United States, and is causing us gradually to cheat ourselves of our own principles. It having been imbibed by many honest, wise, and good men, frauds joyfully unite themselves with the prejudices it inspires, in order to make use of virtue and talents to gratify vices. Thus it has happened that the political provision, called a negative or veto, has been perverted from the original purpose of preserving, to that of destroying, liberty. Tyranny is wonderfully acute in transferring to itself, the weapons of liberty. It has converted charters invented for her use, into pick-pockets for robbing her. It has used even representation to lash her. And we are now sharpening a new instrument, which can only be described by contradictions, namely, an affirmative negative, to stab her outright. Bonaparte first discovered that his previous veto, united with a subservient legislature, was a good instrument for this purpose; and we have discovered that an affirmative negative power, united with a subservient court, is a better. There is something in human nature, wonderfully fond of new inventions, and extremely desirous of improving them, if they bring us either power or money.

The political principle, called a veto or negative, has hitherto been applied to collateral political departments, and wherever it has been given to one, it has been balanced or checked by the same responsive or equivalent power, bestowed on another. In England, the king's veto upon laws is balanced by that of the lords and commons. At Rome, neither the senate nor tribunes could pass a law, against the consent of the other political department; but the judges had no veto restricting the powers of the senate, the tribunes, the tribes, or the centuries, because they did not possess the character of a collateral political department. Both in the Federal and State governments the veto is responsive between departments necessary to concur in legislation. But I recollect no case of investing any man, or body of men, whose concurrence to an act is not necessary, with a veto against that act. The concurrence of the Supreme Court is not necessary either to Federal or State legislation; and therefore, they are not susceptible of the equivalence and reciprocity attached to the political principle of a veto, and of course cannot exercise it, for want of the essential principle, by which it is constituted. The concurrence of the Federal government in making Federal laws, and of the State governments in making State laws, being necessary; the principle of vetos is applicable to both, lest one department should make laws for the other; it is equivalent, reciprocal, and necessary for the preservation of their respective rights: whereas the Supreme Court being no party to the legislative acts of either, have no rights to defend, and no equivalence or reciprocity of restraint, to bestow on either of these governments, to balance an usurped veto upon the political acts of either.

There was, indeed, a time in England, whilst the judges were removable by the king, when he used them so effectually to circumscribe the rights of the other political departments, and enlarge his own, as to produce a long and bloody civil war. Our ancestors, taught by severe experience, that it was a very sufficient mode for introducing tyranny, suppressed it. Are we destined to make the same discovery at the same expense? Their experience plainly informs us, that a judicial power in the hands of one political department, may be effectually used to destroy its rivals, expunge checks, consolidate political powers, and introduce tyranny. It completely exhibits the difference between fairly balanced reciprocal vetoes, and enlisting under the banner of one, a subservient judicial power, so as to destroy the balance. The balanced vetoes keep out usurpations; a destruction of the balance by the judicial ally, is the very mode for letting them in. The first sustains the rights of both the political departments; the second destroys those of one. The first prevents; the second excites civil wars. The king, lords, and commons, now very easily adjust their political powers by equivalent and reciprocal vetoes, and if they cannot agree, the measure dies in peace; but when the judges could act affirmatively on the side of the king, being dependent upon him, they of course fostered usurpations, which could only be killed by the sword. The consequences of a fair, or a foul pair of vetoes; of a veto in one political department, but not in its collateral department instituted also to preserve political liberty;

or of an active affirmative power exercised under the pretext of an uncreating veto; are the items of inconveniences to be computed, in order to ascertain which will be most unfriendly to liberty. On the one hand, we must contemplate a negative power in the States, incapable of making a new constitution; on the other, a power in Congress and the Court, to change the constitution, like the king and his dependent judges. A mutual check between powerful political departments, to be exercised by a reciprocal veto, seems to be the best theoretical principle hitherto discovered for securing liberty, and the only mode by which one can be prevented from swallowing up another; and its absence seems to destroy all constitutions, balances, limitations, and divisions of power, which can be devised.

It is again admitted that, according to our political theory, the judges are invested with a species of political power, not for the purpose of destroying or altering constitutions, nor to disarrange the powers of political departments, but for that of securing the rights of individuals. Constitutions and their divisions were designed for the same end, and it was not intended that one precaution should destroy the other. Both State and Federal judges in the trial of private suits, are obliged to say what is law, and what is not law. And, as unconstitutional laws are not laws, they could not render justice to an individual, by leaving him to suffer without, or against law. If Congress, or the State legislatures, pass unconstitutional laws, it would be no more obligatory than a law passed by a mob, calling itself a Congress or a legislature. Could the Supreme Court force the States to obey the law of a mob? And why not? Only because the States possess an inherent right of self-preservation. The two supposed laws being of equal validity, are equally liable to be met by this right, or it could meet neither. There is no difficulty in reconciling the right of self-preservation mutually possessed by political departments, with the right of dispensing justice, attached to judicial power. Both the rights subsist in England, and one does not invade the other. One ends where the other begins. The rights of political departments are of a different order to those of individuals, and were bestowed as safeguards for these individual rights; but if the rights of political departments are destroyed, they cannot fulfil the intention of preserving individual rights; the purpose for which they were constituted. It is therefore an obvious error to suppose that a judicial power, created as an additional security for the rights of individuals, can destroy or impair the rights of political departments, created also for the preservation of individual rights. The people have confided the custody of their political rights; divided, as they conceived, in the best mode for their security, to the Federal and State departments, prohibiting both from exercising powers intrusted to the other, and no power is given to the judges to compel one department to submit to the encroachments of the other; they have only to leave collisions to be settled by the mutual veto attached to the mutual right of self-preservation, as is done in all other countries by judicial power, and as it does here in all cases of collision between the two legislative departments.

Nothing can be more subversive of acknowledged principles than a habit of inferring from one security for individual liberty, a power to overturn others. Constitutions, so far as they comprise a previous negative for its preservation, are a recent, and have been considered as a happy, discovery; but if they have tacitly blundered into the still newer idea of exalting judicial above political power, and investing it with an irresponsible right of modeling political departments, they have obliterated their chief principles for the preservation of individual liberty, and tacitly expunged what they have expressly enacted. They proceeded upon the principle thoroughly established by experience; that independent, collateral, political departments, mutually able to control the usurpations of each other, were indispensably necessary for the preservation of individual liberty: and to these securities ours have added the new one of a limitation of legislative power, within the sphere prescribed for it by constitutions. But a judicial power in society was also necessary, and out of the constitutional limitation of legislative power, the Supreme Court has very ingeniously extracted for itself, a power to defeat the constitutional limitation of legislative power, by asserting, that their assent to a law, though unconstitutional, will make it obligatory. The liberty of individuals would be infinitely more secure, if independent, collateral, political departments, are safeguards of it, under the conjoined doctrines, that the State and Federal departments should both retain their inherent right of self-defence against their mutual usurpations, and that the judges should have no right to disobey unconstitutional laws; than by uniting in the Supreme Court a right to enforce unconstitutional laws, with a power of destroying or disordering the division of powers between the Federal and State departments. The first policy, however objectionable, would leave to individuals the securities arising both from representation and a division of powers; the second weakens both these securities to a great extent, and also exposes them to the calamities of a civil war.

The four essential principles of our theory for the preservation of liberty, are, that State constitutions ought to be the act of the people; that the Federal constitution ought to be the act of the people and the States, and should not be altered without the concurrence of three-fourths of the State governments; that a definite and permanent division of power should subsist between the State and Federal governments; and that each should possess a right of taxation, which the other cannot take away. The first has been violated by the exercise of a power in Congress, to dictate an article for a State constitution, enforced by the penalty of being excluded from the Union. The second, by the exercise of a joint power, said to reside in Congress and the Supreme Court, exclusively to construe the constitution. The third, by the consequent exercise of a power to usurp or control State rights, and to alter the division of power between the State and Federal departments. And the fourth, by restricting the State right of taxation, as is attempted to be done in the bank case. It is unnecessary to recite minor infractions of our theoretical system for the preservation of liberty, because, sooner or later, a multitude of them must inevitably follow those of a vital nature, if they establish themselves. When the States have lost the right of making for themselves such constitutions as they please; when the right of altering the Federal constitution is transferred from the people and the States to Congress and the Court; when the Federal department have acquired the right of usurping powers confided to the States, and the latter have lost the right of self-defence; and when the State right of taxation is restricted by the comprehensive maxim, that they can pass no law which may obstruct the success of a law passed by Congress, will not all the vital principles of our theory be effectually destroyed? Whether this absolute power in Congress and its Court, was intended to be vested by the constitution, is the first question; if not, then the claim to it is a visible deviation from our political theory, and a visible advance towards tyranny, if that theory is better calculated for the preservation of liberty, than the proposed substitute. This doubt has, however, suggested a second question, which has an illicit influence upon the first to a great extent, namely, whether an absolute power in Congress would not be a better political theory, than that established by the people and the States, with the State and Federal ingredients. I shall presently enter into the consideration of this second question, trusting that the reader will perceive the difference between cheating the people into a new form of government, and openly proposing it for their consideration. The permission of a furtive interpolation, even if good in itself, brings with it the great defect of changing political theories without the concurrence of the people; exposes the new theory to the same artifices used to destroy its predecessor; and renders it impossible to maintain a permanent form of government.

The second point however to be considered, will shed some light upon the opinion, that an absolute power in Congress, will more effectually promote social liberty and happiness, than a mutual check between the Federal and State departments. Congress and the court seem to believe that it will, and the States and the people have been inattentive to the subject. It is not quite impossible, that such an absolute power may produce practical liberty, because absolute monarchies have occasionally done so: and therefore it is contended that a representative Congress may do the same. But the experiment of a consolidated republic, over a territory so extensive as the United States, is at least awful, when we can recollect no case in which it has been successful. If the people had believed it practicable, it would have been preferred to our system of division and union; and even if it had been adopted, from a confidence in the efficacy of representation to sustain a consolidated republic, the reasons against endowing six men with a political power co-extensive with the consolidated territory, would have been still stronger, because it would, to a great extent, have relinquished representation, the only principle relied upon, for sustaining so large a republican empire.

It must yet be admitted, that but little practical tyranny or oppression is to be feared from judicial power. Too feeble to be the source of tyranny itself, in acting oppressively it has been, and must for ever be, the instrument of some stronger power, because it neither wields the sword nor commands the treasury. If judicial power must be subservient to a stronger power, it would be a very imperfect mode of disclosing the origin of oppression, by hiding it under an odium against the Supreme Court. No, let not the tyrant hug himself in his supposed elevation beyond the reach of censure, by leaving crimination to exhaust itself upon his ministers, whilst he is furnishing them with materials, and reaping the fruits of their labours. What can this court do, except as the instrument for enforcing the laws and usurpations of Congress? In this body therefore, and not in the court, lies the source of all the mischiefs of which we complain. By supposing that the court can shield the States against the usurpations of Congress, we should concede to it the power of arranging, preserving, or defeating the division of political powers between the Federal and State departments, and surrender the question of right in the complaints of partiality. Congress forges the weapons, with which the court hack and hew principles, and the court is liable to be punished by Congress if it does not use them. We ought therefore to turn our attention from the judicial to the legislative power; as the latter is the real engineer by whom the pillars of our political system can be undermined or battered to pieces. Congress passed the sedition law, the bank law, the lottery law, and most other laws, which have generated constitutional questions. Perhaps it would have been requiring too much of the Federal court, to expect of it a steady disobedience to all the unconstitutional acts of Congress; even our Presidents, though elected by the people, have but rarely arrested them; or perhaps it conscientiously concurs with Congress, in the opinion, that Congress, as well as itself, possesses a supremacy over the States and the Constitution; a supremacy resulting from an exclusive right of construction; or perhaps it may at least believe that they ought to obtain it. From one of these causes, it has probably happened, that the instances of a bold opposition to unconstitutional laws by State judges, have been so much more frequent than similar proofs of independence on the part of Federal judges. But these considerations do not obliterate truth. It must be admitted that legislative power is the source of nearly all the violations of our political theory. Is it not more magnanimous to assail the principal than his agent? Is it necessary seriously to observe that the English precedent of impeaching the minister for the crimes of the king, is not sufficient to screen Congress by censuring the court? There is a sort of fashionable judicial etiquette, a kind of family pride, which sanctifies precedents, often sustains errors, and deserves the respect to which too long a consistency is sometimes entitled. But legislative bodies never regard this species of decorum, except as an affectation when it accords with their designs, or countenances their encroachments. The argument of consistency is with them as strong as a rock to defend, and as brittle as glass to defeat, acquisitions of wealth and power. As they never entangle themselves in a web of precedents, are quite familiarized to revocation, and are the real sources of our retrocession towards tyranny, both theoretical and practical, it is from them and them only, that redress can be required or obtained.

This remedy is by no means so rare as to be hopeless. From the many instances of its efficacy, I shall select one, which seems particularly applicable to our case. The declaration of rights proclaimed by the English lords and commons, upon the expulsion of James the second, contained a renunciation of pernicious powers, and destroyed several abuses, legislative, executive, and judicial, though sustained by precedents of long standing. Whigs and tories united in recovering the principles of the government. Are they better patriots than federalists and republicans? Is it not possible that a patriotick Congress may also appear, which will, by a similar declaration proclaim the constitutional rights of the States in which they live, and of the people to whom they must return? Will a vanishing power for ever inspire a spirit which causes one Congress to adhere to the errors of another? It would be the best imaginable compromise, for the people to agree to forgive all those of an existing Congress, if it would correct those of its predecessors. Congress can both forbear to pass unconstitutional laws, and also prevent the judges from giving laws an unconstitutional construction, either by provisions in the laws themselves, or by subsequent laws. Thus the bank law might have contained a provision that it should not be construed to impair the State right of taxation; the lottery law, that it should not be construed to extend beyond the ten miles square; and the court law might have forborne to invest the Supreme Court with an unconstitutional jurisdiction. These laws may yet be chastened by Congress of any construction which it condemns. In all cases wherein the Supreme Court has been or may be charged with extending a law of Congress by construction to any unconstitutional object, Congress has the remedy in its own hands; and its silence is therefore a recognition and a confirmation of the court's opinion, of which, advantage will be made for multiplying such constructions. As Congress is both the maker of the law, and the justifier of the court's construction, it is in vain to expect that the court will ever renounce precedents so powerfully sustained; or that they can be defeated, except by a patriotick Congress, or the State right of self-preservation.

That no effort has ever been made by Congress to defend State rights against judicial construction; and that we should be losing sight of its responsibility, by pursuing the pompous, but metaphysical judicial phantom, is an instance of fatuity, which would, without some solution, be inconceivable. It must either be the effect of a conviction in Congress, that the States possess a power to preserve their own rights, and therefore, that there is no reason, and perhaps an impropriety, that Congress should interfere between them and the Supreme Court; or, of the party spirit begotten and fostered by ambition and avarice. The nation has successively attached itself to two parties, called Federal and Republican. How can a majority bear to censure the legislature it has chosen? Is not opposition to any measures of a reigning party considered as an enlistment under the banner of the rival party? Yet no opposition can be of any practical use, but to the measures of a reigning party. Nations are always enslaved by the ingenuity of creating a blind confidence with party prejudices. A reigning party never censures itself, and the people have been tutored to vote under two senseless standards, gaudily painted over with the two words "Federalist and Republican," repeated, and repeated, without having any meaning, or conveying any information. One party passed the alien and sedition laws; the other, the bank and lottery laws; and both, many other laws, theoretically unconstitutional, and practically oppressive; but neither has overturned unconstitutional precedents, though they have often charged each other with creating them, and both have waved the ensigns of a party majority before our eyes, which we have followed to a state of national distress. If a man had successively married two wives, one called Lucretia, and the other Penelope; and should believe in their chastity, after having seen both in bed with several gallants of the worst characters, should we call him a blind cully, or an acute observer?

But there remains a mode of getting over these difficulties. The Supreme Court cannot be considered as the republican party, and therefore, we shall not wound our attachments by resisting its violations of Republican principles. If Congress has foreborne to restrain it from an opinion that the States are able to defend their rights, it only stands aloof and views the combat as an unconcerned spectator, because it knows that the States can bring into the field the competent forces confided to them by the people for their own preservation, to secure a victory. Should Congress condescend to become a partisan for the court, the title of republican party must be surrendered, because the court are not that party; and then we shall no longer be prevented by party prejudices, from considering whether the doctrines of the court tend towards the destruction of a federal, and the introduction of a consolidated republic. Congress may not be incorrect in believing that its interference between the States and the court would be unconstitutional, as implying that State rights were subjected to its protection, and that the States had not a power of self-defence.

In considering whether we are acquiring actual tyranny, our theoretical innovations needed not to have been proved; because as actual tyranny inflicts actual misery, it is unimportant to the oppressed under what theory they suffer. A subversion of the tyranny in fact, and not a war of constructions, is the only effectual remedy. But if a deviation from the principles of our constitutional theory for the preservation of liberty has been proved, and we shall now discover that actual evils have also multiplied, it will demonstrate the connexion between bad principles and bad consequences.

To discover whether actual tyranny is coming or has arrived, let us endeavour to establish some unequivocal evidence, by which tyranny may be known; some characteristick, as obvious to the senses as the difference of colours; and as clear to the understanding, as that two and two make four. The plain good sense of mankind has long since escaped from the intricacy of metaphysical reasoning, and discovered an infinitely more certain mode of ascertaining the existence of tyranny; but the artifices of ambition and avarice have constantly laboured to extinguish a light too luminous for their designs, and to perplex evidence too strong to be denied. When nations are induced, by the dexterities of ambition and avarice, to sear their senses against the plainest of all truths, their situation becomes hopeless, and their subjection to actual tyranny certain. The conviction of the truth of that which I am about to advance, is so universal, that abuses never venture to deny it; but use all their ingenuity to evade its force, by urging that present evils will produce future good. They either endeavour to hide actual tyranny by some eulogized theory, or to draw off the public attention from it, to some distant prospect embellished by the imagination, or to win confidence by ample promises. There is no resource for defeating such artifices, but that of clinging to the universal conviction of mankind.

Money is a more accurate measure of liberty and tyranny, than of property. It is not only the best, but the only permanent measure to which civilized nations can resort, to ascertain their quantum of either, and for discovering whether tyranny is growing or decaying. What was the object of assuming the State debts, and appreciating depreciated paper? Money. What is the object of the banking exclusive privilege? Money. What is the object of the protecting-duty policy? Money. What is the object of extravagant expenditure and heavy taxation? Money. What is the object of the loaning system? Money. What is the object of the enormous pension list? Money. And what suggested the lottery mode of getting power? Money. As a measure therefore of liberty or tyranny, money is infinitely more correct than any other, and mankind are therefore oftener guided by it, than by all others.

Philosophers have observed that the present age contains the rudiments of that which is to follow; and the accuracy with which the observation has been verified by our experience, is remarkable. Funding, banking, loaning, protecting duties, pensions, extravagance, and heavy taxation, have followed each other in orderly succession. When then is the halcyon future, the happy millennium, promised by all money-getting projects to arrive? When a new child of this family is born, he never dies; but lives to see a long line of grand children wallowing like himself, in money. It would be some comfort to the present age if it was certain that its sufferings would secure liberty and happiness for its posterity. This pure philanthropy, the most gratifying compensation to benevolence for its labours and privations, made the hardships of the revolutionary war light. To forget ourselves for the benefit of posterity, is magnanimity; but when we can only preserve posterity from oppression by remembering ourselves, insensibility both for our own sufferings, and those of posterity, deserves a very different character. If it is true that the present age sows the seeds of happiness or misery for future ages, shall we gratify that exalted species of philanthropy, which induced the revolutionary patriots to win and transmit liberty to their descendants, by sowing exclusive privileges, monopolies, and heavy taxation, under a notion, that the relicks of a theory left to us by these venerated patriots, like the bones of a saint, are able to work miracles for its preservation? When cockle is sown with wheat, does it not gradually get the upper hand, and invariably eat it out.

In addressing nations, by conforming to a maxim which they strenuously believe to contain the most perfect definition of liberty and tyranny, we advocate their own opinion, and only give efficacy to their own conviction. All reflecting individuals, except those bribed by self-interest, believe that liberty can only be preserved by a frugal government, and by excluding frauds for transferring property from one man to another. In no definition of it has even its enemies asserted, that liberty consisted of monopolies, extensive privileges, legal transfers of private property, and heavy taxation. In defining a tyrant, it is not necessary to prove that he is a cannibal. How then is tyranny to be ascertained? In no other perfect way that I can discern, except as something which takes away our money, transfers our property and comforts to those who did not earn them, and eats the food belonging to others.

To prevent these convictions from telling nations when tyranny is coming, the generosity which too often flows from the people towards their governments, in a stream so copious as to wash away the foundations of their liberty, is used in modes which have enslaved them. Declamation represents frugality as niggardly and base; and flattery calls extravagance, liberal and exalted. Thus, the purest of all virtues is robbed of her garb to disguise the worst of all vices. Stripped of its stolen feathers, the jay is easily known; and the flatterers of nations will appear as an higher order of parasites, differing only from those who work upon vain and giddy individuals, in having views more extensive, and causing calamities more cruel. What a hopeless doctrine do these declaimers and flatterers preach to nations? Experience has demonstrated over and over again, that a free government cannot subsist in union with extravagance, heavy taxation, exclusive privileges, or with any established process by which a great amount of property is annually transferred to unproductive employments. Such a system is tyranny. How then can it harmonise or live in the same country with liberty? But liberty is always addressed by it, as if she was vain, foolish, and even blind; as if she was only fortune. A free government can only be made lasting by frugality and justice; but it is said that frugality and justice are niggardly and base, and that only extravagance and fraud are liberal and great. Must nations then either lose their liberty, or act basely to preserve it? Have we grossly erred in mistaking Washington for a patriot? His frugality was not liberality to a nation, but niggardly and base. Both he and Jefferson were ignorant of the sublime in politicks, and these two narrow-minded men, only grovelled in the sordid principles necessary to preserve a free government. Are the patriots who have struggled for practical liberty, and devoted their lives to the real good of mankind, already eclipsed by the splendours of extravagance, and the frauds of patronage? A sympathy for general happiness is illiberal, and an abhorrence of all modes by which industry is pilfered, is dishonest. Such is the argument by which the facts now to be urged are attempted to be defeated, and such is the obloquy to which the inferences they furnish are exposed.

By comparing the former with the existing transfer of property, the difference in amount, allowing for the difference in population, will disclose the quantum of our former liberty and our existing tyranny: To come at truth we must take into the computation the expenses of all our governments, and the acquisitions of all our sinecures and exclusive privileges. The difference in amount between the property now transferred, and that transferred in the time of Washington, proves, that we have at least fifty times more tyranny and less liberty than we then had, considering the fall in the prices of products. At that time, less than one fifth of the value of our exported commodities paid all our expenses, or balanced all uncompensated transfers of property; now, these expenses or transfers absorb an amount of property twice or thrice exceeding the value of all our exported commodities. The reader will recollect the former computation to ascertain the respective quotas of liberty enjoyed by the people at each period; and, although like myself, he may not possess the materials for coming at accuracy, yet, by devoting some attention to the computation, he will discover that the difference is enormous.

Taxation disguised in any way, is disguised tyranny, so far as it exceeds the genuine necessities of a good government. It is disguised by giving different names to different taxes, because capitation taxes are allowed to be highly oppressive. But in fact, all taxes are capitation. In every form they are paid by individuals, and ultimately fall on heads. Taxation is also disguised to a great extent, by calling the taxes paid to exclusive privileges, by other names, though there is no distinction between these taxes and those paid to governments, except that the latter are necessary, and the former unnecessary. They both fall on heads, and the heavier they are, the more these heads lose of that erect posture maintained under a light weight. Recollect reader, that you are paying heavy capitation taxes to exclusive privileges, and then boast of your liberty if you can. Is a maniac, who believes himself to be a king, really a king? Are the European nations really free? Yes, if heavy taxation to supply the extravagance of governments, and enrich exclusive privileges, constitutes liberty. Are they oppressed? Yes, if enormous taxes for both purposes constitute oppression. What! are they both free and oppressed? Yes, if money is not a measure of both liberty and tyranny. By rejecting this practical measure, and confining our ideas to the political theory of the United States, we have nearly or quite obtained that kind of liberty enjoyed by the Europeans; theoretical, but not actual. But by measuring tyranny with the correct standard of money, we discern that the kind under which they suffer is near at hand, or already arrived, and may resolve to receive it with open arms or clenched hands, as we choose. To determine which is the case, we have only to compare our taxes paid to governments and exclusive privileges, with those paid by other nations, and we should probably discover that no countries, except Britain and Holland, are equally oppressed by this real species of tyranny. I doubt whether these are, but if they are, numerically, the burden is less oppressive, because they are aided in bearing it by valuable foreign possessions, a highly improved system of agriculture, and a surplus of manufactures; auxiliaries which we are without. If therefore we rival them in taxation, we must excel them in oppression. But this would not be the case, if money was not a correct measure for ascertaining the approach or the arrival of tyranny.

Naples is despised by the world for surrendering her liberty to a physical force; the United States are surrendering theirs to political frauds. To which country will future historians assign the greatest portion of moral degradation? May they not say that Naples could not have maintained her liberty if she wished it, but that the United States could have kept theirs if they would? Naples had to contend with an overwhelming army of soldiers; the United States with only a small unarmed faction. There would be but one excuse for the United States. It might be said that it was as natural to conquer liberty by patronage, taxation, and exclusive privileges, as for tyrants to conquer it by armies; and that there is in fact no difference between the two modes of subjugation, because both terminate in the same result. It may be further urged, that both modes are executed by troops equally merce-nary, equally disciplined, and equally ready to obey orders; and that if a regular army is an overmatch for an undisciplined militia, a government combined with troops of exclusive privileges, must also be an overmatch for the unorganized, unpaid, and unsuspicious militia of equal rights. This is an argument of great force for placing Naples and the United States upon the same ground, and also for justifying efforts to put the weapon of information into the hands of equal rights, to be opposed to the stratagems of a mercenary and disciplined civil army. It is only like putting arms into the hands of the militia, and teaching them their use, for repelling the invasions of the other species of hired troops.

In this great republic, comprising a variety of climates and interests, it is impossible to keep equal rights long asleep, and if they are awakened by violent blows, the consequence will be a revolution. Such blows are already falling upon great districts; and upon all occupations except the privileged. Money will at length be discovered to be the best measure of liberty or tyranny, and when by using this measure it is discerned that some districts suffer more tyranny than others, and that the privileged pecuniary occupations enjoy more liberty than the rest of the nation, a civil war, or a revolution without a civil war, will be the consequence. The inland regions are already more oppressed than the maritime, because they have fewer resources to bear the tyranny introduced by the instrumentality of money; that is, by extravagance, exclusive privileges, loaning, and pensions, for transferring property from the many to the few. Even if the seat of government was removed to an inland situation, these frauds would continue to be chiefly monopolized by a few maritime capitalists; the remedy would be confined to a small circle around the capital; and a great majority of the people every where would continue to be sufferers; because the proportion of individuals, possessing and knowing how to use capital, sufficient to accumulate wealth by the intricate speculations of the property-transferring policy, is quite inconsiderable. In the inland regions this disparity is greatest, and must for ever remain so, from the superior facilities for acquiring capital afforded by maritime situations, and therefore the inland regions must suffer most by this policy. And however indignantly the vast majority of the maritime people ought to receive the suggestion of a partial compensation for the money of which it is defrauded, from the residence among them of a few individuals, in whose hands it is accumulated; the inland people must participate far more slightly even in this most inadequate retribution. Every species of internal taxation, and especially excises, contemplated by the Committee as the resource for sustaining the property-transferring policy into which we have plunged, will conspire with the frauds of this policy to destroy the Union. Pecuniary oppression drives men from republican into monarchical governments; it will more easily induce them to dissolve the Union, and try some other republican form. Frugality, a suppression of frauds for transferring property, and light taxation, or a great mercenary army, are therefore the only means for preserving the Union, and between these we must choose. The avarice and ambition of individuals would be nothing in a conflict with a love for the government, which would be inspired by a system of frugality and justice, diffusing equal liberty and general happiness. But the inequalities and oppressions attending heavy taxation and exclusive privileges, create materials for ambition; and laws for fostering avarice complete a system contrived for gratifying the two passions, by which governments are either overthrown or made despotick.

In about twenty years the French revolutionary government passed, it is said, between seven and eight thousand laws; of which, about one hundred now remain in force. I know not a better proof of bad government than a perpetual flood of time-serving laws. To this flood of legislation is justly ascribed much of the concurrent dissatisfaction which subverted theory after theory, and terminated in an impetuous recurrence to a military despotism. In the United States about four thousand laws are annually passed, amounting in forty-five years to one hundred and eighty thousand. When there were fewer States, the annual number of our laws may have been less, but now it is probably more. In future, if the rage for legislation continues, the number of laws will considerably exceed this computation. A great majority of these laws are passed for the purpose of transferring property from the people to patronized individuals or combinations. They are annually shaving and shaving the fruits of industry, and have greatly contributed towards reducing it down to its present state. It is at length nearly drowned by this deluge of legislation. What must be the consequence of a perseverance in this pernicious habit? If it is an evil of portentous and present magnitude, ought not its cause to be sought for and removed, by all those who prefer a good to a bad government? Have the individuals who compose legislative bodies no such preference? Ought they to pervert money from the office of multiplying enjoyments, to that of contracting them; from the end of exchanging and increasing comforts, to that of transferring them? Is not this tyranny?

If our inundation of laws fosters real and practical tyranny, it ought to be checked, and the check is suggested by the cause. This is undoubtedly high legislative wages, which have fostered a habit of transferring property, in order to reap pay. It is not contended that the wages of public officers, the legislative excepted, are too high; or that their rate has had any pernicious effect towards introducing the

oppressive system of transferring property by law; of nurturing extravagance, and of increasing taxation. Let the distinction between legislative,
and other public officers, arising from the difference between employing
one's time occasionally in public service, or devoting a whole life to it,
be waved; and the consideration of the two cases to be confined to the
consequences of high salaries to legislative and other public officers.
The wages of other public officers are limited; legislative wages are not
only increased by a prolongation of sessions; but this prolongation
causes also an increase of expenditure, because it can only be effected
by patronizing the frauds of individuals. The former salaries being
defined, are kept within reasonable bounds by public attention; the
latter are incidentally increased without attracting the public attention,
by wasting time in transferring property, and thus doubly aggravating
taxation; evils which other public officers cannot introduce for the
purpose of increasing their wages, and uniting to aggravate pecuniary
oppression. The argument in favour of high legislative wages, is, that
poor merit is thereby enabled to serve the public; but if they have the
effect of corrupting this merit, and inducing it for the sake of pecuniary
acquisitions, to hurt the public by an inundation of laws for transferring
its property to individuals and combinations; the argument entirely
fails unless it can be proved, as the transferring policy seems to suppose,
that the public has no property; and though legislatures have no moral
or constitutional right to give one man's property to another; yet that
by combining the property of all men under the appellation "public,"
they acquire both a moral and constitutional right to give the property
of all men, to one man. To corrupt legislation by sordid motives, is a
mode of obtaining individual merit, from which nations reap no
benefit, but much oppression. Patriotism is legislative merit. But if it
is induced by high wages to inundate a country with laws, and especially
with those for transferring property, it is transformed into avarice, and
a plunderer of the people. If the eminence and honour of legislative
power ceases to be the only compensation to a legislator, beyond his
bare expenses, he ceases to be chaste; because if he feels the inducement
of money, he will feel for himself, and not for the community. He
must legislate from motives entirely patriotick and unselfish, or he
will legislate fraudulently; and nations must elect between legislatures
actuated by one, or the other motive. High wages are incompatible

with disinterestedness; and low wages the only security against the influence of avarice in obtaining a seat, or exercising legislation. The existing *furor* for legislating, is a formidable foe to a true, honest, and liberty-sustaining system of political economy, from its necessity for new objects upon which to exercise itself. There are two kinds of political economy. One consists of a frugal government, and an encouragement of individuals to earn, by suffering them to use; the other of contrivances for feeding an extravagant government, its parasites and partisans, its sinecures and exclusive privileges; one makes a nation rich and happy; the other creates enormous capitals in a few hands, at the national expense; one requires but few laws, and few tax gatherers; the other requires a multitude of both; one must have penalties and petty officers without number, to enforce its own frauds; the other being founded in justice, has no use for these instruments to prevent or punish treasons against fraud; one demonstrates the existence of a politick people, who know how to keep their property; the other demonstrates the existence of a political combination, which knows how to get their property; one kind of political economy, is liberty; the other is tyranny. When we see the bad kind cultivated with zeal, and the good kind treated with contempt, we are forced to conclude that selfishness has inspired the ardour, otherwise inexplicable. Economy is frugality. How can the economy which teaches governments to extort all they can from the people, and to accumulate their burdens by loans, bounties, exclusive privileges, and extravagance, be distinguished from the economy of the landlord who grinds his tenants, that he may be a prodigal? The frugality of transferring property by partial laws; a wasteful frugality, a fraudulent frugality, is the European species of political economy, by which real tyranny is inflicted upon the people, under any form of government. Can it be admired by a politick nation? Our deluge of laws proves, that our legislatures have been tempted by some motive to run into this European species of political economy. Is it worth the increase of legislative wages, which we have paid for it? Few laws are necessary to preserve property; a multitude are required for transferring it. The last intention furnishes endless employment for legislatures, and the multiplication of laws is an evidence of the intention. The design and effect of four thousand new laws annually in the United States, is no longer matter for conjecture. If it cannot be seen, it must be felt. Their operation in transferring property has produced general distress, and exorbitant individual wealth. This is tyranny, if tyranny can be measured by money; and the question seems to be, Whether it is good policy in a nation to pay high legislative wages for the purpose of purchasing tyranny?

The present fashionable art of defeating the essential principles of the Federal constitution, sometimes by adhering to, and at others by amplifying its letter, is a formidable accomplice of the tyranny-bearing species of political economy. As governments mould manners, this disastrous constructive taste has tinctured the plain good sense of the people, and diverted it from the only effective, to the most frivolous, temper, for preserving their liberty. By exchanging the great principles established to secure it, for verbal constructions which prove any thing or nothing, the reservation of State powers is easily destroyed; and by the aid of an inundation of laws, the people are made the prey of exclusive privileges. Thus, the right of the States to tax, is taken from the States and transferred to bankers, who are empowered to tax a State to enrich themselves, whilst the State is prohibited from taxing them to support its government. Thus, also, the right of taxing States by lotteries is bestowed, and a power of taxation for public good is withheld, to confer powers of taxation for fostering private avarice. Thus, the preservation of good manners is taken from the States, and entrusted to combinations, whose own manners want improvement. And thus Congress has invented by the judicial law, a process by the name of a writ of error, equivalent to the odious writ of *quo warranto,* once used in England by the king and his judges, to destroy the rights of corporations. By our substitute the end is effected, as if Congress had empowered the judges to issue a writ of *quo warranto* directly against the State governments. The only difference between the cases is, that the English *quo warranto* destroyed all the rights of corporations at a blow, and that ours destroys the rights of State governments by degrees. But the end of both proceedings is the same; in England, it was to make corporations subservient to royal pleasure; here, it is to make State governments subservient to Federal pleasure. A dependence of corporations upon the will of the king, was evidently a subversion of the principles of the English government. If a dependence of State rights upon the will of Congress is also a subversion of the principles of our form of government, may not our *quo warranto* process, under a new name, be a tendency towards tyrannical government; if the true principles of our form of government are as good as those of the English form for the preservation of liberty? The security of State rights may be as essential to our liberty, as the security of corporate rights was supposed to be in England; and a consolidation of States subservient to Congress, as dangerous to it, as a consolidation of corporations into a subserviency to royal sovereignty; especially if a consolidated republic over our vast territories, should turn out to be impracticable. These writs of error are as good instruments for establishing the property transferring policy, as the *quo warranto* was in England. For this purpose they have been used in the bank and lottery cases to come at the money or property of the people.

Political economy measures itself by money, and it therefore admits, that like money it may be used to establish either liberty or tyranny. To introduce the latter, it constantly asserts that contributions for creating great individual capitals, or taking away their money, is in fact, giving money to the people. Yet all writers agree, that capital can only be created by the industry and frugality of individuals. In governments, however, where the design is to transfer the capitals thus earned and saved, cause and effect are cunningly transposed, and it is pretended, that capital begets industry and frugality, instead of their begetting capital. Having taught the people to adopt this egregious error, the false species of political economy is freed from restraint, and entrenched against detection. It then launches into many contrivances for transferring property, under pretence that capital creates industry; and for impoverishing the people to create an order of rich capitalists, under pretence that this order will enrich the people. Writers, subject to this fraudulent species of political economy, are objects of compassion. They writhe under the effort to find natural causes for its effects, or to convert artificial phenomena into effects of natural causes. Hence they form complicated systems about labour, stock, profits, wages, rents, capital, and wealth, compounded of facts, without distinguishing those which may be called natural, from those which are artificial. By excluding from their systems an exposition of the artificial and fraudulent modes, used to produce the facts with which they build their theories, they have relinquished the true causes of the apparent phenomena, and assumed the artificial and legal causes of the existing European system of political economy, as being the legitimate children of nature. They have shrunk from the facts, that no one system of European economy regards natural rights; that all are merely artificial; that none are bottomed upon the freedom of industry and the safety of property; that no one enables individuals who earn capital, to save and employ it for their own use; that it is the object of all to transfer as much as possible of individual earnings to capitalists; to monopolize and not to diffuse capital; that these stratagems are fluctuating; and that their success is tyranny to a vast majority of every nation. How can these systems of political economy be relied upon, when they have excluded the consideration of the artificial modes by which the effects have been produced from which they reason; and of all those natural rights which a true and honest system of political economy will respect and preserve? Is it true, as they assert, that natural causes and not fraudulent laws, produce the transfers of property by which capital is accumulated, and nations enslaved? Were the feudal, the hierarchical, the banking, the funding, the lottery, and the protecting-duty modes of accumulating wealth in a few hands, all forged in nature's workhouse? Instead of detecting fraudulent laws, and then reasoning from the principle, that free will, industry, demand and supply, would naturally regulate the acquisition of capital; all the European systems of political economy, finally draw their conclusions, however copiously they may be sprinkled with just principles, from legal abuses. Their facts being chiefly delusive, as flowing from corrupted sources, their conclusions are all accommodated to the policy of transferring property by law.

Our protecting-duty system, borrowed from fallacious European theories, is only defended by the same mode of reasoning. The report previously examined has entirely excluded a consideration of natural rights; and wholly neglected to enquire what are the effects of the legal modes which we have adopted for transferring property and accumulating capitals, upon these rights; whether they have been good or bad, and whether they have both accumulated a few great capitals, and also enriched the people, as they have long been promising. Has political economy nothing to do with the legal and artificial causes which have conspired with unavoidable but temporary circumstances, to produce our distresses? Can it discover no difference between the payment of five or an hundred millions annually; taking into the account the fall in the price of products; by productive to unproductive labour? Is it unable to discern, that if money appreciates and prices fall, the distresses of productive labour must be correspondently increased by legal or artificial transfers of property, remaining, as measured by money, numerically the same? What becomes of its pretended sympathy for the general distress, when it shuts its eyes upon the chief circumstance by which it is caused? How can it cure evils which it will not see? It will not see that enormous transfers of property from industry to capitalists, is tyranny to the rest of the nation. It will not see that an appreciation of money and a depreciation of products has aggravated this tyranny. It will not see that the remedy is only to be found in a repeal of the legal modes for transferring property. It will not see that the oppression ought at least to be softened by reducing these transfers to the value meditated by the laws imposing them, instead of leaving them to be doubled or trebled in value, contrary to the intention of these laws, by suffering casualties to become legislators. But it can see that contributions to capitalists, though accidentally doubled or trebled, ought to be further increased by new laws. Is this species of political economy, blind to phenomena so glaring, blind to the general benefits resulting to the community from leaving capital in the hands of industry, and awake only to the policy of transferring it to a few capitalists, to be mistaken for a patriot upon its own word and honour? Or is it the very species of political economy adopted by European governments to plunder the people, and defended by European writers, to court the favour of wealth and power?

If I was examined upon oath, *in perpetuam rei memoriam,* my deposition would be as follows: This deponent saith, that he was twenty-one years of age at the commencement of the revolutionary war, from whence to this time he has paid all the attention in his power to the progress of public affairs, and to the prosperity and happiness of individuals, for which his opportunities have been considerable. That he believes both national prosperity and private happiness to have been considerably greater in the times of Washington and Jefferson than at present, and that he thinks the difference is entirely owing to the difference between the rates of taxation, the amounts of property transferred by exclusive privileges, and the restrictions upon commerce, at the respective periods.

To the truth of this deposition the report of the Committee bears ample testimony. It declares "that no national interest is in a healthful condition." Capitalists are made sick by a plethora, and the people by too much evacuation. Do not these diagnosticks prescribe the remedy? We may trace these maladies from a few historical causes. A very extensive predilection for the English form of government existed at the commencement of the revolution, embracing a multitude of men of great talents, distinction, and virtue. Of these a small number became tories, as they were called; that is, they conscientiously preferred the English, and were adverse to a republican form of government. But by far the greater number, yielding to public opinion, were dragged by it to independence. Many of these, however, retained buried in their bosoms, an affection for the English form of government, and only transferred the predilection from its existence in England to its existence in this country. It certainly arose from an honest conviction, but this conviction was as certainly produced by former habits of thinking, and not by an unprejudiced estimate of the principles, most likely to produce national prosperity and individual happiness here. It is well known that at the termination of the revolutionary war, an intrigue was formed; not by the tories, who remained excluded from public confidence and public affairs; but by gentlemen of great influence, talents, and integrity, to introduce something like the English form of government; that a strenuous and ingenious effort was made to gain the army; that a crown or something like it was offered to the general; and that he magnanimously rejected the temptation. This rejection is a proof that Washington preferred our Federal policy, imperfect as it was, both to the English form of government, and to the consolidated republic. Shall we follow or renounce his example? Shall we receive a consolidated republic or a monarchy from pecuniary combinations and the supreme court, which he could not be induced to approve of by the most brilliant temptation, nor by the authority of many of his compatriots? We cannot all be made kings.

The defects of the old union soon suggested its improvement, and the convention for this purpose took place, before the predictions which had suggested the experiment upon the popular leader of a veteran army, were diminished. They were not effaced, because they could not find a Bonaparte, and being still alive, they naturally produced propositions for introducing a consolidated republic, by reducing the States to corporations, entirely dependent on the Federal government. These were probably sustained by the same arguments which had recently been urged to Washington to effect a similar purpose; but they were finally rejected. This rejection discloses a disapprobation of a consolidated republic by a majority of the convention, and subjoins to the opinion of Washington, the solemn judgment against this form of government, of a body of men as enlightened as any which were ever assembled. The weight of authority, patriotism, and talents, was thus so far opposed to a consolidated republic which is attempted to be introduced, without having recourse to any similar tribunal. But the respectable minority which then attempted by fair means to introduce it, caused an alarm. The secret leaked out, and suggested amendments to the constitution, for the purpose of preventing future indirect attempts to introduce a consolidated republic. "The powers, not delegated to the United States by the constitution, nor prohibited by it to the States, are reserved to the States respectively, or to the people." If such was not the sole intention of this amendment, it had no intention at all; if it was to defeat this intention by absorbing these reserved State powers into a consolidated republic, it is unconstitutional.

The constitution came into operation when the predilection for the English form of government, or for a consolidated republic, still subsisted, and the respectable minority by whom it was conscientiously entertained, were soon reinforced by powerful auxiliaries. The partial funding system suddenly created a mercenary faction, fearful of losing a vast unearned acquisition, and well qualified as partisans for the power which bestowed and could only secure it. The old tories gradually re-instated themselves in public confidence, and brought an accession of principles favourable to a consolidation of power. Exclusive privileges for getting money were invented, and concurred with a gradual but vast increase of taxation, to bring over many detachments of mercenary troops, to a consolidating policy. And these successive reinforcements more powerful and less virtuous than Washington and his army, have united indirectly to introduce a consolidated republic positively rejected by the convention.

In favour of this old project entertained at the conclusion of the revolutionary war, and renewed in the convention, the old arguments then secretly urged, are now openly repeated. The States, it is said, will obstruct or defeat the measures of the Federal government, unless they are subjected to a negative on the part of that government upon their own internal measures; and also to an affirmative power, by which Congress and the Court may make internal local laws. A single State may make local laws contrary to the will of all the other States. Ambitious men may use their State influence, to disorder Federal affairs, and even to destroy the Union. The checking power of election is more to be relied on, when exercised by all the States, than when exercised by one. And a supreme federal power over all, is necessary to prevent these inconveniences. Such arguments were undoubtedly urged and refuted in the convention. They defend the proposition made and rejected in that body for establishing a consolidated, in preference to a federal, republic. But the existing attempt to introduce the former, is infinitely more objectionable, than that made in the convention. There, it was proposed to invest Congress with a negative or restraining power over the State governments; now, it is proposed to invest the Supreme Court with it. The difference between these remedies manifestly involves an essential contrariety in principle. The combined elective power of all the States may reach one chamber of Congress, and might check, in some degree, a negative or restrictive power in that body over the State governments; but it cannot reach a single member of the Court, nor influence in the least degree such a power in that body. The elective check would have been attentive to a negative or restraining power in Congress over the States, because it could reach and control it; but it must be wholly inattentive to that power in the Court, because it can neither reach nor control it. The elective check, relied upon to defend a sovereign controlling power in Congress over the States, yields no defence against the same power in the Supreme Court; and therefore, though the minority which proposed, in the convention, to invest Congress with this power, might have contended that it would be in part subjected to this indispensable principle for the preservation of liberty, the same minority would have allowed, that a similar power in the Court would have been founded in the principle which defines tyranny, as being a great political power, without any elective responsibility. It conclusively results, that the mode of consolidation by the instrumentality of the Supreme Court, is infinitely more adverse to the great principle necessary to preserve a free government, than that proposed and rejected in the convention.

But passing by the claim of the Supreme Court, to a negative or restrictive power over the State governments, in the exercise of their reserved powers, as too inconsistent with the representative principle, even to have been proposed by the admirers of the English policy themselves, the project of investing Congress with this power, though rejected by the convention, is again forced upon our consideration. It is said, that it is safer to rely upon the elective principle, when exercised by all the States, than when exercised by one. I deny that this assertion is either constitutionally or logically maintainable. Not constitutionally, because the elective principle is co-extensively used and relied upon for the preservation both of State and Federal rights, and instead of intending that one moiety of this principle shall swallow up the other, each moiety had a distinct office assigned to it; one half was to superintend Federal powers, and the other half State powers. The elective principle in one State, never had a moral or actual right, to control the elective principle in another State, and having no such power itself, it could not convey such a power either to Congress or the Supreme Court. The people of all the States, far from claiming a power over the elective principle in each State, have themselves, if they are to be considered as collectively the authors of the constitution, explicitly reserved it to themselves, for the regulation and superintendence of the State powers also reserved. If such was not the case, if the State powers reserved and the elective principle were bestowed by the people of all the States, the people of no State would have a right to alter their constitutions, or control their governments, because these constitutions, and the powers of the State governments were established by the supreme authority of the people of all the States. The supreme authority which reserved State powers, could only modify or take them away,

and, until this is done, each State government would have a right to
hold and exercise under the authority of the people of the United
States, exactly the powers, neither more nor less, reserved to it by this
supposed supreme power of the people of all the States, over the people
of one State; because the inferior elective principle could have no right
to undo that which the superior elective principle had established. But
of this supreme elective principle in the people of all the States, over
the elective principle in each State, as to reserved State rights, never
did exist, and never was recognised, then as to these reserved rights,
the elective principle in one State remains independent of the elective
principle in every other, and possesses the inherent moral right of
individual self-defence.

But how can the posture masters of words, dispose of the clear and
explicit term "respectively" used in amendment of the constitution?
Could a plainer [word] have been found in the English language to
express its meaning? Powers are reserved to the United States "respectively." Whatever these were, they were reserved by this expression
separately and not collectively to the States. Either the right of internal
self-government was among them, or no State has any such right.
Among them, also, was the unimpaired right of election in the people
of each State, for the purpose of local State government, or the people
of no State have any such right. The people of each State held no other
power which the reservation could secure. The reservation of this right,
would have been quite nugatory, coupled with a power in Congress
and the Supreme Court to render it inoperative. State local rights,
being reserved separately to each State, cannot be either preserved, or
taken away by the States collectively; and a right of separate preservation
must attend each separate reservation, or the reservation is void. Many
men have no authority to defend one man's title to his estate. Massachusetts could not resist the aggression upon the local law of Virginia by
the Supreme Court in the lottery case, nor that upon the local law of
Ohio in the bank case. It was for this unanswerable reason, that the
right of internal self-government was reserved to the States separately
or respectively. There existed no medium between this separate reservation, and a consolidated republic which was proposed and rejected.
Had the constitution, after having reserved the right of internal self-

government to the States, or the people "respectively," added, "but Congress or the Supreme Court shall have a power to control this reservation to the States or to the people, respectively," it would have been an absurd contradiction, and the same absurdity attends such a construction of the constitution. If the States respectively, cannot resist aggressions, respectively or separately made upon the separate right of each to internal self-government, they cannot be resisted at all; because the right being separate, the resistance must necessarily be separate also, or a consolidated republic must ensue. To prevent this, the reservation was to the States "respectively." The elective power in all the States, had no original right to control the elective power in each State, or to regulate its government either externally or internally. As to the former only, the separate elective powers of the States were united; but as to the right of internal self-government, the separate elective power of each State was left untouched by the limitation of powers confided to the Federal government; and also by the positive reservation. With respect to local State government, the States were left in the same relation to each other, which existed previously to the Union; and since this relation never invested the people of all the States, with any power to regulate the internal government of one State, the people of all the States could not invest Congress or the court with a power which they had not themselves; nor could Congress by a judicial law, invest the Supreme Court with the same power. It seems therefore, quite certain, that this project for introducing a consolidated republic, is literally inconsistent with the amendment, intended to preserve a federal republic.

The expediency of investing Congress or the court, or both, with a negative power over the local acts of the State governments, opens a wider field for reasoning. If it is conceded that fellow-feeling and responsibility bestow on representation all its honesty and all its value, it must inevitably follow, that the principle of election, as exercised by all the States in reference to the Federal government, does not possess either of these essential characters of representation, in reference to the State governments. These do not exercise their reserved rights in one mode, nor adopt the same internal regulations. It cannot therefore often happen, that a conflict will take place between federal and reserved powers, which involves all the States equally; and it will but seldom happen that more than one State at a time will have occasion to resist an aggression upon its reserved rights, on account of the dissimilarity between the laws of the States respectively. In such cases the people of the other States possess neither of the essential characters of representation as to the State attached; and, therefore, by their election, they could not infuse these characters into their representatives. By considering the people of the other States or their representatives, as a representation of the people of the injured State, the great principles of election and representation for the freedom and security of internal State government, would be completely destroyed. It is obvious that sympathy and responsibility as to internal laws would be thus obliterated, or at least too feeble to repel particular aggressions upon the right of internal self-government, and that if some inoperative sympathy might exist, there would not exist a vestige of responsibility in the people of the other States, or in representatives chosen by them, to the people of the injured State. Neither of them feel an internal State law. By substituting this fungus of representation, this metaphysical prolusion, this oyster-like substratum, without an organ of active vitality, as a foundation for State rights, and the solitary security for a federal government, instead of State election and representation, the constitution is supposed to have created two of the most effectual weapons for the destruction of both which could have been devised. One is a maxim—Divide and conquer. Division is an inevitable security for victory, if the Federal government should be prudent enough to assail State rights successively, as indeed it must generally be, from the unconnectedness of State legislation. But as if this weapon was not sufficient for their demolition, it is rendered inevitably fatal by the superadded doctrine, that no one of these divisions, no single State when assailed, shall possess the right of self-defence, but must stake its existence or liberty on volunteers uninfluenced by fellow-feeling or responsibility, and who may possibly be influenced by an adverse local prejudice. If it is admitted that a division of Federal and State powers can alone prevent a consolidated republic, that this species of government threatens us with a worse, and that a genuine representation of local State rights is necessary to sustain this division; it is evident that this representation must be of the States

"respectively," or that the end cannot be effected. A proof of this
conclusion results from considering the nature of the united representation of the States. There is great ingenuity in eluding this proof. We
are told that it is the people of all the States; and that the people of all
may be more safely relied upon to preserve both State and Federal rights,
than the people of one. This is very plausible. Federal representation is
the people, therefore we have already a consolidated republic; because
the people of all the States are sovereign, representation is the people,
and sovereignty can do any thing. The guardianship of State rights,
reserved to the people of each State respectively, is thus transferred
exclusively to Congress, which may again transfer it to the Federal
court, and the work of introducing a consolidated republic is dexter-
ously finished. But what were the powers which confederated? If they
were not both something and also distinct, they could not have confederated. If they were any thing, they were different societies of people.
The existence of societies supposes a sovereignty in each society, and
this sovereignty can only be found in the people of each State as
associated. If the Constitution is not a confederation, but the work of
all the people of all the States, acting individually and not in an
associated capacity, they yet thought it expedient for the preservation
of their own liberties, to establish a Federal government for some
purposes, and State governments for others; and resorted to representation for effecting both objects; but it is now urged that in this they
acted unwisely; and thus we are brought back to the old question of a
consolidated republic, considered and rejected by the people themselves; if the convention was the people, and the project secretly proposed is now openly advocated, not in a convention, but by unknown,
avaricious, or ambitious individuals.

The most recondite artifice and contradiction, and yet the most
effectual for destroying the division of power once thought to be
expedient and wise, couches under the great argument used to effect
this object. Shall the people of one State construe the constitution for
the people of all the States? The ingenuity of this argument consists in
its capacity for receiving, from the advocates of a consolidated republic,
the answers both no and yes. If the question is divided, and they are
first asked, whether one State can defend its reserved rights, they answer

No; but if they are asked whether Federal powers can be extended, through the instrumentality of one State, they answer Yes. In this case one State may construe the constitution for all the States, because it will advance the project of a consolidated republic; but not in the other, because it will sustain a federal republic. Thus, if one State submits to have one of its reserved powers questioned, tried, and abolished by the Federal court, this submission and decision becomes a precedent for construing the constitution, though the act of one State only; and is binding on all the States in the eyes of the consolidating project, though they were not parties to this species of political or constitutional law-suit, any more than they would be parties to a political collision between the Federal and a State government. Accordingly the bank suit of Maryland is to bind Ohio, and the lottery suit of Virginia is to bind all the other States. It might even happen that some interested but secret motive might, by these law-suits, bring in question State powers, with an apparent affectation of defending them, but a real intention of losing them; and that thus these State powers might be gradually retrenched and finally destroyed by the collusions of individuals. In point of wisdom, safety, and expediency, which is best—to depend upon ex parte or collusive law-suits for the construction of the constitution, which may alter it without the consent of the people or the States; or to depend upon the elective power of the people of each State, to keep their representatives within the bounds of the constitution? By one mode of construing the constitution, the right of internal self-government is lost to all the States; by the other, all retain it, because the resistance of one State to an unconstitutional aggression, leaves the rest free to use their own judgments, and to resist or not, according to their own will, should they also be attacked. But the mode of making constitutions as common law is made, by precedents made by judges, is conclusive upon the States, without any exercise of their judgments at all. If inconveniences may attend the right of a State to construe the constitution; which are however more speculative than real; yet it may be better to suffer them, than to incur the misfortune of a consolidated republic; or at least inferiour to those which will arise from suffering the Supreme Court by the instrumentality of one State, or some faction, or some individual fraud, to splinter the constitution. Election is a powerful remedy against inconveniences arising from the former policy; it is none against those arising from the latter. It would be strange, whilst we cling to the idea of representation in making laws, that we should imagine it to be unwise in making constitutions. Ambition however has always thought it highly inconvenient. Here, as is commonly observable in the freest countries, it is particularly ingenious. It proposes to destroy a real and active majority, by the idea of an imaginary and inactive majority; and a representation in fact, by pretending that it will produce more inconveniences than no representation at all. According to this recent doctrine, no one political department can vindicate the powers committed to it by the conventional majority, because no one department represents a majority of people in all the United States. This conventional majority being dead, and incapable of current use, is however made to furnish an idea with which to destroy the rights of the political departments created by it when alive. But the argument proves too much for those who use it. The climax by which it is brought out is this. The constitution is the act of the people of the United States; those representing a majority of these people, have the exclusive right of construing it; but the State governments do not represent this majority; and therefore they cannot construe it at all. If the argument is sound, the conclusion is, that as no political department represents a majority of the people of the United States, none can construe the Constitution. The legislative Federal department is far from doing so, from the construction of the Senate; and the House of Representatives is only one constituent of that department, of itself, imbecile. The argument, however, is unsound under any policy, by which a majority establishes divisions of power, because the checks and balances of such a policy are exercised, not by departments representing a majority, but by departments acting under the authority of the majority which created them; and if these divisions are deprived of the right of self-preservation, by which only such checks and balances can effect the objects intended, it is, under a feigned submission, an actual rebellion against the majority by which they were established. Therefore the powers of the States being bestowed or reserved by a majority of the States or of the people, no matter which; any State would disobey the majority, and thus betray the national right of self-government in the federal form, by suffering itself to be deprived of these powers. A division and a consolidation; checks and no checks; cannot exist together. Political checks are designed to counterpoise each other, and the majority which creates them, never intends that a pretended veneration for an inoperative idea of itself, should defeat its own precautions to preserve its own liberty. The majority which made the Federal Constitution, defined the only modes by which a majority for altering it could be brought into operation, and this definition proves that an inoperative idea of a speechless majority, was not contemplated as sufficient to destroy the divisions of power, established by an articulating majority. The provision for an articulating majority, was suggested by the consideration, that political divisions of power were not subjected to any other tribunal. Loyalty was expected from these divisions of power by the majority which created them, in exercising and defending their respective trusts; and by providing a mode for supervising them, by a majority only both of the people and of the States, it disclosed an intention that they should be supervised in no other mode. The specified supervising political tribunal would have been unnecessary, if the supreme court had been contemplated as such a tribunal. Suppose it had been proposed in the convention "that, for the preservation of the Union, no political department, not representing a majority of the people of all the United States, should have a right to defend and maintain the powers allotted to it." Would the adoption of this amendment have been wise or expedient? Yet its adoption would have been exactly equivalent to the chief argument, by which the right of defending themselves individually is denied to the States.

This argument is enforced by the most exquisite derision of the States, of the people, and of human nature itself; the derision of contempt under an affectation of fear. It is gravely suggested that the Union is endangered by the ambition of the States. And what are the proofs of this tremendous ambition which meditates the destruction of the confederation? One State prohibits within its own territory an exclusive banking privilege, and another, the sale of lottery tickets. Is it not a broad grin at common sense to tell it, that such local State powers will destroy the Union? It was once asserted that the alien and sedition laws, like banking and lotteries, were necessary to preserve the Union. They are dead and the Union lives. Had the States resisted those laws successfully, by judicially liberating the persons unconstitutionally prosecuted under them, a great outcry would have been uttered by the consolidating party, that the Union was destroyed; yet it would have stood exactly where it now does. If the banking and lottery laws were also dead, might not the Union still live? Did either of these State resistances touch any of the Federal powers necessary to maintain the Union, or disclose the least symptom of ambition in any State to obtain any active power? The general interest was excited, though slowly, by the alien and sedition laws; because, though partially executed, they were of a general import, and produced a remedy, of which encroachments interesting only to one State are not susceptible. The laws were consigned to the grave, and the party which made them dislodged from power. Was this destructive of the Union, or did it teach a consolidating faction, that it was safer to assail the States in detail, than by general attacks? Two observations of great force present themselves; one, that as the Federal government was designed to operate generally upon all the States for the sake of union, its partial operation upon one or a few, dismembers the intended combination and reinstates separate inimical interests; and is therefore radically unconstitutional, as defeating the very end and design of the Constitution; the other, that these frivolous charges of ambition, though egregiously magnified by all the arts of misrepresentation, only demonstrate that no such ambition exists, or that the States do not possess the means for gratifying it.

But the same frivolity furnishes very different evidence against the Federal government. By exercising or assailing trifling local powers, having no force able to destroy the Union, and not weakening the great powers with which the Federal government is invested to preserve it, an intention of gradually establishing a consolidated republic, by which the very term "federal" will be substantially effaced from our political code, and the Union radically destroyed, is demonstrated. I know a rich man, having a large estate of fertile land, whilst his poor neighbour owned only one hundred adjoining acres of inferior quality. Upon this hundred acres, however, the rich man cast his eye; but as his neighbour did not choose to part with his land, the rich man by various little aggressions involved the poor one in successive vexatious law-suits; forced him to part, first with one acre, then with two, at length with three or four; and finally, the rich man got the whole hundred acres. Yet his partisans all along, loudly insisted, that the rich man was not avaricious, and had no design to get the poor man's land.

To advance a similar transfer of political property, it is said that the States have no original rights, and never possessed any character beyond that of mere corporations; and the inference is, that having no such original rights, their reservation had nothing to operate upon. Admitting the assertion to be true, the inference does not follow. If the people had a right to establish a government, they had a right to establish corporations. Suppose they had established a bank in each State, previously to a Federal constitution, with charters specifying the powers and rights of such corporations, and had declared by the confederation, that these powers and rights should be reserved to these existing corporations; could the Federal government have rightfully taken them away? The State constitutions are at least as good as such charters; and admitting that the convention was a meeting of the people of the United States, though such a people have never yet met, even by representation, since the Senate is not a representation of them; and that the pre-existing elements of political power were all dissolved by this ideal meeting; yet this meeting might certainly revive these elements, and divide political power among them, for the purpose of establishing a free government, or a federal republic.

I deny, however, that any such dissolution of existing political elements took place. So far from it, the political element of election and representation in the States respectively and separately, was that to which the Federal constitution was referred, and by which it was established. Did the meeting of the convention dissolve this political element? If so, it could not possess any right to establish or reject the constitution. Did the establishment of the constitution destroy both this political element and the State governments; if so, as the constitution does not re-create either, both these elements wrongfully exist. If they exist rightfully, not being created by the constitution, they exist separately and independently of the constitution, and of course independently of the people of the United States, even supposing that they made the constitution in a consolidated character.

The dissolution of the existing political elements could never have been contemplated, because the constitution from beginning to end, recognises their existence, and makes them the foundation of a confederation. If they were dissolved in any mode, nothing is left for the Federal government to stand upon. Were they however, first dissolved and then revived, this doctrine would still leave them invested with the same powers and rights. But it would be an egregious violation of an established political principle; since if our State constitutions and governments were both dissolved and revived by the people of all the States, the conclusions would follow, that the people of all the States may create constitutions and governments for each State; and that the people of each State have no moral right to create constitutions or governments for themselves. What does the right of self-government say to this doctrine?

Nor is it true, that the State governments had no original powers, except by supposing that "original powers" means powers which had no origin. As to political powers, the word "original" is not susceptible of this meaning, and it is sufficient that the State governments did possess political powers originating from the people, to confirm their reservation. This soundest origin of power, can never be overturned by any power originating in construction. The powers of the Federal government are only good, so far as they also originate from sources possessing a moral or natural right to confer them; and if political powers are obtained in any other mode; if they can be conferred by the words "sovereignty, construction, necessity, and convenience" as originally appertaining to them, the idea of self-government is not applicable to a community, and only to its government.

The most formidable weapons used for destroying a federal, and introducing a consolidated republic, are flattery, falsehood, and scurrility. The people are first flattered, by being told, that they are very wise and very watchful, and will therefore elect good Federal representatives, and also control their usurpations. Then they are reproached with being both foolish and heedless, to prove that they will elect State representatives, who will be lawless, ambitious, and ignorant; that these

State representatives insult them by vindicating State rights, reserved by the people, to be preserved and exercised by these same representatives; that by such vindications they are endeavouring to deprive the people of self-government; that these insolent rulers of particular States, especially of large States, are endeavouring to destroy a Federal form of government; and that these same people, so wise and watchful, as to be a perfect check upon their Federal representatives, are so stupid and blind as to be no check at all upon their State representatives.

Similar declamations are invariably used to destroy every species of political check or division, to concentrate power, and to rob nations of liberty. Ambition can resort to them in every case. Does the President retain or use his legislative negative? It is a silent insinuation that the people are incapable of self-government, and unqualified for controlling Congress themselves. Does the Senate control the House of Representatives? It is an arrogant assumption of the rights of the people, by whom that House is elected. Do the judges control unconstitutional laws? They commit treason against the majesty of the people. Does a particular State resist a particular aggression upon its internal right of self-government? If it is large, it is ambitious; if small, it is contemptible; and either large or small, it behaves arrogantly to the people. Are Federal rulers ambitious? The people will control them. Are State rulers ambitious? The people will not control them. What are the people? Acute statesmen for introducing a consolidated republic, but egregious blockheads for preserving a Federal republic.

The use made of such contradictions, falsehoods, and flatteries, though fraudulent, unconstitutional, and illogical, requires great attention. Self-government is flattered to destroy self-government. It is not true that the people do govern themselves. They are governed by the governments which they have instituted for that purpose, and the essence of their right of self-government, consists in their reserved power to supervise and control these governments. Limited governing powers have been assigned to the Federal and State governments, reserving to the people in the former case a great portion, but not the whole, of this essence of the right of self-government, and in the latter, its complete essence, as the best security for civil liberty. If the control of the State governments is taken from the people by the Federal government, both their right of internal self-government is lost, and a power is raised up able to suppress, at its pleasure, the residue of the right. Various concentrations of power have proved able to do this, in a monarch, in an aristocracy, and in representative bodies. In France, the accumulation of powers in representative bodies, hoarded up a treasury of ambition and avarice, which proved to be an ample fund for introducing a despotism. Against the danger of an accumulation of power at one point, to their birth-right of self-government, the people established the division of powers between the Federal and State governments, reserving to themselves the control of both by election. One half of this control, constituting the essence of the right of self-government, is lost, if the Federal government should usurp the power of controlling the State governments, or if the State governments should usurp the power of controlling the Federal government. Will sovereignty, or the right of self-government, in the people, remain entire, after one half of it is taken away? How happens it that this principle is so excellent for the preservation of civil liberty in reference to Federal powers, and so detestable for the preservation of civil liberty in reference to State local power?

The flattery bestowed on the right of self-government, in order to transfer one moiety of its controlling power to the Supreme Court, still more evidently discloses the enmity of the consolidating doctrine towards it. How can the people, either by State or Federal elections, prevent the subversion of the division of powers, made to preserve their right of self-government, if this court can alter it? It may be answered, by a convention. To this it is replied, that the same remedy will reach State governments, but that their usurpations may be also reached by the easy and current remedy of election, so that the principle of self-government is infinitely more applicable to the State governments than to the Supreme Court. It is also more perfectly applicable to the State governments than to Congress, because the Senate is not a representation of the people of the United States, nor exposed to any influence from the right of self-government, unless such a right is admitted to reside in the States respectively. I cannot discern how the right of self-government can exist in relation to internal State measures, by transferring its control over these measures, either to the Federal Senate and House of Representatives, or to the Supreme Court.

It is however said that this transfer will be wise, because State functionaries are or will be ignorant, ambitious, and avaricious. This argument is neither philosophical nor founded in truth. It is inconsistent with sound reasoning to suppose, that one set of men invested with power, will be exposed to these bad qualities, and another not. The inconsistency is moreover aggravated, by supposing, that the influence of ambition and avarice will be least, where the temptation is greatest. Our system of government is founded upon sounder principles. It evidently believed in two very different suppositions; one, that the community contained materials for both the Federal and State governments; the other, that the men invested with the powers of either, would be liable to the frailties of human nature. The reproaches of ignorance, ambition, and avarice, exclusively applied to the State functionaries, are therefore a direct attack upon the principles of self-government itself. What confidence can be placed in that principle, if the people cannot, or will not furnish individuals capable of executing a political system, deemed by them necessary for preserving the principle itself? And what more contemptible character can be given of the people, than that they are unable to discern the difference between concentrating and dividing the highest provocative of the lusts of ambition and avarice? If the erect and manly principle of self-government can be taught to believe, that the community will be exhausted of its talents, virtue, and patriotism, by supplying functionaries for the Federal government that those to whom the State rights are confided must be drawn from a moral wilderness; and that a monopoly of power will chasten men of ambition, just as a monopoly of money will chasten them of avarice (as it is also desired to believe) this great principle cannot be either a good theoretical or practical politician; it must be admitted to know nothing of human nature, and it is of course unable to preserve human liberty. Is it not notorious that a monopoly of power is at least as pernicious to human happiness as a monopoly of money; and that the capitalists of the first absorb, steal, or seize human rights even more atrociously, than the capitalists of the last do property?

   If the Federal court can prohibit State legislation by injunctions; can sequestrate State treasuries; and can imprison State functionaries for contempts in obeying State laws; I know not what can prevent it from exercising the same powers over the Federal government; or why it may not imprison both Congress, the President, State legislatures, Governors, and Judges. Such a power over State functionaries only, enables it to stop the wheels of government, in spite of the self-governing right, and is as hostile to that right, as any concentrated power can be.

Until men are cleansed of ambition, it is to be expected in both the Federal and State departments. Self-government thought it best to make the ambition of one department, a counterpoise and check to the ambition of the other. It is now told that it will be made safer, by giving to one a monopoly of ambition, and enabling Federal ambition to enlist State ambition as an ally. But will not the right of self-government be more secure, by leaving to the people of each State the control of State ambition, than by converting it into an instrument for Federal ambition? If State legislatures shall usurp an unconstitutional share of power, election can control them. It is more frequently resorted to for this purpose in the States, than in the Federal government. Why will the people detect ambition in one department and not in the other? Why is the remedy good for every thing in one case, and good for nothing in the other? The people have two rights of self-government, one for Federal or general purposes, the other for State or local purposes. But a new idea is invented to destroy one right, under pretence that the destruction of one is necessary to preserve the other. It is contended that the Federal government must either be considered as an alien to the people; or, that it must have the right of the people to control the State governments in their internal regulations. If the word alien is applicable to the subject at all, it is in the relative situations of the States to each other, as to their local governments; and in the relation between Federal and State powers. The States may be called aliens to each other, with regard to their separate internal governments, as to which, no combination of States, in or out of Congress, have any right to dictate to one; and Federal and State powers, so far as they are divided, are alien to each other in the same way. If either of these aliens gains a right belonging to another, it must be by conquest or usurpation; and one or the other right of self-government must be taken from the people.

To flatter them out of one, they are told, that if their State governments should presume to defend it, they arrogantly intimate that the people are incompetent to defend it themselves. The same sophistry might, with equal propriety be urged against an attempt by their Federal legislature to defend the Federal right of self-government, as established by the Union. Must the garrison stationed in the political local fortress, called State self-government, be either traitors or calumniators of the people if they are faithful and brave?

In addition to the artifice of praising the Federal government in order to reflect contempt upon the State governments, the poorer trick is resorted to of calumniating entire States, which happen to be large, by charging them with a design of subjecting the rest, as a reason for increasing the power of the Federal government to guard against a danger so formidable. A great State is compounded of a great population, and the charge must either be true or false, applied to this population. There has not appeared the least symptom of a temper in the people of any State to infringe the rights of the rest. The number of the States is an insurmountable obstacle to such a speculation, and it is obviously fraudulent to use the petty struggles of individuals for offices or money, as evidence of so preposterous an idea in the people of any State. But the absurdity of this expedient for enlarging the power of the Federal government, even exceeds its destitution of truth. An increase of the power of the Federal government is the only mode, and exactly the best mode, for exciting the dormant ambition of the large States. Let that become supreme over State rights, and it bestows greater influence on the numerical superiority of the large States in the only branch of the Federal government, elected by the people. The reservation of State rights was dictated for the special purpose of preventing this numerical superiority from introducing a consolidated republic, by which the large States would acquire an unchecked jurisdiction over the small. It is by Federal, and not by State powers, that the smaller States are in danger of being swallowed up. The small States fixed their apprehension upon this danger, when the constitution was formed, and considered the reservation of State powers, and the limitation of Federal powers, as the only securities against it. If they were then right, by an extension of Federal power now, the power of the large States would be also increased, and the danger then feared, revived. If any great States are to be suspected of ambition, it must be those which pursue this policy, and not those which adhere to the policy of preserving State rights, originally suggested as a security against the ambition of the great States. The bank case did not proceed from the great States, nor the lottery case from the largest; and neither have any aspect capable of being tortured into the least proof of having proceeded from State ambition. Both these cases however illustrate the inattention naturally to be expected from States not directly assailed; and the ease with which the State right of self-government may be destroyed in detail, if it cannot defend itself. If the State right of taxation had been assailed in all the States, or if an emanation of internal power had been darted from the ten miles square, so as to be felt by every State, the opinion and sensation of every State in the Union, would have been the same with the opinion and sensation of the States particularly attacked. The impossibility of resistance where there is no practical injury, demonstrates a necessity for it where there is one, or there can never be any resistance at all. Virginia could not resist the aggression upon Ohio's right of internal taxation, nor Ohio the aggression upon the right of Virginia to prohibit the sale of lottery tickets. There are no rights where there are no remedies, or where the remedies depend upon the will of the aggressor.

To contend that the elective or self-governing right is sufficient to control the usurpations of the Federal courts, though limited to the House of Representatives; but that it is not sufficient to control the usurpations of State legislatures, though extended to both the Houses of which they consist; that it is wise and virtuous for one purpose, but weak and vicious for the other; that it is awake to its interest in one case, and asleep to it in the other; and that the more it is restricted, the freer it becomes; is not less profound than curious. In such doctrines the cloven foot of the old English prejudices, which made tories of many respectable men, which suggested the intrigue suppressed by Washington, and which produced the efforts for a consolidated republic in the convention, is plainly discernible. The elective right of the people is limited in England to the House of Commons, as it is here to the House of Representatives, and the effort now making to confine all its efficacy within the bounds of this Federal restriction, will reduce it to the British model. This restriction was suggested by the purpose of securing, in the construction of the Senate, the existence of the small States, and not by the purpose of surrendering the perfect elective or self-governing right as to local State government, to the imperfect English model. As to the powers reserved to the States or to the people respectively, the perfect right of self-government was retained; but as to the powers bestowed on the Federal government, an imperfect right of self-government was submitted to; not for the purpose either of destroying the perfect right retained, or of forming a government by the English standard; but for the sake of effecting the union. It was never intended that the imperfect should swallow up the perfect principle, nor did the people or the States intend to transfer the custody of local rights as well as Federal powers, from the latter to the former. They have never expressed an opinion, that the representation in the British House of Commons is better for preserving the right of self-government, than the complete influence of election applicable to the reserved powers; and the eulogies on their virtue, wisdom, and capacity, for preserving the right of self-government, by electing only one legislative chamber, is like telling a pugilist that he will be a better match for his adversary by tying his right hand behind him.

To draw the people into the absurdity of considering their elective power over only one legislative branch, as the best security for all their rights both State and Federal, unbounded applauses of the Federal government are offered as proofs, that an unlimited confidence in that government, is better than the limited confidence reposed in it by the constitution. In biography, compounded only of encomiums, we perceive flattery and suppression of truth. If the Federal government has committed no errors, it must be super-human; but if it is administered by men, that, as well as the State governments, must be liable to mistakes. The present State of the country discloses the probability that errors have been committed by both, and the object of this treatise is to prove it. Instead of plunging into the endless war of commercial restrictions, may it not be better to adopt a system of neutrality? Might not a neutrality in wars of avarice be as beneficial to us, as a neutrality in wars of ambition, although we should be exposed to inconveniences from the commercial regulations of the belligerents? Might not our active and intelligent merchants often make those regulations beneficial to themselves? Would not the spoliations of cunning be more avoidable than those of force? Are belligerent exclusive privileges fighting for money at home, more avoidable than belligerent commercial restrictions fighting for money abroad? Is it wise in an individual to curtail half his expenses, when half his income is lost? Are not nations in this respect like individuals? If so, does not the question apply more strongly to governments which suffer the same expenses to remain, though doubled or trebled by a fall in the price of produce? Is there no similarity between a council of appointment to gratify factions with offices, and a Supreme Court to gratify factions with powers and money? Are such councils a better check upon ambition and avarice, than a genuine influence of the self-governing right? Are there not in every society, men who prefer a splendid and expensive government, as a fine market for their talents, to the general happiness of the nation; and will not these men constantly endeavour to repay the people for the money extracted from them, by approving the measures of a government which will gratify their lusts, and take away the comforts of the people, to buy talents or partisans at extravagant prices?

But the strongest argument in the eyes of those who are for introducing a consolidated republic, and the weakest in the eyes of those who are for maintaining a federal republic, is, that the first policy will preserve, and the second destroy the Union. To me it seems that these assertions ought to be reversed. The strength or weakness of a government ought to be graduated by the good or bad principles intended to be enforced or obstructed. A government well constituted for securing the principles of liberty, may be strong for that purpose, and if so, it must be weak for the purpose of oppression; and a government so constituted as to be able to oppress, must on the contrary be weak for the object of preserving liberty. Nations must construe the terms "strong and weak," according to this distinction, or cease to be free. It is a sound distinction for obtaining a correct idea of liberty or tyranny. Every innovation which weakens the limitations and divisions of power, alone able to make a government strong for the object of preserving liberty, makes it strong for the object of oppression. A government strong to preserve liberty, and weak for introducing tyranny, is that best calculated for preserving the Union. Both this strength and this weakness, are admirably provided for by the division of powers between the Federal and State governments. To the Federal government is assigned the powers of peace and war, of taxation, of raising armies, and of commanding the militia. They were given that it might be strong enough to preserve the Union, but not to make it strong enough to change it into a consolidated republic. To the State governments are assigned the powers necessary to make them strong enough to sustain a Federal republic, but not to destroy the Union. The powers entrusted to the State governments, are too weak to destroy the Federal government, and those entrusted to the Federal government being by far the strongest, require a greater degree of watchfulness. How are the powers of the Federal government weakened, in relation to the preservation of the Union, by leaving to the States the minor powers of making roads and canals, of excluding banks and lotteries, of providing for the poor, of exchanging their local productions freely, and of imposing internal taxes? May not the Federal government preserve the Union, though the States shall exercise these powers? Why then should the Federal government fish for the minnows reserved to the State governments? Why should the strong David covet the poor Uriah's ewe lambs? If he gets them, will he love Uriah the better, or kill him through fear of his resentment? Is this the way to preserve the Union?

The British Parliament attempted to preserve the integrity of the empire by the same consolidating policy, now proposed for preserving the Union; but its effect was disunion. Had it pursued the contrary policy of respecting local provincial rights, of trifling importance compared with great Federal objects; the division of the empire would not have been accelerated. It is in vain to reply to this admonition, that the people of the Provinces were not represented in the British House of Commons, because it does not remove the causes for State dissatisfaction, which provoked Provincial dissatisfaction, if the right of internal State government is obstructed. It was foreseen that even the members of our House of Representatives would bring with them some portion of the local prejudices, local ambition, and local avarice, which caused the division of the British empire; and therefore they were inhibited from exercising the local powers reserved to the States, to avoid the risk of State dissatisfactions, as likely to produce a similar division. The dissimilarities between the customs, climates, and occupations, of the States, rendered Federal representatives almost as unfit for local legislators, as the British Parliament; and suggested a prohibition against their becoming such, as the best, and probably the only policy by which the Union could be preserved. But what shall we say to the construction of the Senate? If the construction of the House of Representatives could not exclude those qualities of human nature, which led to the dismemberment of the British empire, can it be supposed that the same qualities would be eradicated, without the application of popular election; that the members of the Senate will bring with them no local predilections; and that they will therefore be qualified for exercising local governing powers, without any risk of exciting local dissatisfactions? Would not a minority of the people by a local legislative power in the Senate, govern a majority of the people as to their internal State affairs; and might not a majority of States, by means of such a power, disorder or abolish local rights, contrary to the will of a majority of the people? Would this have a tendency to preserve the Union? In this view also, the alleged distinction between the British Parliament and Congress loses its force; and the reasons which suggested the preservation of local provincial rights for preventing the division of the British empire, suggest the most careful preservation of local State rights, to prevent the dissolution of the Union. The object of the British Parliament, in attempting to make the Provinces tributary, was great, however unjust; it risked much to gain much; but the attempt of Federal government to make the State governments tributary in little powers; in banks, lotteries, roads, canals, and exclusive privileges; is exposed to the same risk without the same temptation: it is like a child's crying for poisonous fruit; and it risks the Union without a chance of any compensation, adequate to the risk. Could not the Federal government go on without craving such trinkets? To what can an eagerness for baubles be ascribed, but an intention to weave a net of precedents, to catch, hereafter, higher game than butterflies? A greediness for the insects of power, evinces a taste for its ortolans. Cannot the Union subsist unless Congress and the Supreme Court shall make banks and lotteries? Will the States long endure the doctrine, that their homely fare ought to be made worse to pamper exclusive privileges? If one painter could draw so true a picture of monarchy, as to cause a general shriek of abhorrence, and make an impression on the mind sufficient to break the iron sceptre of British despotism; may we not expect from another, a declaration of independence against the vampires of private property, sufficient to break the necromantic wand of political conjurers used to transfer power and money; the very objects, in attempting to gain which, British lost about an eighth part of the habitable world? Can it be supposed that the policy of drawing from industry those earnings by which she improves agriculture, encourages commerce, nourishes manufactures, extends knowledge, and fosters useful professions; in order to feed idleness, nourish luxury, extend corruption, and introduce tyranny; will be a better security for the continuance of the Union, than an expulsion of fraudulent money changers from the temple of liberty? Or are we ready to adopt the motto of dying Rome *"omnia erant venalia?"*

About fifty years past I read a description of a British ministry (Bute's, I believe) by Edmund Burke. As well as I recollect, he likened it to a tesselated pavement; a Mosaick work composed of different coloured shells; a motley assemblage of discordant materials; so that when the members met, they stared at each other, and each wondered how he could have gotten into such company. Let us see if we are not compounding a government according to the heterogeneous model of this corrupt administration.

The people of the United States, and not the people of the States, made the Federal government; and therefore the Federal government has a right to exercise the powers reserved by the people to the State governments.

The States have no original rights, therefore they could not confederate; nor could the Federal government make the State governments, before it was made itself. Both being nonentities when the constitution was made, and being created at the same time, the Federal government became heir to all the powers of the people, as their more bulky production, though not the first born; and thus obtained a supremacy over State rights, though it did not create them.

Election is a complete security against Federal unconstitutional acts. It is not security against State unconstitutional acts; because all the States will elect wisely, and each State will elect foolishly.

As the same people will elect good men to represent them in one legislative chamber of Congress, and bad men to represent them in two legislative chambers of each State, the one House of Representatives, not having a power to make laws, is a safer guardian of the State local right of self-government, than the two houses.

Powers are divided between the Federal and State departments to restrain ambitious men in both. They are accumulated in the hands of ambitious men in one.

A federal republic is the best for maintaining a republican form of government over a country so extensive as the United States. A consolidated republic is better.

Confederation is union. Consolidation is union.

Each State has a right to make its own constitution. Congress has a right to make a constitution for each State.

Each State has a right to make its own local laws. Congress and the Court can repeal them, and make local laws for the States.

The people of the States had a right to make the Federal constitution, and to prohibit its alteration, except with the concurrence of three-fourths of the legislatures of the several States. Congress and the Supreme Court may make alterations without the concurrence of a single State, or of a majority of the people of all the States.

Powers are divided by the terms of the Union between the State and Federal departments. A portion of one department may make a new division.

The people have two rights of self-government, State and Federal. It is expedient to take away, or neutralize one.

Election is the best security against unconstitutional laws for usurping powers withheld either from the Federal or State governments. The Supreme Court is a better.

A mutual right of self-preservation, both in the Federal and State departments, is the next best. Such a right in one, is indispensable; in the other, pernicious.

The protection of property is an end of government. Its transfer by fraudulent laws is another end.

Government has no right to take away the property of one man and give it to another. It has a right to take away the property of all men and give it to one.

Taxes ought to be imposed for national use. They ought also to be imposed to enrich corporations and exclusive privileges.

The States have a right to impose local taxes for State use. Congress may make corporations with a right to tax the States, and prohibit the States from taxing them.

State functionaries cannot discharge their duties, unless they are free. The Federal courts may put them in prison.

The Federal department cannot constitutionally invade State rights. It may do so if it pleases.

The English parliament may alter their government, because the people elect the house of commons. Congress and the Supreme Court may alter our government, because the people elect the House of Representatives.

State judges take an oath to be loyal to the State right of internal self-government. Federal judges who take no such oath, may force them to break it.

Legislative and judicial powers are divided by the Federal and State constitutions. Federal and State legislatures may exercise judicial powers.

Congress may establish post roads. It may make all roads. It may make war; that is, it may make canals.

It may dispose of public lands; that is, it may give them away. It was instituted for common defence, general welfare, and to preserve the blessings of liberty. It was also instituted to establish monopolies, exclusive privileges, bounties, sinecures, pensions, lotteries, and to give away the public money.

It is prohibited from taxing exports. It is allowed to invest a capitalist interest with a power to tax them very highly and very partially for its own benefit, by means of commercial restrictions which diminish their exchangeable value, and foster a monopoly enhancing the prices of those necessaries which the raisers of these exports must consume.

It is empowered to govern ten miles square. It may therefore govern all the States internally, with the concurrence of the Supreme Court. This closes the drama by a catastrophe reaching all powers whatsoever.

Such is the chaos which is obscuring the original effulgence of our system of government, and gradually intercepting the genial warmth it imparted, whilst inspired by home-bred principles.

It seems to me, that the property-transferring policy is the true cause of all the collisions which have occurred between the State and Federal governments; and that if this policy was abandoned, these collisions would cease. That it is also the chief cause of the existing hard times. Money has been the sole object of funding, banking, capitalist monopolies, lotteries, and pensions. The alien and sedition laws were also dictated by the design of retaining offices and money, but they were infinitely less oppressive than the other money-getting projects. I cannot see how such projects will preserve the Union; on the contrary, a conviction that this property-transferring policy subjects industry and liberty to avarice and ambition, suggested this humble effort against their deadliest foe, in my eyes. Nothing is advanced from the least antipathy towards individuals, or from any selfish motive; and nothing is suppressed which seemed necessary for sustaining my convictions. If the property-transferring policy has been unfelt by the community, my labour is only lost; and whatever may be my opinion, it must be left to the reader's better judgment, whether this treatise is calculated to advance or diminish the happiness of the people.

Is it enthusiasm or reason which causes me to behold the finger of God conducting the United States into a situation happily contrived to try and place at rest for ever, the doubt, whether human nature is able to maintain a fair, free, mild, and cheap government? No other people ever were, or ever will be in so good a situation to settle this question affirmatively; and their practical testimony will therefore be considered as conclusive. A great nation was made to nurture them up to independence. A despotick government was made an instrument towards effecting it. Their soils and climates bestow subsistence and energy, without possessing the exuberant fertility or alluring softness, by which conquerors are invited and the mind is enervated. They cover the largest space of the whole world, in which one language is spoken; so that ideas may be exchanged, prejudices encountered, and opinions examined, by one easy, rapid and familiar mode of communication throughout all their territories. A surprising concurrence of circumstances excluded orders and exclusive privileges; and the experience of two centuries taught them that they could do without these remnants of barbarous ages, and instruments of civilized tyranny. Various sects of Christians were wafted into them, without being actuated by the intention of establishing religious freedom, which yet it sprung out of this circumstance without man's agency, except as the humble instrument of an overruling providence. Had all emigrants been of one faith, this half of human liberty would probably have been lost for ever. Apparently, accident also produced a division of States, not less efficacious in favour of civil liberty, than are different sects in favour of religious. The wonderful concurrence of circumstances for effecting both ends, admonishes us to behold the division into States as also the work of providence. We have been taught that religion flourishes best, without oppressing the people by expensive establishments, as if to disclose to man the next great truth, that civil liberty does not require them. Make religion rich, and she becomes the patron of vice. Let a government become expensive, and it becomes the patron of ambition and avarice. In neither case can self-government exist, because both are founded upon a supposed necessity, that men must be robbed of their property to preserve social order; and this policy invariably terminates in despotism. Providence seems to have shielded us against it, by producing the division of religious sects, and of a vast territory into separate States; and as if still more securely to protect us against the endless pretext for exposing nations to enslaving privileges and impoverishing expenses, drawn from the contiguity of powerful governments, so often used to destroy both religious and civil liberty; it has blessed us with a geographical position, apparently, that our understandings might have the fairest opportunity to detect impositions framed with national antipathies, but directed against private property; and increased our population, so as to place us beyond the reach of fear. In these circumstances I behold a miracle, worked for the salvation of liberty, and creating an awful responsibility on the people of the United States. They seem to have been selected to evince the capacity of man for sustaining a fair and free government; and if by their failure, with such pre-eminent advantages, they shall renounce the favours of heaven, and consign a whole world of endless generations to the tyranny of expensive governments, they will be reprobated as another infatuated and rebellious people, who have rejected benefactions visibly flowing from an Almighty source.

The commissions to overturn political idolatry thus entrusted to the United States, like that to overturn religious idolatry entrusted to the Jews, requires only that portion of sagacity, sufficient to discover a fact, of universal notoriety, incapable of contradiction, and acknowledged by every honest man, learned or unlearned. It is, that no species of property-transferring policy, past or existing, foreign or domestick, ever did or ever can enrich the labouring classes of any society whatever; but that it universally impoverishes them. To this fact not a single exception appears in the whole history of mankind. What then can be more absurd, than that the agricultural and mechanical classes, or either of them, should conceive that they will be benefited by such a policy? What except labour, can permanently supply the property transferred? The mercantile class, as merchants only, must be impoverished by this policy; but a few individuals of this class, more frequently evade its oppression, than of other labouring classes, by blending the capitalist with the mercantile character; and becoming bankers, lenders to government, or factory owners. So far also, as the agricultural and mechanical classes, are interspersed with individuals endowed with pecuniary privileges, such individuals derive emolument from the property-transferring policy, not as mechanicks or agriculturists, but in their privileged characters. Those who gain more by banking, by the protecting-duty monopoly, or by loaning to the government, than they lose by these property-transferring machines, constitute no exception to the fact, that the property-transferring policy invariably impoverishes all labouring and productive classes. A few individuals are enriched by every species of tyranny, as its essence in civilized countries consists of transferring property by laws. If the general good is the end of self-government, and if the property-transferring policy defeats the general good, it also defeats self-government. Therefore the United States cannot fulfil the great purpose to which they seem almost to have been destined, except by a degree of sagacity sufficient to discern, that the property-transferring policy in all its forms, however disguised, is a tyrannical imposition, only sustainable by the same species of political idolatry, which has blinded mankind to their interest, and is yet enslaving most or all civilized nations.

The United States "are the light of the world. Ought their light to shine before men, that they may see their good works, or to be put under the bushel" of the property-transferring policy.

"Seek, and ye shall find; knock" down this policy, and the blessing of a free and fair government "will be opened unto you."

"When the blind lead the blind, both fall into the ditch." Let us not follow then at the tail of the Europeans.

"Beware of false prophets, which come in sheep's clothing, but inwardly are ravening wolves. Every good tree bringeth forth good fruits, but a corrupt tree bringeth forth evil fruits. By their fruits ye shall know them." The United States have tasted the fruits of the property-transferring policy. Are they sweet or bitter?

The freedom of property "is an easy yoke and a light burden." But the property-transferring policy galls our necks and bears heavily on our shoulders.

Let us no longer "sow our seed for the fowls to devour." Is it better to be governed by the costly pageants of the property-transferring policy, than by the free animating principle of fair exchanges and unplundered industry?

Index

Absolute power, 101, 220
  See also Consolidation of power;
    Corruption; Limited power;
    Monarchy; Monopoly; Tyranny
Adams, John
  administration of, 7–8
Africa, 10, 156
Age, xxvii–xxviii
Agricultural interests, 13, 15–16, 23,
    97, 267
  capitalists at war with, 48–49
  capitalists legally restrict, 102–3
  industry opposed to, 108
  oppressed by taxation, 62, 130–31
  silent in Congress, 74
  subservient to manufacturing, 34–
    35
  See also Agriculture; Landed in-
    terests
Agriculture
  connected with commerce and
    manufactures, 4
  protecting-duty advocates pretend
    to favor, xxvii
  protecting-duty system destroys,
    147–91
  staples, 23–24
Alabama, 24
Alien and Sedition Acts, 99–100,
    209–10, 221, 223–24, 248–49
Ambition. *See* Avarice
Amphictyonic council, 121–22, 213
Areopagus, 213
Aristocracy, 12–13, 85
  concentration of power in, 253
  similar to mobs, 41

Army, 9–11, 52, 97
Arts, 152–54, 181, 189–90
Asia, 10, 153
Avarice, 7–9, 20, 73, 230–31, 261, 265
  ambition linked to, 49
  cause of legislative corruption, 135
  liberty threatened by, 147
  politics driven by, 76, 253–59
  of republics, 26–27
  tyranny based on, 194, 225

Balance of trade, 18–19, 69–70
  Committee of Manufactures advo-
    cates, 87
  dominated by manufacturers, 89–
    90
  not regulated by money, 55–56
  as oppressive governmental policy,
    53, 54
  problems of ascertaining, 57
  protectionism masked as, 52
Balances, doctrine of, 47
Banking interests, 14, 94, 225, 248–49
  benefit from governments, 30, 43
  and currency, 21, 32, 59–60, 68–69
Bank law, 22, 221–24, 235, 242, 246,
    249, 257
Bank of the United States, 37
Bankruptcy, 5, 37
Banks, 62, 261, 265
  abuses of, 7–8, 46, 80
  bankruptcy of, 21, 66–68
  expansion of, 21
  nature of, 33
  promise to foster commerce, 168

A Note on the Type

The text of this book is set in 11-point Adobe Garamond, a modern adaptation of the typeface originally cut around 1540 by the French typographer and printer Claude Garamond (d. 1561). Garamond, with its small lowercase height and restrained contrast between thick and thin strokes, is a classic "old-style" face, and has been one of the most influential and widely used typefaces since its creation..

Printed on paper that is acid-free and meets the requirements of the American National Standard for Permanence of Paper for Printed Library Materials, z39.48-1992. ∞

Editorial services by BooksCraft, Inc., Indianapolis, Indiana

Book design by Binns & Lubin/Martin Lubin, New York, New York

Typesetting by Monotype Composition Company, Inc., Baltimore, Maryland

Index by Scholars Editorial Services, Inc., Madison, Wisconsin

Printed and bound by Edwards Brothers, Inc., Ann Arbor, Michigan